THE ACOUSTIC MIRROR

Theories of Representation and Difference

General Editor: Teresa de Lauretis

KAJA SILVERMAN

THE ACOUSTIC MIRROR

The Female Voice in

Psychoanalysis and Cinema

INDIANA UNIVERSITY PRESS

Bloomington and Indianapolis

Portions of chapters 1, 2, and 5 have appeared in somewhat different form in *Wide Angle* 8, nos. 1 and 2 (1985), *Iris* 3, no. 1 (1985), and Mary Ann Doane, Patricia Mellencamp, and Linda Williams, eds., *Re-vision: Essays in Feminist Film Criticism* (Los Angeles: AFI, 1984).

MANUFACTURED IN THE UNITED STATES OF AMERICA

Library of Congress Cataloging-in-Publication Data

Silverman, Kaja.
   The acoustic mirror.

   (Theories of representation and difference)
   Bibliography: p.
   Includes index.
   1. Women in motion pictures.   2. Moving-pictures—
Psychological aspects.   3. Psychoanalysis.   4. Voice.
I. Title.   II. Series.
PN1995.9.W6S57   1988   791.43'09'09352042   87-45834
ISBN 0-253-30284-6
ISBN 0-253-20474-7 (pbk.)
1   2   3   4   5   92   91   90   89   88

C O N T E N T S

For Michael and Philosophy on the Telephone.

Acknowledgments

Anne Friedberg, Barbara Miller, Tania Modleski, Elizabeth Weed, Anne Norton, Joan Scott, Stephen Heath, Mahara Ranger, Karen Newman, Roswitha Mueller, Margaret Mchugh, Laura Mulvey, Lorette Clement, Jackie Rose, Rey Chow, Mary Ann Doane, Elena Feder, and my colleagues in the Women's Studies Program at Simon Fraser University all contributed in some vital way to the intellectual and social milieu in which I wrote this book, and have taught me to think in new ways about feminist theory and practice. The generous support of the Brown University Pembroke Center made it possible for me to write chapters 1 and 2. Judith Mayne read *The Acoustic Mirror* in manuscript, and offered wonderfully helpful suggestions for improving upon it. I also owe particular thanks to Peter Wollen and Naomi Schor, with whom I talked over crucial parts of this book, and to whose friendship it is a small tribute. Teresa de Lauretis helped to pull me through many a conceptual impasse, and has been a constant source of intellectual, political, and emotional support. Mary Russo is, quite simply, the best of everything that a friend can be, and most of the thoughts in this book have been in some way filtered through her. But above all I want to thank Michael Silverman, who has always "been there," even when he couldn't actually be in the same country, and who always knows how to make even a good thing better.

Providence
April 1987

Preface

"No matter how many times I do this, I still get the same thrill," confides one of the doctors in Curtis Bernhardt's *Possessed* (1947), as he injects a woman played by Joan Crawford with a drug which will induce her to "confess" her past upon demand, and without her conscious participation. He waits with ardent anticipation for each new installment of his patient's story, repeating the injections whenever her voice falters. The scene is strikingly—indeed uncannily—reminiscent of a scene from George Cukor's *A Woman's Face,* a film made six years earlier by another director and for a different studio, but which also takes place in a hospital room, also theatricalizes the exchange between a male doctor and his female patient, and also casts Joan Crawford in the role of a patient: the scene, that is, where the doctor removes the bandages from the female face which he has surgically reconstituted.

However, the uncanny similarity is undermined from within by a critical difference—whereas *A Woman's Face* stages its drama at the surface of the female body, *Possessed* derives its narrative coherence from the female voice. In the later of those two films, the doctor's desire is engaged not by the possibility of constituting woman as spectacle, but by the possibility of extracting speech from her. *Possessed* is by no means an isolated moment in the history of Hollywood. Films as historically diverse as *Johnny Belinda* (1948), *Singin' in the Rain* (1952), *Marnie* (1964), and *Blow-Out* (1981) testify to its continual fascination with the sounds and meanings generated by the female voice. Like the doctor in *Possessed,* classic cinema could be said to "get the same thrill" each time that voice is produced.

It is curious in light of this institutional obsession that the feminist critique of classic cinema has focused primarily upon the image track and the construction of woman as the object of the male gaze—upon the spectacle which is revealed, as it were, when the bandages are removed from Joan Crawford's face, rather than upon the "confession" which is medically extracted from her. It has somehow escaped theoretical attention that sexual difference is the effect of dominant cinema's *sound* regime as well as its visual regime, and that the female *voice* is as relentlessly held to normative representations and functions as is the female body.

This book derived its initial impetus from my desire to extend the feminist critique of Hollywood into the area of the voice. However, as I wrote, that latter concept became increasingly flexible and commodious, capable of subsuming not only a wide variety of recorded vocalizations, but the whole problematic of authorship. My theoretical investigation of the female voice also opened decisively onto a range of "subjective" issues, from castration, projection, disavowal, and fantasy to narcissim, melancholia, and the negative Oedipus complex.

My target of study underwent a similar expansion. It proved impossible to limit the category of classic (sound) cinema to a fixed period of Hollywood history, since the auditory regime I uncovered in films from the 1940s and 1950s is still operative in films as late as *Klute* (1971) and *Blow-Out,* and can be detected in non-American films such as *Darling* (1965) and *Diva* (1981). (Within the context of this book, classic cinema designates less a formal system of the sort exhaustively codified by David Bordwell, Janet Staiger, and Kristin Thompson[1] than a textual model which holds the female voice and body insistently to the interior of the diegesis, while relegating the male subject to a position of *apparent* discursive exteriority by identifying him with mastering speech, vision, or hearing. The psychic and ideological underpinnings of this model are discussed at some length in chapter 1. Its sonorous dimensions are outlined in chapter 2. I should add that while the system of classic [sound] cinema is an abstraction gleaned from repeated viewings of numerous films, all individual films exceed that system in at least some respects, and often in many. No film, in other words, is reducible to the category of classic cinema, no matter how that category is conceived.)

But even stretching the category of classic cinema in this way left it too restrictive for my purposes. I wanted to include a discussion of two films which exceed its paradigm in a number of very striking ways, but which are in some sense "about" it—*Peeping Tom* (1960) and *The Conversation* (1974). I also wanted to look closely at a Hollywood film—*Three Women* (1977)—and an avant-garde British film—*Riddles of the Sphinx* (1976)—which are libidinally unassimilable to classic cinema. Finally, I wanted to examine authorship in the work of the Italian director Liliana Cavani, and to include in my larger analysis of the voice a group of experimental films by women which have effectively dismantled Hollywood's sound/image regime. As a result, only the first three chapters deal with classic cinema. The remaining three address films which challenge that model, particularly at the level of voice.

The investigative field of *The Acoustic Mirror* also expanded to include a range of texts drawn from psychoanalysis, film theory, and feminism. At times these texts are given a metacritical function, but more often they too are read "symptomatically," shown to be motivated at least in part by the same psychic and ideological forces as the films with which they are grouped. Chapter 1, for instance, is predicated on the assumption that Freud's essays on anatomical difference and fetishism enact a similar projection to that effected by classic cinema, and are part of the same undertaking—the construction of an "adequate" male subject. Chapter 3 attempts to show that Michel Chion's theoretical account of the maternal voice is structured by an identical fantasy to that which informs *Sorry, Wrong Number* (1948), a fantasy which is very different from the one which informs Guy Rosolato's account of the maternal voice, or *Diva* (1983). And chapter 4 pursues the libidinal traces of the negative Oedipus complex not only in *Riddles of the Sphinx*, but in Kristeva's writings on motherhood. A number of chapters—1, 4, and 6—are indeed *primarily* organized around theoretical texts, the first of these seeking through a "diagnostic" reading of Freud and film theory to redefine what is generally understood to be the castration crisis, the second mounting an exhaustive search within key essays from *Polylogue* and *Histoires d'amour* for the libidinal economy of feminism, and the third tracking authorial subjectivity in a wide range of essays dating from the 1960s through the 1980s. Another, chapter 5, gives equal attention to Irigaray and the feminist avant-garde, in addition to elaborating its own theory of femininity, and expanding further upon the negative Oedipus complex. The result of all these textual intersections is as much an anatomy of female subjectivity as a study of the female voice.

THE ACOUSTIC MIRROR

[1]

LOST OBJECTS AND MISTAKEN SUBJECTS:

A PROLOGUE

Lost objects are the only ones one is afraid to lose. . . .
                                           Christian Metz

Acknowledgement of castration prevents murder;
it is its opposite and opposes it.
                                           Julia Kristeva

THIS CHAPTER WILL attempt to demonstrate, with Lacan, that there is a castration which precedes the recognition of anatomical difference—a castration to which all cultural subjects must submit, since it coincides with separation from the world of objects, and the entry into language. However, it will also venture something which psychoanalysis has not as yet undertaken, which is to articulate the relationship between that castration—symbolic castration—and the traumatic discovery anato-mized by Freud. It is my assumption that the former as well as the latter can be uncovered in certain of his texts, and I will to that purpose perform symptomatic readings of "Some Psychical Consequences of the Anatomical Distinction between the Sexes" and "Fetishism."

But the scope of my investigation will extend beyond psycho-analysis. I will endeavor to show that classic cinema has the poten-tial to reactivate the trauma of symbolic castration within the viewer, and that it puts sexual difference in place as a partial defense against that trauma. I say "partial" both because no system of defense is impreg-nable, and because this one serves to protect only the male viewer. It has very different consequences for the female viewer, at least assuming that identification in any way follows gender, since it projects male lack onto female characters in the guise of anatomical deficiency and discursive inadequacy.

Although it might seem odd to mount such an argument without a series of detailed analyses of prototypical Hollywood films, I will be looking instead at a range of "secondary" texts which might be said to register the symbolic castration anxiety that classic cinema is capable of generating at the site of male subjectivity. The texts to which I refer constitute the dominant tradition within film theory, from Munsterberg

1

to the present. They will be supplemented by Michael Powell's *Peeping Tom*, a film whose metacritical relation to Hollywood focuses precisely upon the system of projection and disavowal through which the latter denies male lack.

This chapter will specifically address the female voice only in its concluding section. It is, nonetheless, the necessary preface to the chapters which follow, since in each one of them that category will be shown to open decisively onto both sexual difference and subjectivity.

Film theory has been haunted since its inception by the specter of a loss or absence at the center of cinematic production, a loss which both threatens and secures the viewing subject. When Jean-Louis Comolli suggests that "the whole edifice of cinematic representation . . . finds itself affected [by] a fundamental lack,"[1] he speaks for Munsterberg and Bazin as well as Metz, Oudart, Dayan, and Mulvey.

This fundamental lack reveals a remarkable propensity for displacement. Sometimes the absence which structures cinema would seem to be the foreclosed real. At other times it is equated with the concealed site of production. On yet other occasions, lack would appear to be inscribed into cinema through the female body. Random as they seem, these displacements follow a very specific trajectory. The identification of woman with lack functions to cover over the absent real and the foreclosed site of production—losses which are incompatible with the "phallic function" in relation to which the male subject is defined.[2]

What I am proposing is that film theory's preoccupation with lack is really a preoccupation with male subjectivity, and with that in cinema which threatens constantly to undermine its stability. This obsession with the coherence of the male subject informs the debates on realism and suture as well as those on sexual difference and representation. Moreover, as early as Munsterberg and Bazin, disavowal and fetishism are marshaled to protect that coherence.

Although Hugo Munsterberg's chief concern is to establish the affinities between human psychology and cinematic articulation, he devotes considerable time to the question of realism. However, far from privileging the relation of the cinematic image to the phenomenal world, his *Photoplay* places the two in binary opposition. For Munsterberg the fundamental condition of the cinema is that the viewer be "distinctly conscious of the unreality of the artistic production, and that means that [this production] must be kept absolutely separated from the real things and men, that it must be isolated and kept in its own sphere."[3] Film, in other words, is defined by the distance that separates it from the phenomenal order—by the absence of the object or referent. Its pertinent relationships are discursive, not existential. Munsterberg writes enthusiastically about inserts, cross-cutting, and other devices that draw attention to movies as constructed entities.

Andre Bazin, of course, adopts a very different position toward both the referent and cinematic syntax. He argues that the camera not only records but *traces* the profilmic object—that an existential bond links the cinematic image to the phenomenal world. The transition from one shot to another threatens to disrupt this privileged relationship, to replace it with one which is arbitrary and artificial. Montage transforms "something real into something imaginary";[4] it substitutes absence for presence.[5]

Despite Bazin's assertion that the photographic image "is the object itself,"[6] and his conviction that the continuum of image and object is interrupted only by syntax and metaphor,[7] he occasionally concedes that lack is somehow intrinsic to the cinematic operation. In "An Aesthetic of Reality," he speaks of the "loss of the real" which is "implicit in any realist choice," and which "frequently allows the artist, by the use of any aesthetic convention he may introduce into the area thus left vacant, to increase the effectiveness of his chosen form of reality."[8] Elsewhere Bazin suggests that one of the sacrifices cinema thus necessitates is the physical presence of the actor—and, by extension, that of any other profilmic event.[9]

Christian Metz makes much of this particular absence. Because the spectator and the actor are never in the same place at the same time, cinema is the story of missed encounters, of "the failure to meet of the voyeur and the exhibitionist whose approaches no longer coincide."[10] Moreover, unlike theater, which employs real actors to depict fictional characters, film communicates its illusions through other illusions; it is doubly simulated, the representation of a representation. For Metz, cinema is not only invaded by but synonymous with the loss of the profilmic event:

> What distinguishes cinema is an extra reduplication, a supplementary and specific turn of the screw bolting desire to the lack. First because the spectacles and sounds the cinema "offers" to us (offers at a distance, hence as much as *steals* from us) are especially rich and varied: a mere difference of degree, but already one that counts: the screen presents to our apprehension, but absents from our grasp, more "things." (p. 61)

Despite their divergent theoretical positions, Munsterberg, Bazin, and Metz all conceptualize the transition from referent to cinematic sign as a surgical incision. Munsterberg speaks of the necessity for film to "cut off every possible connection" with the phenomenal order—to frame its spectacle in such a way that all links with the object are "severed" (p. 64). Bazin, who opposes the usurpation of the referent by the sign, and who sees montage as the agency of usurpation, characterizes the editing procedure as one which chops up the world into "little fragments," disrupting the unity "natural to people and things."[11] Metz uses the term *castration* to describe cinema's structuring lack, thereby foregrounding the viewer's very personal stake in the loss of the object, and adding a new dimension to the metaphors of cutting and chopping deployed by his predecessors.

Metz not only refers to the loss of the object as a castration, but he suggests that the viewer protects him- or herself from the trauma of that castration through defensive mechanisms similar to those adopted by Freud's male child—disavowal and fetishism. Metz's spectator is divided between the one-who-knows and the one-who-doesn't-know:

> Any spectator will tell you that he "doesn't believe it," but everything happens as if there were nonetheless someone to be deceived, someone who really would "believe in it." . . . This credulous person is, of course, another part of ourselves, he is seated *beneath* the incredulous one, or in his heart, it is he who continues to believe, who disavows what he knows. . . . (p. 72)

Like the little boy who sees the female genitals for the first time and who disavows the absence of the penis, this viewer refuses to acknowledge what he or she knows full well—that cinema is founded on the lack of the object.

Although Metz was the first to situate this epistemological division within a psychoanalytic context, he was by no means the first to note it. Munsterberg writes that "we are never deceived" about the flatness of the cinematic image, and yet we credit it with three-dimensionality (p. 23). Bazin makes a similar observation about filmic illusion in "The Virtues and Limitations of Montage":

> If the film is to fulfill itself aesthetically we need to believe in the reality of what is happening while knowing it to be tricked. . . . So the screen reflects the ebb and flow of our imagination which feeds on a reality for which it plans to substitute. (Vol. 1, p. 48)

The ebb and flow of the Bazinian imagination enacts the double movement of disavowal, the "I know very well, but all the same . . ." of a subject split down the axis of belief.[12]

Metz suggests that the disavowal of destabilizing knowledge is facilitated in the cinema, as it is in the situation described by Freud, by the construction of a fetish. The viewing subject protects him- or herself from the perception of lack by putting a surrogate in place of the absent real. That surrogate becomes the precondition for pleasure. Curiously, however, Metz argues that the cinematic fetish is most often technical virtuosity or formal brilliance—a demonstration, as it were, of the "goodness" of the apparatus (p. 74). He proposes, that is, that the lost object is replaced by an overt display of artifice. What is puzzling about this argument is that it posits a fetishistic situation in which there is no suspension of disbelief. The cameramen, directors, critics, and spectators of whom he speaks, whose love of cinema is a love of technique, have already acceded to the loss of the real, and find nothing traumatic about that loss. Their investment is not in the ontological relation of image to object, but in the productive relation of machine to image.

Comolli provides a much more convincing articulation of cinematic fetishism when he proposes that what stands in for the absent real is a simulated real—what he calls "an impression of reality" (p. 133). This formulation echoes that advanced by Bazin in "An Asthetic of Reality," where he spells out the conditions which make possible the "ebb and flow" of the viewer's imagination:

> We would describe as "realist" . . . all narrative means tending to bring an added measure of reality to the screen. . . . At the conclusion of this inevitable and necessary "chemical" action, for the initial reality there has been substituted an illusion of reality. . . . It is a necessary illusion but it quickly induces a loss of awareness of the reality itself, which becomes identified in the mind of the spectator with its cinematographic representation. (Vol. 2, p. 27)

Bazin here describes the paradigmatic fetishist operation, one where a construction not only substitutes for the absent object, but is confused or identified with it.

The cinematic fetish is nowhere more flamboyantly displayed than in Bazin's assertion that the photographic image "is the object itself." However, it manifests itself in other ways, as well, most frequently through the viewer's or theoretician's emphasis upon the existential and analogical bonds tying the image to the object. Comolli suggests that "the extreme eagerness of the first spectators to *recognize* in the images of the first films—devoid of color, nuance, fluidity—the identical image, the double of 'life itself' " came precisely from a "lack to be filled"— from the lack of the object or referent (p. 124). In other words, the desire to perceive similitude where there was as yet scarcely a discernible image speaks to the imperative of finding a surrogate with which to cover over the absent real.

Munsterberg deflects attention away from the object to the subject of the fetishistic exchange when he stresses the necessity for the cinematic text to exist in "perfect isolation" from the viewer. The fetishist relies, as fully as the voyeur, on the maintenance of a distance from that which secures his or her pleasure. Indeed, even outside the cinema, the fetishist always begins as a voyeur, requiring of the erotic prop that it function as a spectacle prior to any tactile convergence. The fetish, as Stephen Heath remarks, is "a brilliance, something lit up, heightened, depicted, as under an arc light, a point of (theatrical) representation; hence the glance: the subject is installed (as at the theatre or at the movies) *for* the representation."[13] Within cinema there are, of course, no tactile convergences, and the gap between viewer and spectacle remains irreducible.

That gap not only promotes fetishism; it also enables the fetishist to ignore his or her stake in the cinematic representation—to conform to Munsterberg's stricture that "the relation of the work to us as persons must not enter into our awareness of it" (p. 69). As I will attempt to demonstrate in a moment, that stricture casts considerable light both on the cinematic fetishist's relation to the "impression of reality" which stands in for the lost real, and on the relation of the male fetishist to woman-as-spectacle.

Castration, disavowal, fetishism: What are we to make of film theory's reliance upon psychoanalysis to account for the absence of the object within the cinematic experience, as well as the viewer's defenses against that absence? And why the constant return to concepts in psychoanalysis which derive their seeming value from the founding moment of sexual difference?

The first of these questions is more easily answered than the second. There is no problem of the object which is not simultaneously a problem of the subject, no loss within cinema which is not also a loss within the viewer. If crisis surrounds the discovery that filmic construction is organized around absence, that is because the spectating subject is organized around the same absence.

The history of the subject who rediscovers him- or herself within cinema unfolds through a series of "splittings" or divisions, many of which turn on the object. Indeed, the case can be even more forcefully stated: These splittings or divisions produce both subject and object, constituting the one in opposition to the other. The child's entry into the symbolic order is made only at considerable cost, not merely through the loss of numerous "parts" of itself, which are relegated to the status of objects, but through the sacrifice of its own being.

The first of these divisions occurs at the mirror stage, where the child arrives at an initial perception of self. That perception is induced through a culturally mediated image which remains irreducibly external, and which consequently implants in the child a sense of otherness at the very moment that identity is glimpsed. At least within the account Lacan offers in "The Mirror Stage,"[14] in which the child catches sight of its actual reflection, that otherness would seem to be compounded by the fact that the child makes its self-discovery through a process of subtraction—through the understanding that it is what is left when a familiar object (e.g., the mother) has been removed. Subjectivity is thus from the very outset dependent upon the recognition of a distance separating self from other—on an object whose loss is simultaneous with its apprehension. (These losses are, of course, experienced only retroactively, from a position within the symbolic. Insofar as the mirror stage could be said to have any emotional "content," it would be that "jubilation" of which Lacan speaks, a "jubilation" which is itself based upon an illusory unity, or—as Jane Gallop encourages us to see it—upon an *anticipation* of self-mastery and a unified identity.)[15]

The child's as yet unsteady grasp of its own boundaries becomes firmer with the severance of various objects it previously experienced as parts of itself—the breast, the feces, the mother's voice, a loved blanket. However, these objects retain their aura of presence even after they have absented themselves, and are consequently described by Lacan as *objets petits autres* (objects with only a little "otherness"). Since these objects are carved out of the subject's own flesh, they attest with unusual force to the terms under which the subject enters the symbolic—to the divisions through which it acquires its identity, divisions which constitute the world of objects out of the subject's own self. Although its full impact will not be felt until later, with the entry into language and the Oedipal matrix, the partitioning off of the part objects from the infant subject is experienced as a castration. Lacan stresses that the *objet (a)* is always "bound to the orifices of the body."[16] It is "something from which the subject, in order to constitute itself, has separated itself off as organ," and which consequently "serves as a symbol of the lack."[17]

The object thus acquires from the very beginning the value of that without which the subject can never be whole or complete, and for which it consequently yearns. At the same time, the cultural identity of the subject depends upon this separation. Indeed, it could almost be said that to the degree that the object has been lost, the subject has been found. Because at this point in the child's history, the object enjoys only a little "otherness," the subject enjoys only a little identity. Further divisions and losses will be necessary before the child can emerge as a coherent cultural subject.

The entry into language is the juncture at which the object is definitively and irretrievably lost, and the subject as definitively and almost as irretrievably found. It is also the occasion for a further sacrifice, that of the subject's own being. These losses are determined by the fact that although signification takes the place of the real, it is in no way motivated by or reflective of what it supplants. The signifier is a non-representative representation.[18]

When we say that language takes the place of the real, we mean that it takes the place of the real for the subject—that the child identifies with a signifier through which it is inserted into a closed field of signification. Within that field of signification, all elements—including the first-person pronoun which seems transparently to designate the subject—are defined exclusively through the play of codified differences. Not one of those elements is capable of reaching beyond itself to reestablish contact with the real. The door thus closes as finally upon the subject's being as upon the object. Lacan conveys the extremity of the opposition between language and the phenomenal realm when he describes it as a choice between meaning and life.[19]

It is this irrecoverability of object to subject, this irreducible distance separating representation from the real, that cinema has often seemed destined to overcome. Siegfried Kracauer describes the "inveterate moviegoer" as someone alienated from the phenomenal world, who hopes to find in the darkened theater what he or she has lost elsewhere—the "crude and unnegotiated presence of natural objects."[20] This imaginary figure, who is a kind of distillate of not only Kracauer's but Bazin's realist aspirations, "traces his suffering . . . to his being out of touch with the breathing world about him, that stream of things and events which, were it flowing through him, would render his existence more exciting and significant. He misses 'life.' And he is attracted to cinema because it gives him the illusion of vicariously partaking of life in its fullness" (p. 169).

The life for which this spectator yearns is, of course, his or her own. Kracauer makes that clear not only through his emphasis upon the cinephile's self-alienation, but through the natal metaphor by means of which he articulates the ideal relationship between the cinematic apparatus and the profilmic event. Films, he writes, conform most rigorously to our dreams when the camera seems as if it has "just now extricated [its objects] from the womb of physical existence and as if the umbilical cord between image and actuality [has] not yet been severed" (p. 164). Kracauer's viewer longs not only for the restoration of this "actuality," but for the return to a presubjective condition, as well. Significantly, the life line leading back to fusion and nondifferentiation is the indexical relation of the camera to its object.

The indexical relation of the camera to the profilmic event has always provided the most reliable guarantee that cinema is in fact capable of restoring the object to the subject. When Bazin celebrates the camera's ability to reproduce what is placed in front of it, and when he argues for the elimination of any human intervention, he leans with all his weight upon that guarantee:

> For the first time, between the originating object and its reproduction there intervenes only the instrumentality of a nonliving agent. For the first time an image of the world is formed automatically, without the intervention of man. . . . All the arts are based on the presence of man, only photography derives an advantage from his absence. Photography affects us like a phenomenon in nature, like a flower or snowflake whose vegetable or earthly origins are an inseparable part of their beauty.
>
> This production by automatic means has radically affected our psychology of the image. The objective nature of photography confers upon it a quality of credibility absent from other picture-making. In spite of any objections our critical spirit may offer, we are forced to accept as real the existence of the object reproduced. (Vol. 1, p. 13)

Despite its utopian fervor, this passage from "The Ontology of the Photographic Image" reveals a complex understanding of the binary relation of subject to referent—of the fact that the presence of the one necessitates the absence of the other, since the former belongs to the symbolic order and the latter to the phenomenal realm. On this occasion Bazin opts for brute materiality over meaning; his nostalgia for the lost object is so intense that he is willing to sacrifice subjectivity in order to secure its restitution. However, lack returns via the route it invariably takes in Bazin—through the recollection that films are edited, and that shot-to-shot relationships usurp those which obtain between the camera and the profilmic event. He is obliged to conclude his essay-dream with the admission that "cinema is also a language" (p. 916).

Cinema thus revives the primordial desire for the object only to disappoint that desire, and to reactivate the original trauma of its disappearance. Since the loss of the object always entails a loss of what was once part of the subject, it is—in the strictest sense of the word—a castration. Metz's use of that concept is consequently neither idiosyncratic nor hyperbolic. Indeed, Serge Leclaire maintains that *castration* is the only correct term with which to designate the break with the real induced by language, since it alone is equal to the task of marking "the radicality of the division between the order of the letter (signifier) and the alterity of the object."[21]

If *castration* is the only word which can properly be applied to the loss of the object induced by signification, and if film is (as even Bazin acknowledges) a language, then disavowal and fetishism would seem as accurately to name certain strategies deployed by classic cinema for concealing that loss. Metz's reliance upon those signifiers has the additional virtue of drawing attention to the fact that when a film covers over the absent real with a simulated or constructed reality, it also makes good the spectating subject's lack, restoring him or her to an imaginary wholeness.

As I suggested at the beginning of this chapter, the lack which haunts film theory proves surprisingly mobile. At the same time, its displacements follow a precise trajectory—a trajectory which proceeds from the loss of the object, to the foreclosed site of production, to the representation of woman as lacking. These orchestrated displacements have as their final goal the articulation of a coherent male subject. Before addressing the second of the questions posed above—the question, that is, as to why film theory accounts for cinema's structuring loss with concepts drawn from Freud's work on sexual difference—some remarks must be made about the foreclosed site of production.

We have seen that the object is definitively lost (and the subject definitively found) at the moment of linguistic access. Cinema replays that drama of phenomenal loss and cultural recovery. Its "unaccustomed perceptual wealth"[22] instills in the viewer the imaginary sense of possession described by one of Kracauer's interviewees, who said that at the cinema "one is, so to speak, like God who sees everything and one has the feeling that nothing eludes you and that one grasps all of it."[23] However, this pleasure of possession is in constant jeopardy; not only are cinema's objects fantasmatic, but they belong to the order of the signifier. Here as elsewhere the operations of meaning exclude the real; the moment the viewer reaches out to claim the profilmic event, it fades to black.

The theoreticians of suture make much of this usurpation—of the transition from a mythical moment in which the spectator enjoys a "dyadic relationship" with the cinematic image, and in which space is "still a pure expanse of *jouissance*," to the congealing of that image into a "frozen letter, which signifies an absence during its advent."[24] However, the theoreticians of suture also take the semiotic analysis one step further, pointing out that cinematic signifiers, like their linguistic counterparts, are activated only within discourse, and that discourse always requires an enunciating agency. Jean-Pierre Oudart and Daniel Dayan emphasize, in short, that films are necessarily spoken.[25]

In the wake of auteurism, and in a reaction against the privileging of the individual voice, film theory has been at pains to distinguish cinema's enunciating agency from the figure of the director or scriptwriter. The result has been a much greater emphasis upon both the productive role of the technological and ideological apparatus, and the strategies for concealing this apparatus from the general view.[26] Filmic articulation has been traced in part to the complex of machines without which it would remain only an abstract possibility, and in part to the specific and nonspecific codes responsible for generating meaning. Since this creative dispersal runs counter to the dominant humanist view of authorship, it is often covered over (both in films and in writing about films) by a harmonizing representation. Because of its close identification with human vision, the camera most often supplies that harmonizing representation,[27] although films as diverse as *Double Indemnity, The Conversation,* and *Blow-Out* suggest that the tape recorder can perform a similar function by virtue of its association with human hearing. Together, these two privileged machines make possible a certain anthropomorphism of the cinematic apparatus, its conceptualization in terms of a transcendental viewer and listener.

However, as Dayan and Oudart stress, not even this reassuring fiction can conceal the fact that cinema's enunciating agency is absent from the filmic construction—that it, like the profilmic object, occupies a different scene from that inhabited by the viewing subject. The point of discursive origin is hidden or veiled; it exceeds the spectator, who lacks any access to it. Oudart refers to cinema's unseen "speaker"—to the foreclosed site of production—as the "Absent One."[28]

This second exclusion manifests itself even before the cut. It is implicit in the single shot—in that element most central to Bazin's theory of realism. Dayan and Oudart argue that as soon as the spectator notices the frame-line, he or she becomes aware of visual constraint, and hence of an unseen agency of control. The spectacle is evacuated of its fullness, becoming an empty signifier for the invisible enunciator. Thus, rather than affecting the viewer "like a phenomenon in nature," the cinematic image attests to artifice and coercion.

The absence of the site of production from the diegetic scene is as potentially disruptive of the viewer's pleasure as is the absence of the object. Dayan suggests that the discovery of a field beyond his or her gaze is experienced as a "dispossession"—as a diminution or loss of visual potency. As I will argue below, that discovery is also conducive to the viewer's sense of auditory insufficiency. Classic cinema's success can be measured by the degree to which it manages to substitute fictional fields for the irretrievably absent one—by the extent to which it manages to construct adequate surrogates.

The shot/reverse shot is generally deemed to be particularly well suited to this purpose, since the second shot purports to show what was missing from the first shot; together the two shots seem to constitute a perfect whole. Moreover, typically one of those shots depicts someone looking, while the other seems to provide the object of the gaze. The shot/reverse shot formation thus simulates the scopic exchange behind the production of cinematic images. It not only supplies an imaginary version of the absent field, but it associates authoritative vision with a fictional character—a character who stands in for the invisible enunciator. The viewer is in this way repossessed of visual (and auditory) potency, assured that his or her gaze suffers under no constraints.

By now it should be apparent that the theoreticians of suture rely as heavily as do Bazin, Metz, and Comolli on the paradigm of castration, disavowal, and fetishism. However, they displace attention away from the absent real to the symbolic order, and the distribution of power within that order. Whereas Bazin, Metz, and Comolli are primarily concerned with the suppression of the object, Oudart and Dayan focus instead on the viewer's exclusion—on his or her alienation from the site of cinematic production. For them the trauma of castration occurs whenever the viewer recognizes his or her discursive impotence, understands that he or she is "only authorized to see what happens to be in the axis of the glance of another spectator, who is ghostly or absent."[29] The disavowal of this lack is always an ideological operation, since it restores the viewer to his or her preordained subject-position and re-secures existing power relations.

We can say, then, that film theory's preoccupation with castration, disavowal, and fetishism is motivated not only by cinema's exclusion of the object, but by its subordination of the spectator to a transcendental Other. It is not merely that classic cinema drops a curtain between the scene of production and the scene of consumption (there are, after all, ways of rewriting the already said and the already shown at the point of reception), but that filmic enunciation is so highly dispersed as to exceed even the authorial subject. Like the symbolic order, only much more palpably, cinematic meaning always carries the trace of the Other. The absence to which film theory almost obsessively returns finds its locus in the viewing subject, a subject who lacks both "actuality" and symbolic mastery.

The first of these losses is disavowed through the "impression of reality" which substitutes for the foreclosed object. The second loss—

what Dayan calls the subject's discursive "dispossession"—is also concealed through a fetish, at least in classic cinema. The viewer's exclusion from the site of cinematic production is covered over by the inscription into the diegesis of a character from whom the film's sounds and images seem to flow, a character equipped with authoritative vision, hearing, and speech. Insofar as the spectator identifies with this most fantasmatic of representations, he or she enjoys an unquestioned wholeness and assurance. What has not yet been adequately acknowledged by the theory of suture is the degree to which the compensatory representation is coded as male.

For Freud, who provides the founding formulation, castration is something the little boy learns to fear only after he has seen the female genitals. Since until that moment he assumes that everyone has a penis, woman's anatomical difference impresses him as a lack or absence. He disavows what he has seen until some later point, when he is threatened with castration if he persists in a forbidden activity. He then recalls and acknowledges the earlier spectacle, resolving the violent emotions it arouses in him through "horror of the mutilated creature or triumphant contempt for her."[30]

The fetishist is described by Freud as a man who remains incapable of accepting woman's lack, and who continues to disavow what he has seen. He substitutes for the missing penis an adjacent object—something which was part of the original "picture" (a shoe, a garment, another part of the female anatomy). As long as this fetish is in place, woman is adequate to his pleasure. She constitutes no challenge to the sexual potency of the male subject because her "difference" has been covered over. However, although the fetish conceals female lack, its presence testifies to the male subject's knowledge of that lack.[31]

It comes as something of a shock to return to the anatomical literalism of the Freudian account of castration, disavowal, and fetishism after exploring the paradigms advanced by film theory. Most startling of all is the sublimation those three concepts undergo in their transfer from the former to the latter—their diversion away from an analysis of sexuality to an analysis of cinema.[32] That sublimation is most striking in Metz, who provides a careful summary of the Freudian argument, but who chooses nonetheless to establish his own formulation on the base of what might be called the Lacanian "revision"—to conceptualize castration, that is, in terms of the various splittings through which the subject is constituted. Moreover, even here Metz appropriates selectively, focusing primarily on those splittings which precede the Oedipal juncture, and hence sexual difference. As we have seen, for him castration designates the loss of the object induced by the cinematic signifier, a loss which catches up and gives meaning to the divisions induced in the subject by the mirror stage, the loss of the object, and the entry into language.

Jacqueline Rose has sharply criticized Metz and Comolli for what she considers to be their misappropriation of the concepts of castration, disavowal, and fetishism, suggesting that it is a strategy for avoiding the whole issue of sexual difference in cinema. She insists upon a return to the Freudian formulation as a means of rectifying this situation:

> To redefine [the concept of disavowal] as the question of sexual difference is necessarily to recognize its phallic reference, how woman is structured as image around this reference and how she thereby *comes to* represent the potential loss and difference which underpins the whole system (and it is the failure to engage with this that is the problem with Metz's and Comolli's work). What classical cinema performs or "puts on stage" is this image of woman as other, dark continent, and from there what escapes or is lost to the system. . . .[33]

Rose here gestures in the direction of a critically important argument for feminism—an argument which has yet to be fully elaborated. She proposes that the lack which preoccupies Metz and Comolli (and by extension Munsterberg and Bazin) is somehow related to the lack which preoccupies Freud—that woman functions within classic cinema as a representation of the losses which precede sexual difference as well as those through which sexual difference is established. Rose intimates, in other words, that the absence which cinema locates at the site of the female body has its origins elsewhere, in the operations of the signifier and the foreclosure of the real.

However, her critique of Metz and Comolli's treatment of cinematic castration overlooks its deconstructive potential—its potential for dislodging woman from the obligatory acting out of absence and lack. By focusing so exclusively on the losses inflicted by the signifier, and by insisting that these losses constitute a castration, Metz and Comolli provide us with the necessary critical distance from the Freudian paradigm to see what it attempts to conceal. They permit us to understand the equation of woman with lack as a *secondary construction,* one which covers over *earlier sacrifices.*

Looking at Freud's theory of castration from the position provided by Metz and Comolli, one is struck by its single-mindedness, its refusal to accommodate any lack except that which it attaches to the female genitals. This refusal seems all the more remarkable in light of the symmetry Freud establishes between the terms *faeces, baby,* and *penis* in "History of an Infantile Neurosis," and his description of each of those objects as " 'a little one' that can be separated from one's own body."[34] This abbreviated account of the *objet (a)* is supplemented by a 1923 footnote to "Analysis of a Phobia in a Five-Year-Old Boy," where Freud once again insists upon restricting the meaning of castration to the absence of the penis:

> It has been urged that every time his mother's breast is withdrawn from a baby he is bound to feel it as a castration (that is to say, as the loss of what he regards as an important part of his own body); that, further, he cannot fail to be similarly affected by the regular loss of his faeces; and, finally, that the act of birth itself (consisting as it does in the separation of the child from his mother, with whom he has hitherto been united) is the prototype of all castration. While recognizing all of these roots of the complex, I have nevertheless put forward the view that the term "castration complex" ought to be confined to those excitations and consequences which are bound up with the loss of the *penis*. (Vol. 10, p. 8)

I would like to suggest that this refusal to identify castration with any of the divisions which occur prior to the registration of sexual difference reveals Freud's desire to place a maximum distance between the male subject and the notion of lack. To admit that the loss of the object is also a castration would be to acknowledge that the male subject is already structured by absence prior to the moment at which he registers woman's anatomical difference—to concede that he, like the female subject, has already been deprived of being, and already been marked by the language and desires of the Other.

Freud's emphasis upon the delayed nature of the castration crisis can be read in a similar way, as a device for protecting the male subject from a painful and culturally disruptive confrontation with his own insufficiency. By granting a retroactive status to the little boy's "recognition" of woman's lack, and by making that recognition the effect of prohibition and threat, Freud implies that the idea of lack is so alien to male consciousness that it must be installed through paternal admonition.

We recall that Freud grants the little girl no such reprieve. At the moment of anatomical unveiling, she "makes her judgement and her decision in a flash. She has seen it and knows that she is without it and wants to have it."[35] However, since she (no more than the little boy) has undergone the loss of the penis, the responses attributed to her by Freud remain inexplicable. It can only be through a cultural intervention analogous to that to which the male subject is exposed that the female subject comes to perceive herself as lacking a privileged organ. Freud admits as much in "Female Sexuality," when he comments on the

female subject's epistemological recalcitrance: "When the little girl discovers her own deficiency, from seeing a male genital, it is only with
hesitation and reluctance that she accepts the unwelcome knowledge"
(vol. 21, p. 223).

The sense of crisis and lack which permeates the little scene described by Freud in "Some Psychical Consequences of the Anatomical
Distinction between the Sexes" and "Fetishism" must consequently be
traced to another source—to the various pre-Oedipal castrations cata-
logued by Lacan, castrations which are realized only retroactively, with
the entry into language. These castrations produce a subject who is
structured by lack long before the "discovery" of sexual difference, a
subject whose very coherence and certitude are predicated on division
and alienation.

Freud's insistence that the little girl experiences a direct and immediate apprehension of what the little boy is obliged to confront only
indirectly and at a later date is extremely telling. So is his stress upon the
defensive mechanisms—disavowal and fetishism—whereby the male
subject can further protect himself from the knowledge of loss. Perhaps
most revealing of all, though, is the malice Freud himself exhibits
toward the female subject in the course of his essay on anatomical
difference—the "triumphant contempt" he encourages the male subject
to entertain for the "mutilated creature" who is his sexual other. This set
of emotions attests to nothing so much as a successfully engineered
projection, to the externalizing displacement onto the female subject of
what the male subject cannot tolerate in himself: castration or lack. As
Freud himself observes elsewhere, once the subject establishes the cause
of anxiety as external to the self, he or she then reacts against it "with
the attempts at flight represented by phobic avoidance."[36]

Significantly, projection is a form of defense closely related to disavowal, in that it is a "refusal to recognize" something which gives
unpleasure. However, whereas within the Freudian scheme disavowal
involves the refusal to recognize an unwanted quality in the other,
projection involves the refusal to be that which evokes unpleasure.[37]
The subject protects itself against this ontological dilemma by separating
off "a part of its self, which it projects into the external world and feels as
hostile."[38] In other words, it undergoes another of those splittings so
necessary to its sense of consistency and wholeness.

Freud's work on paranoia, in the context of which most of his
random remarks about projection are made, suggests that vision and
hearing play a key role in the relocation of an unwanted quality from
the inside to the outside. Visual and auditory hallucinations have a
critically important projective function in "Psychoanalytic Notes on an

Autobiographical Account of a Case of Paranoia" and "A Case of Paranoia Running Counter to the Psychoanalytic Theory of the Disease." In both instances, the projecting subject protects itself against unpleasure by placing the unwanted quality at a visual and/or auditory remove—by making it the object of the scopic and invocatory drives.

Freud's account of the male castration crisis conforms with startling precision to the defensive operation just described. To begin with, that crisis is the occasion of the most dramatic of all the divisions in the history of the subject—of the differentiation of the sexes. For the first time, the little boy apprehends woman as radically and unpleasurably other, as the site of an alien and unwanted quality. He insists upon that otherness by renouncing his Oedipal desires and identifying with the father.

Second, vision provides the agency whereby the female subject is established as being both different and inferior, the mechanism through which the male subject assures himself that it is not he but another who is castrated. As in the case of paranoia, the threatening spectacle is initially unreal and easily disputed (the little boy "begins by showing irresolution and lack of interest; he sees nothing or disavows what he has seen"),[39] but gains authenticity as its exteriority becomes more firmly established.

The exteriority of the alien and unwanted quality is initially in doubt because that quality in fact belongs to the little boy as much as to the little girl. Freud inadvertently points his reader toward this conclusion when he describes the revelation of woman's lack as "uncanny and traumatic,"[40] since in an earlier essay he defines the uncanny as "that class of the frightening which leads back to what is known of old and long familiar."[41] According to the terms of Freud's own argument, if the spectacle of female castration strikes the male viewer as "uncanny," he himself must already have experienced castration; far from functioning merely as an "innocent" (albeit horrified) onlooker, he too inhabits the frame of the unpleasurable image. In other words, the recurrence of the word *uncanny* in the essay on fetishism reminds us that even before the so-called castration crisis, the male subject has an intimate knowledge of loss—that he undergoes numerous divisions or splittings prior to the moment at which he is made to fear the loss of his sexual organ. Thus, what seems to confront him from without, in the guise of the "mutilated" female body, actually threatens him from within, in the form of his own history.

It is hardly surprising, then, that at the heart of woman's otherness there remains something strangely familiar, something which impinges dangerously upon male subjectivity. From the very outset, the little boy is haunted by this similitude—by the fear of becoming like his sexual other. That fear speaks to the "doubling, dividing and interchanging of the self"[42] out of which sexual difference emerges. It indicates that what is now associated with the female subject has been transferred to her from the male subject, and that the transfer is by no means irreversible.

The male subject responds to this threat of (re)contamination with phobic avoidance—by insisting upon the absoluteness of the boundaries separating male from female. Nevertheless, as Kristeva suggests, he will continue to be marked by "the uncertainty of his borders and of his affective valency as well; these are all the more undermining as the paternal function was weak or non-existent, opening the door to perversion or psychosis."[43] Sometimes the male subject is even unable to tolerate the image of loss he has projected onto woman, and is obliged to cover it over with a fetish. However, whether he insists upon sexual difference through phobic avoidance or attempts to conceal that difference with a fetish, he fortifies himself less against the female subject's castration than against his own. The "normal" male subject is constructed through the denial of his lack; he is at all points motivated by a "not wishing to be." In short, what he disavows is his own insufficiency, and the mechanism of that disavowal is projection.

Freud is at great pains to anchor fetishism to female lack—to establish fetishism as a male defense against the female condition of castration. Indeed, he makes the former equation the guarantor of the latter, recommending the study of fetishism to anyone "who still doubts the existence of the castration complex or who can still believe that fright at the sight of the female genital has some other ground—for instance, that it is derived from a supposed recollection of the trauma of birth."[44] However, the use of the adjective *uncanny* to describe the spectacle of woman's castration is not the only symptom of divided authorial belief in the essay on "Fetishism," or the only signpost pointing in a very different direction from the manifest argument.

The famous case history with which the essay begins, for instance, provides a vivid dramatization of that defensive operation whereby the female subject is obliged to bear a double burden of lack. Freud tells us that the fetish in question, a shine on the nose, is actually a disguised reference to a "glance at the nose" (p. 152), and that the substitution of the former for the latter was made possible by the overlapping sounds of the German word *glanz* (shine) and the English word *glance*. However, he fails to remark the externalizing displacement this substitution effects, the shift of attention away from the subject to the object, the look to the spectacle, as the flash of the glance becomes the shine on the nose. A remarkable narrative is elided here, in which male lack is projected onto the image of woman, but returns, "uncanny and traumatic," to trouble his gaze—a narrative, in other words, in which the male subject is shocked into a visual confrontation with his own lack. This return of the repressed necessitates further defensive operations on behalf of male subjectivity, defensive operations designed to construct once again the illusion of an absolute divide separating the viewing subject from the viewed object.

Here, too, Freud's account proves curiously elliptical. The only one of these defensive operations that he is prepared to acknowledge is the fetishistic transaction, and he even moves quickly to close off analysis of it. After a brief summary of the patient's linguistic history, he abruptly concludes that "the nose was the fetish." The conviction with which Freud makes this diagnosis is as surprising as its naive simplicity, since within the preceding discussion the nose figures only as a term which is so complexly mediated by the glance/shine as to be indissociable from it:

> The patient had been brought up in an English nursery but had later come to Germany, where he forgot his mother-tongue almost completely. The fetish, which originated from his earliest childhood, had to be understood in English, not German. The "shine on the nose" [in German *"Glanz auf der Nase"*]—was in reality a *"glance* at the nose." The nose was thus the fetish, which, incidentally, he endowed at will with the luminous shine which was not perceptible to others. (p. 152)

Freud offers an even more exaggerated display of hermeneutic self-assurance in the next paragraph, where he asserts that the fetish itself must always be understood as "a substitute for the woman's (the mother's) penis that the little boy once believed in and—for reasons familiar to us—does not want to give up," and characterizes his interpretation as "natural" and "compelling" (pp. 152–53). This declaration of faith seems especially odd in the context of a disquisition upon the divisions and contradictions to which belief is prone. It is very much in keeping with that disquisition that Freud finds himself impelled, in mid-certitude, to respond to objections that can come only from an internal scene, although he himself attempts to displace them on to an external one ("When now I announce that the fetish is a substitute for the penis, I shall certainly create disappointment; so I hasten to add that it is not a substitute for any chance penis, but for a particular and quite special penis that had been extremely important in early childhood but had later been lost" [p. 152]).

In the face of Freud's own defensive logic—in the face, that is, of such a web of disavowals and projections—I feel impelled to stress once again that the fetish classically functions not so much to conceal woman's castration as to deny man's, and that this goal can be achieved only by identifying lack with what is exclusive to woman, i.e., with her anatomy. Even if we are to assume, with Freud, that in the present instance the fetish is in fact the nose, it does not necessarily follow that the function of this fetish is to compensate for woman's lack. In fact, I would go so far as to suggest the contrary—to argue that the nose-as-fetish functions to secure lack on the side of the female subject. But let us return for a moment to the shine.

As I have already remarked above, the substitution of the *glanz* or shine for the glance shifts attention—and affect—away from the subject to the object, the viewer to the spectacle. It also transfers a certain value from the male to the female subject, so that she comes to occupy the place formerly occupied by him—to stand in for him, and in so doing to cover over his lack. It is thus woman herself who represents the "original" fetish, woman herself who is required to conceal from the male subject what he cannot know about himself. The nose is only a secondary or supplementary fetish, although it remains an important and necessary testament to woman's supposed anatomical "lack," and consequently an additional "buffer" between the male fetishist and his own castration.

Unfortunately for the classic male fetishist, this supplementary fetish is emblazoned with the mark of his own divided belief and, like all fetishes, announces what it attempts to conceal. It is, after all, to paraphrase Freud, not any chance nose, but a particular and quite special nose—a nose lit up with a "luminous shine" which is the mirror image of the gaze that imparts it, and which consequently never stops speaking to the absolute reversibility of male viewer and female spectacle, and hence to the shared lack of subject and object.

The loss of the patient's native English is another symptom pointing to male castration, testifying as it does to the massive repression of his own infantile history, and to the disavowal of those manifold divisions early suffered by both the male and the female subject (one thinks once again here of Freud's reference in the succeeding paragraph to the all-important part played in fetishism by childhood losses, losses which he shows himself so determined to circumscribe within the boundaries of the female body). The phrase with which Freud refers to that language—"mother-tongue"—effects yet another externalizing displacement of castration along lines of sexual difference, and one of profound significance to the present study. With that externalizing displacement, the male fetishist attributes to woman sole knowledge of that language within which lack can be experienced and known. I will have occasion to return to this last projection many times in the next chapter, as I examine the strategies whereby classic cinema divests the female subject of any claim to discursive authority.

Freud attempts to increase the distance between the male subject and castration by associating the fetishist's look with "will," i.e., with volitional creativity, and thus with mastery. However, he collapses this distance—which he produces only by disavowing his own most fundamental discovery, that of the unconscious—through a curious foreclosure. Remarkably, there is not a single reference to woman, either in the abstract or in the particular, throughout the entire paragraph devoted to this unusual fetish; the female subject is completely excluded from Freud's cryptic account of the displacement from the "glance" to the "glanz," in an account within which "the nose" dangles like a disembodied and anonymous organ, unclaimed even by the female possessive pronoun. This exclusion testifies eloquently both to the closed economy and ultimate self-referentiality of male fetishism, and to Freud's own implication in that perversion.

Male lack is even more overtly implied by two of the other fetishes Freud mentions in his essay on that topic—so much so that he comes perilously close to revealing what he is at such pains to conceal. The first of these fetishes is an athletic support-belt, about which Freud has this to say:

> There are many and weighty additional proofs of the divided attitude of fetishists to the question of the castration of women. In very subtle instances both the disavowal and the affirmation of the castration have found their way into the construction of the fetish itself. This was so in the case of a man whose fetish was an athletic support-belt which could also be worn as bathing drawers. This piece of clothing covered up the genitals entirely and concealed the distinction between them. Analysis shows that it signified that women were castrated and that they were not castrated; and it also allowed of the hypothesis that men were castrated, for all these possibilities could equally well be concealed under the belt—the earliest rudiment of which in his childhood had been the fig-leaf on a statue. (pp. 156–157)

This remarkable fetish does more than simultaneously avow and disavow female lack; as Freud himself admits, it also speaks to the possibility of male lack, and it does so in ways that affirm the fundamental identity-in-castration of the male and female subjects. By concealing the genital zone of its female wearer altogether, the athletic belt eliminates the only "evidence" by means of which the fetishist is able to naturalize the relation between woman and lack, and so to disavow his own lack. The abolition of this "distinction" is tantamount to an acknowledgment of male castration.

The second of these examples, with which the essay on "Fetishism" concludes, clearly gives the lie to the notion that the fetish functions to conceal female lack. Freud brings this example forward by way of illustrating a most startling premise—the premise that in some situations the fetish speaks as much to the desire to castrate woman as to deny her castration: "Another variant . . . might be seen in the Chinese custom of mutilating the female foot and then revering it like a fetish after it has been mutilated. It seems as though the Chinese male wants to thank the woman for having submitted to being castrated" (p. 157). There can be little remaining doubt as to what this castration signifies, or what it effects. The foot-binding example foregrounds the motivating desire behind conventional fetishism—the desire to inscribe lack onto the material surface of the female body, and in so doing to construct a fetish capable of standing in for all those divisions and losses suffered by the male subject in the course of his cultural history. That fetish, as must now be perfectly obvious, confers plenitude and coherence only on the male subject. Gratitude, even if it attaches itself erotically to all of woman's "wounds," seems a meager recompense.

Laplanche and Pontalis suggest that one of the psychoanalytic meanings of projection is comparable to the cinematic one, since in both cases "the subject sends out into the external world an image of something that exists in him in an unconscious way." They add that "projection is defined here as a mode of refusal to recognize *(méconnaissance)* which has as its counterpart the subject's ability to recognize in others precisely what he refuses to acknowledge in himself" (p. 354).

At first glance, the comparison seems rather puzzling, since the activities of viewing and projecting are sharply differentiated within the classic cinematic regime. The former are on the side of reception, and the latter on that of (re)production. The spectator is consequently not "responsible" for what he or she sees, at either a conscious or an unconscious level, despite the fact that his or her desires may be quite fully engaged. He or she relies upon an unseen apparatus for the flow of images—upon "a flickering vibration whose imperious thrust grazes our head from behind," and whose "beam of light seems to bore a keyhole for our stupefied gaze to pass through."[45]

It is also unclear how cinema—in either its technological or ideological operations—can be said to involve the viewer in an externalizing displacement of the sort described above. In other words, it remains to be established precisely how the classic filmic text participates in the

projection onto others of those qualities which constitute an unacceptable part of the viewer's own self, particularly since the latter in no way
determines which qualities shall be so projected.

The first of these difficulties vanishes as soon as we remember that
the spectator is always caught up in the flow of cinematic images—as
soon as we recall that films are produced not only for but through the
spectator. Implicit in the reception of the cinematic spectacle is the
viewer's identification not only with the camera, but with the projector
and the screen:

> During the performance the spectator is [a] searchlight . . . duplicating the
> camera, and he is also the sensitive surface duplicating the screen, which
> itself duplicates the film-strip. . . . When I say that "I see" the film, I mean
> thereby a unique mixture of two contrary currents. . . . Releasing it, I am the
> projector, receiving it, I am the screen: in both these figures together, I am
> the camera, which points and yet which records.[46]

The viewer is held in the "pincers" of the cinematic apparatus, and thus
inserted into its technology. Even at the most "primary" level—the level
of the spectator's perceptual relation to the text—watching a film is a
constant process of projection and introjection, of sending out "a sort of
stream called the look" so that "objects can come back up the stream in
the opposite direction."[47]

Film theory has also noted that introjection plays a vital role in
determining the viewer's relation to the diegesis, since "secondary"
identification is effected in large part through the incorporation of
character representations. Those representations are taken into the self,
and provide the basis for a momentary subjectivity—a subjectivity
which is sometimes in contradiction to the spectator's previous structuration, but which is more often sufficiently compatible so as to create
the illusion of continuity. The function of projection within secondary
identification has received less attention. However, I would like to
suggest that it occupies as prominent a place within the representational
system of dominant cinema as does introjection.

Regardless of whether cinematic projection is understood in its most
technological or its most ideological sense, it always both implicates and
exceeds the viewer. In short, it is activated for him or her by an external
agency (the projectionist, the textual system). Cinematic projection
consequently provides an invaluable metaphor for conceptualizing the
involuntary nature of the sexually differentiating projections discussed
above. The latter are no more "willed" than the former. They are the
effect of a constantly renewed Oedipal structuration, which resituates
the loss of the object at the level of the female anatomy, thereby
restoring to the little boy an imaginary wholeness. This externalizing

displacement is further secured through the forced identification of woman with lack. The female subject bears the scar of the castration by which both she and the male subject enter language, granting him the illusion of an as yet intact being.

This is not the only cut the female subject is obliged to display. The coherence of the male subject is threatened as much by the distance that separates him from the phallus as by the distance that separates him from the real. In the former instance, as in the latter, his integrity is established through the projection onto woman of the lack he cannot tolerate in himself. The male subject "proves" his symbolic potency through the repeated demonstration of the female subject's symbolic impotence.

One of the aims of the present discussion is somehow to reverse these displacements—to read the loss and difference associated with the female subject as a symptom of the male condition.[48] Another is to show that classic cinema entertains more than a metaphoric relation to the operations which construct sexual difference: to suggest that dominant film practice actually initiates and orchestrates the burdensome transfer of male lack to the female subject by projecting the projections upon which our current notions of gender depend.

Of course, I do not mean to suggest that cinema constructs sexual difference all by itself. However, I do mean to propose that Hollywood plays more than a reproductive role in the construction of sexual difference. It is no coincidence that the history of cinema has coincided with the ever-increasing specularization of woman. Indeed, I would argue that cinema has contributed massively to what might be called the "revisualization" of sexual difference.

I say "revisualization" because the insistent equation of woman with spectacle and man with vision marks a shift in the general terms of cultural reference which occurred between 1750 and the present. This shift manifests itself in a variety of nineteenth-century discourses, from painting and the novel to psychoanalysis and photography. However, J. C. Flugel suggests that if we want to understand the stakes involved in that transformation, we might well look even earlier, at late-eighteenth-century fashion, which inaugurated a major change in clothing customs.

This change, described by Flugel as "the Great Masculine Renunciation," turned upon the despecularization of the male subject, and consequently (as I will argue below) upon the hyperspecularization of the female subject. After evolving for centuries in the direction of richness and elegance, male clothing underwent a kind of visual "purification," from which it and its wearers emerged chastened and subdued:

At about that time there occurred one of the most remarkable events in the whole history of dress, one under the influence of which we are still living, one, moreover, which has attracted far less attention than it deserves: men gave up their right to all the brighter, gayer, more elaborate, and more varied forms of ornamentation, leaving these entirely to the use of women, and thereby making their own tailoring the most austere and ascetic of arts. . . . Man abandoned his claim to be considered beautiful. He henceforth aimed at being only useful. So far as clothes remained of importance to him, his utmost endeavours could lie only in the direction of being "correctly" attired. . . . henceforward, to the present day, woman was to enjoy the privilege of being the only possessor of beauty and magnificence. . . .[49]

Since Flugel's account of fashion would seem to have more than a little relevance to cinema, it would seem useful to remain with it for a moment or two, and to examine some of his hypotheses.

Flugel explains that "the Great Masculine Renunciation" involved more than the renunciation of male finery; it also entailed the collapse of a whole system of social and class distinctions which both differentiated and separated men from each other. Male clothing underwent a process of democratization, becoming both simpler and more uniform; it ceased to have as its primary function the designation of rank and privilege, and began instead to signify the solidarity between one male subject and all others. Male clothing also came increasingly to signify allegiance to the larger social order, and man's privileged position within that order. As a consequence, writes Flugel, "modern man's clothing abounds in features which symbolize his devotion to the principles of duty, of renunciation, and of self-control. The whole relatively 'fixed' system of his clothing is, in fact, an outward sign of the strictness of his adherence to the social code (though at the same time, due to its phallic attributes, it symbolizes the most fundamental features of his sexual nature)" (p. 113).

In its own way, this passage anticipates the lesson Lacan spent so many years delivering, the lesson that the phallus is not the penis. It does this obliquely, through the statement of a seeming contradiction—through the observation that although over the past two centuries male clothing has aspired increasingly to ideological rectitude, and has consequently detached itself more and more from the male body, it nonetheless continues to construct male sexuality. Modern male sexuality would thus seem to be defined less by the body than by the negation of the body.

Flugel's formulation points to the ways in which that sexuality has been sublimated into a relation with the phallus. The phallus, which at an earlier historical moment seemed to fit as smoothly over the penis as a condom, has undergone a similar abstraction. It no longer seems merely a theatricalization or hyberbolization of the organ it indisputably represents, but has instead become a signifier for symbolic knowledge, power, and privilege. Access to the phallus is still predicated upon possession of the penis, but the relation between the two is increasingly arbitrary, in Saussure's sense of the word, and must be constantly mediated by ideal male representations. All of this is another way of saying that over the past two centuries, the male subject has increasingly dissociated himself from the visible, attempting thereby to align himself with a symbolic order within which power has become more and more dispersed and demuterial.

This dissociation has been no easy matter, for the equation of woman with lack follows only from the identification of man with specularity. The female genitals, in other words, can be defined as a "nothing-to-see" only by contrast with the "strikingly visible" male organ, so that it would seem almost impossible to maintain the former definition while denying the latter. However, through an extraordinary sleight of hand, woman has been made the repository not only of lack but of specularity. She has also come to be identified with two other qualities, narcissism and exhibitionism, which would seem more compatible with male subjectivity—qualities which are almost synonymous with organ display.

According to Flugel, the identification of woman with narcissism and exhibitionism is the result of a series of defensive activities calculated to shield the male subject from himself. He suggests that the male subject protects himself from the specularity which defines him in part by converting it into its opposite, scopophilia, and in part by projecting it onto woman. An erotic contract is thus put in place which binds the male subject complexly to the female subject; not only is she the mechanism by which he establishes his phallic wholeness and adequacy, but she provides the means by which he continues to derive pleasure from what he has ostensibly renounced:

> What has happened to the psychological tendencies (Narcissistic, exhibitionistic, etc.) which formerly found expression in the decorative aspects of [male] dress? . . . In general, it would seem that, when a satisfaction is denied, the desires connected with the satisfaction are either inhibited or displaced. . . . in the case of the exhibitionistic desires connected with self-display, a particularly easy form of conversion may be found in a change from (passive) exhibitionism to (active) scoptophilia . . . the desire to be seen being transformed into the desire to see and know. It is perhaps no mere chance that a period of unexampled scientific progress should have followed the abandonment of ornamental clothing on the part of men at the beginning of the last century.
> Another subtle psychological change may consist in the projection of the exhibitionistic desire on to a person of the opposite sex. . . . In such cases there is clearly some element of identification with woman. (pp. 115–19)

Voyeurism, exhibitionism, narcissism, identification: we are back in familiar territory. This passage from *The Psychology of Clothes* points as emphatically to the continuity between late-eighteenth-century fashion and classic cinema as it does to the discontinuity between late-eighteenth-century fashion and what preceded it. It also encourages us to understand the Great Masculine Renunciation in terms of the female subject it constructs—a female subject who is the mirror reflection not only of the male subject's castration, but of his specularity, exhibitionism, and narcissism.

Cinema challenges the imaginary plenitude of the viewing subject whenever it reveals the fantasmatic basis of its objects—whenever it reenacts the foreclosure of the real from representation. I have indicated how fully this loss absorbs film theory, and the emphasis which is placed there upon the substitution of an "impression of reality" for the absent real. Even more threatening to the subject's coherence is the disclosure of the cinematic signifier, since that disclosure not only finalizes the rupture with the phenomenal realm, but draws attention to the invisible enunciator—to the fact, that is, that films and their spectators are spoken by an unseen Other. Film theory has shown itself to be equally sensitive to this absence, and to the strategies developed by classic cinema to cover it over.

However, at no point in either of these extended theoretical discussions has it been noted that the lack which must somehow be disavowed not only structures male subjectivity as much as female subjectivity, but poses a far greater danger to the stability of the former than to that of the latter. Since the female subject is constructed through an identification with dispossession, her exposure to further castrations jeopardizes nothing. The male subject, on the contrary, is constructed through an identification with the phallus. That identification may be threatened by the disappearance of the object, but it is capsized by any reminder of the male subject's discursive limitations. It is impossible for a subject who knows himself to be excluded from authoritative vision, speech, and hearing to sustain a pleasurable relation to the phallus.

Nor has either of these theoretical explorations suggested that there might be an important connection between the losses which structure cinema and the representation of woman as lacking. This omission is particularly striking in the case of Oudart and Dayan, since the system of suture works precisely through the articulation of sexual difference. As I have argued elsewhere,[50] the most paradigmatic of all shot/reverse shot formations is that which aligns the female body with the male gaze. This two-shot not only covers over the absent site of production, but places the male subject on the side of vision, and the female subject on the side of spectacle. Moreover, insofar as the apparatus is anthropomorphized (insofar as the camera is associated with human sight and the tape recorder with human hearing), it assumes a paternal shape. The complex involvement of classic cinema in the articulation of sexual difference can best be demonstrated through a brief examination of yet another corpus of film theory preoccupied with the notion of lack.

Since the publication of Laura Mulvey's "Visual Pleasure and Narrative Cinema" in 1976, feminist film theory has focused a good deal of attention on the coding of the female subject as inadequate or castrated within dominant cinema.[51] That theory has also looked closely at the potential for trauma contained within the spectacle of woman-as-lack, and at the defensive mechanisms made available to the viewer as a shield against that lack.

Curiously, the scenario described by Mulvey conforms much more rigorously to the original psychoanalytic paradigm of castration and crisis than do those of Metz and Comolli, or Oudart and Dayan. Like Freud's little boy, cinema's male viewer finds the vision of woman's lack threatening to his own coherence, and fears that he will become the victim of a similar deprivation. According to Mulvey, classic cinema offers two possible resolutions of this crisis: disavowal through fetishism, and avowal accompanied by disparagement. According to the first of these resolutions, an item of clothing or another part of the female anatomy becomes the locus of a compensatory investment, and substitutes for the organ which is assumed to be missing. The second of these resolutions has a very different end result, since instead of deflecting attention away from one part of the body to another, it shifts the focus from woman's "outside" to her "inside." That transfer is effected through an investigation, which "reveals" that the female subject has either committed a crime for which she has to be punished, or suffered from a crippling illness. Since in either case woman's castration can be traced back to her own interiority, this resolution of the male viewer's anxiety permits him to place a maximum distance between himself and the spectacle of lack—to indulge in an attitude of "triumphant contempt" for the "mutilated creature" who is his sexual other.

Its greater conformity to the Freudian formulation is not the only way in which Mulvey's account of cinematic castration deviates from those of the other theoreticians discussed here. An equally important and closely related deviation is that whereas Metz, Comolli, Oudart, and Dayan all emphasize the suturing effects of narrative—its capacity for covering over or making good cinema's various organizing absences— Mulvey locates the moment of loss inside the narrative. She displaces attention away from the extradiegetic castrations recounted by the others to one that occurs within the diegesis. Mulvey proposes, in other words, that the "impression of reality" with which dominant cinema compensates for the absent real and effaces its own status as discourse relies upon a restaging of the drama of loss. What are we to make of this compulsion to repeat, this return of the repressed? And how are we to account for the paradoxical recourse to representations of lack with which to dispel the specter of an existential lack?

The first thing that must be said is that the narrative formulation is a repetition with a number of striking differences. The most important of these differences is that Mulvey's viewer, unlike that presumed by Metz, Comolli, Oudart, and Dayan, occupies a specifically masculine position. This viewer—whether in fact a man or a woman—identifies with the look of the male protagonist, experiencing with him the anxiety of castration and the pleasure of its neutralization.[52] Another difference within the narrative repetition is that whereas the spectator described by the other theoreticians disavows the loss of something which was earlier perceived as part of the self, whether it be the object or discursive potency, that described by Mulvey seems to disavow another's lack. The source of unpleasure is externalized in the form of the female body. It can be seen (and heard).

However, despite its apparent exteriority, this lack proves profoundly disturbing to the male viewer, in whom it inspires anxiety and fear. He experiences woman's wound as an assault upon his own subjectivity, a threat of like retribution. The violence of this reaction and the extremity of the measures which must be taken to neutralize it suggest that the image of woman reflects "something which ought to have remained hidden but has come to light." Far from exposing the male viewer to the "new and alien," that image would seem to confront him with "something familiar and old-established [in his mind] . . . which has become alienated from it through the process of repression."[53]

We would seem to be face to face with another sexually differentiating projection—with an externalizing displacement of the kind unwittingly articulated by Freud's writings on the castration crisis. Here, as there, an unwanted part of the self is shifted to the outer register, where it can be mastered through vision. And here, as there, the projected image returns to trouble the male subject. However, the situation elaborated by Mulvey occurs well after the subject's entry into the symbolic, and is precipitated not only by the loss of the real and the renunciation of Oedipal desire, but by the "encumbrance" of the phallus—by the weight of that signifier in relation to which the male subject can never be adequate.

Although the phallus is naturalized through its imaginary alignment with the penis, it is never more or less than a distillate of the positive values at the center of a historically circumscribed symbolic order. Those values stubbornly resist embodiment, designating a grammatical rather than an existential position—the place occupied by the name rather than the body of the father. Each of the dominant discourses which make up the larger symbolic order helps to define and localize the phallus by "imagining" or "fantasizing" a speaking subject—a subject authorized to command that discourse's power-knowledge. The phallus is in effect the sum of all such speaking subjects.

Like the phallus, the speaking subject is a symbolic figuration which always exceeds the individuals defined by it. That is particularly evident in the case of classic cinema, where enunciation is as much an effect of the ideological and technological apparatus as of any human intervention. Indeed, as I have already noted, the theoreticians of suture refer to classic cinema's enunciating agency not as the director but as the "Absent One."[54] The speaking subject—and so by implication the phallus—is here equivalent to this unseen enunciator, and to the attributes (transcendental vision, hearing, and speech) by which it is defined.

The exclusion of classic cinema's viewer from the point of discursive origin is thus simultaneously an isolation from the phallus. Every reminder of the foreclosed site of production draws attention to that isolation, revealing the gulf separating the male spectator from the paternal signifier upon which he relies for his cultural identity. Indeed, since every frame-line and cut constitute potential reminders of that hidden scene, the classic film poses a constant threat to the very subjectivity it wishes to consolidate.

I would argue that the castration crisis diagnosed by Mulvey can proceed only from this source—that in the final analysis it is the male viewer's own exclusion from the site of filmic production rather than the spectacle of woman's anatomical "lack" which arouses such anxiety and fear in him. As with the foreclosed real, classic cinema musters numerous defenses against this castration, both "primary" and "secondary." (To the former category belong all those defenses mounted directly against the male subject's lack. The second category contains all those defenses which, like those discussed by Mulvey, seem to bear upon woman's lack, but which in fact bear indirectly upon male lack.)

Ideal representations play a key role here. The male subject is protected against the knowledge of his discursive insufficiency through the inscription into the diegesis of phallic characters with whom he is encouraged to identify—characters equipped with the phallic attributes of the "Absent One" (i.e., with the capacity to look creatively, speak authoritatively, and capture and coerce the speech of others). However, projection plays an even more important part, since the male viewer can effect these pleasurable introjections only if he is able to disburden himself of the various losses which organize his subjectivity—if he is able to displace his discursive lack onto woman.

Once again, classic cinema engineers this projection for him. Through its endless renarrativization of the castration crisis, it transfers to the female subject the losses which afflict the male subject. It also arms him against the possible return of those losses by orchestrating a range of defensive operations to be used against the image of woman, from disavowal and fetishism to voyeurism and sadism. In this way the trauma which would otherwise capsize the male viewer is both elicited and contained.

But what does all of this entail for the female viewer, presuming that she, like the male viewer, is structured by secondary identification, and that secondary identification at least to some degree proceeds along lines of sexual difference? Above all, I want to stress that although woman's castration is always anatomically naturalized within Hollywood films, what this castration in fact entails is her exclusion from symbolic power and privilege. That exclusion is articulated as a passive relation to classic cinema's scopic and auditory regimes—as an incapacity for looking, speaking, or listening authoritatively, on the one hand, and with what might be called a "receptivity" to the male gaze and voice, on the other. Thus, the female subject's gaze is depicted as partial, flawed, unreliable, and self-entrapping. She sees things that aren't there, bumps into walls, or loses control at the sight of the color red. And although her own look seldom hits its mark, woman is always on display before the male gaze. Indeed, she manifests so little resistance to that gaze that she often seems no more than an extension of it.

Woman's words are shown to be even less her own than are her "looks." They are scripted for her, extracted from her by an external agency, or uttered by her in a trancelike state. Her voice also reveals a remarkable facility for self-disparagement and self-incrimination—for putting the blame on Mame. Even when she speaks without apparent coercion, she is always spoken from the place of the sexual other.

Classic cinema's female subject is the site at which the viewer's discursive impotence is exhumed, exhibited, and contained. She is what might be called a synecdochic representation—the part for the whole— since she is obliged to absorb the male subject's lack as well as her own.

The female subject's involuntary incorporation of the various losses which haunt cinema, from the foreclosed real to the invisible agency of enunciation, makes possible the male subject's identification with the symbolic father, and his imaginary alignment with creative vision, speech, and hearing. Indeed, not only is woman made to assume male lack as her own, but her obligatory receptivity to the male gaze is what establishes its superiority, just as her obedience to the male voice is what "proves" its power.

The diegetic drama of castration described by Mulvey is thus a simulation of the crisis which occurs whenever the male viewer is reminded of his visual and verbal subordination to cinema's absent enunciator—a simulation which covers over that other scene of castration with its representations of phallic men and wounded women. Because it restages what happens elsewhere, in both the history of the subject and the production of the cinematic text, Hollywood's diegetic organization can perhaps best be characterized by a phrase from Bazin: it is "a mirror with a delayed reflection, the tin foil of which retains the image" of earlier losses.[55] It is scarcely necessary to add that woman is the foil.

It would seem a not altogether implausible assumption that among that category of films generally deemed "reflexive," there might be one or two in which this mirror relation is reversed—in which the obsessive self-referentiality works to uncover the pathology of male subjectivity. Hitchcock's *Rear Window* (1954), Antonioni's *Blow-Up* (1967), and Jim McBride's *David Holzman's Diary* (1967) are titles that might be invoked here. However, it is through the mediating details of a fourth film, Michael Powell's *Peeping Tom* (1960), that I would like to pursue my diagnosis.

Peeping Tom gives new emphasis to the concept of reflexivity. Not only does it foreground the workings of the apparatus, and the place given there to voyeurism and sadism, but its remarkable structure suggests that dominant cinema is indeed a mirror with a delayed reflection. It deploys the film-within-a-film trope with a new and radical effect, making it into a device for dramatizing the displacement of lack from the male to the female subject.

There are, in fact, two films-within-the-film. The first, which was completed by the now-deceased Dr. Lewis (Michael Powell) some twenty years prior to the diegetic present, offers a "scientific" record of his son's childhood, with particular emphasis on moments of fear, loss, and sexual crisis. Completely traumatized by his father's experiments, Mark Lewis (Carl Boehm) attempts as an adult to master that trauma by making a film of his own, which constitutes the second film-within-the-film.

Although both films purport to be documentaries, each is shown to be elaborately staged. Not only does Dr. Lewis orchestrate the crises he then photographs, but these crises are all key moments within the Oedipal narrative (the castration threat, the primal scene, the loss of the mother, and access to the paternal legacy, here represented by the gift of a camera). Throughout these various episodes, the emphasis falls on the father's punishing power and on the son's lack (this is true even at the moment of seeming phallic transmission, since the father's camera remains conspicuously trained on the son's). That lack is dramatically figured here by Mark's exclusion from the site of discursive production—by the evident fact that his meaning comes to him from elsewhere. By constantly turning his camera on his son, Dr. Lewis firmly locates him on the side of the spectacle, within the boundaries of the filmic fiction. Although Mark's position is thus analogous to that of any diegetic character within classic cinema, it is clearly shown to be incompatible with the "phallic function,"[56] and to necessitate extreme defensive measures. Here those measures take the form of Mark's own "documentary," which performs an analogous displacement to that engineered by Hollywood, obliging woman once again to assume a double burden of lack.

This second film is consequently equally constrained by Oedipal imperatives—by the imperatives of male adequacy. It casts an inverted reflection of the first, manifesting the same obsessive interest in trauma, but now situating Mark outside the fiction, on the side of apparent discursive control. This shift is effected by inserting a series of prostitutes and models into the specular position Mark occupies in Dr. Lewis's film, and by subjecting them to a lethal castration.

Mark's relationship with these women is insistently mediated by the camera; from the moment that he first sights one of them as a bridge to phallic identification, he never looks away from the view finder, thereby indicating the central role played by the cinematic apparatus in the desired psychic transaction. In each case, he films his victim in an attitude of erotic display which facilitates the inscription of lack onto the female body at precisely that point where Freud would have it be found. (Thus, the key moment in the erotic display of the nameless prostitute is when she separates her legs to remove her stockings. In the case of Vera it is the spreading of her trousered legs as she dances. Millie proves even more cooperative by wearing a corset whose *v*-shaped lower edge sharply demarcates the looked-for site of absence.)

Mark then films his victims as he kills them. The conflation of these two actions is reiterated by the murder weapon, which is itself a part of the apparatus—a knife at the end of one of the tripod legs. Significantly, Mark forces the women to look at their own faces in a mirror as he stabs them in the throat—to see their own fear, pain, and loss, just as his father's films have obliged him to see his own.[57] The mirror also functions to disavow male lack even further by suggesting that the female subject reflects only herself, and so denying the place of the male subject within the mimetic circuit.

The scene in which castration is most successfully localized at the female body, and in which the fiction of the coherent and intact male subject is consequently best promoted, is the one where Mark encounters a woman with a grotesque harelip. This encounter takes place during a pornographic photography session, and it generates an eroticism which has until then been conspicuously missing. As soon as Mark sees Dora, the deformed model, he exchanges his commercial camera for the one with which he always shoots his "documentary" footage, and begins rhapsodically interrogating her face with it. Earlier in the same session, Millie, the other model, asks Mark to shoot her in such a way as to conceal her bruises, and he automatically complies. Now, however, the "bruise" is the site of libidinal investment, and Mark has eyes for nothing but it and the psychic pain it elicits in its wearer. Significantly, the facial contortion caused by Dora's harelip makes her look very much like the twisted faces reflected in the mirror attached to Mark's camera. Confronted with this spectacle, he is like the Chinese fetishists of whom Freud speaks, transfixed with gratitude to Dora for thus openly displaying the "mark" of castration.

The opening shot of *Peeping Tom* introduces what will be a recurrent motif in the murder sequences—a series of images seen through the cross hairs of the view finder. This motif conveys the usual message that we are looking at a "subjective shot," but it also functions as a powerful metaphor for the barrier Mark tries to erect between himself and his victims so as to dissociate himself from them, and thereby consolidate his own claim to the paternal legacy. Here, too, Mark's project converges with classic cinema, which also turns upon the fiction that an irreducible distance isolates the viewer from the spectacle. As Heath points out, what is at stake in both cases is a "structure of fetishism":

> Separation is the mode of . . . classic cinema; the very mode of representation. The structure of representation is a structure of fetishism: the subject is produced in a position of separation from which he is confirmed in an

imaginary coherence (the representation is the guarantee of his self-coherence) the condition of which is the ignorance of the structure of his production, of his setting in position.[58]

Peeping Tom makes abundantly clear that this structure works to conceal male rather than female lack, and to promote the imaginary coherence of the male rather than the female subject. It does this by indicating the permeability of the barrier Mark sets in place, and the precarious instability of his projections.

Perhaps the most striking demonstration of the reversibility of Mark's projections occurs during the scene in which he gives Helen a lizard brooch, thereby attempting to locate her in the position he occupied as a child when his father dropped a live lizard into his bed. As Helen tries to decide where to pin the brooch, moving it around on her dress, voyeurism gives way to identification, and Mark fascinatedly mimics her gestures. However, it is while screening his "documentary" footage that he most consistently crosses the barrier he has been at such pains to construct, slipping over to the side of the victim.

Twice while watching that footage, Mark literally crosses the imaginary dividing line separating viewer from spectacle; rising from his chair, he walks over to the image of a woman experiencing the anguish of death, and places his face against the screen. This physical relocation dramatically attests to the collapse of the fetishistic structure of classic cinema. Far from maintaining the requisite distance from the image of woman-as-lack, Mark recognizes himself in that image, and tips over into it. As he does so, a remarkable transformation occurs, which is more than a little reminiscent of the glance/*glanz* example. Suddenly the beam of the projector lamp no longer irradiates the spectacle for the viewing subject (Mark); it illuminates him, as well. In so doing it functions much like the flashlight his father used to turn on him as a child. When Mark cries out that "the lights faded too soon," he speaks not only to his failure to produce technically good footage of Vera's murder, but to his failure to sustain that externalizing displacement which converts the paternal flashlight into the son's projector lamp, and the image into the gaze. He speaks, in other words, to his inability to project the projections necessary to disburden himself of lack—to his inability to transfer "the shine" from himself to woman.

On two different screening occasions, Mark tries to protect himself against the return of his own lack by directing his klieg lights onto a female companion's face, and by supplementing the projector with the camera. On the first of these occasions, Helen is the companion, and Marks tells her that he wants to film her watching his father's "documentary." His action would seem to be motivated in part by the desire to shift Helen from the side of vision to the side of visibility, and so to assert his sole claim to the former position. It would also seem to be prompted by the desire to capture on Helen's face that expression of fear for which he searches in his victims' faces.

However, he employs a very different "mirror" for that purpose here than he does on the other occasion. As I suggested a moment ago, the reflecting device Mark attaches to his camera shows his female victims only the image of their own fear, and so seems to deny any external point of reference. In this scene, on the contrary, Helen is presented with that image of which the others are only delayed reflections. Although Mark attempts to photograph her watching face rather than the footage of his own childhood, and so to repeat the by now all-too-familiar pattern of deflecting attention away from male to female pain and distress, it should also be noted that in so doing he opens to her a possibility he denies all of the other women in the film—the possibility of understanding her own status as a symptom of male lack. Finally, one would have to say that this scene, like the one involving the lizard brooch, attests as profoundly to Mark's identification with Helen as it does to his desire to differentiate himself from her. Not only does he admit her into the screening room, and place her in his customary viewing seat, but his unsuccessful attempt to film her watching face is obviously motivated at some level by his desire to film his own watching face. (This reading is reinforced by a subsequent scene, in which Helen also figures centrally—a scene in which Mark probes his own face with the lens of his camera.)

Helen's mother, Mrs. Stephens (Maxine Audley), is the second woman to be subjected to the klieg lights in Mark's screening room. She goes there in search of information about the films he watches every night, but since she is blind, her search is necessarily mediated by language. "Take me to your cinema," she commands Mark, who literally complies by leading her over to the screen upon which he is projecting the images of Vera's death. Once they arrive there, however, he becomes too engrossed in his film to attend to her increasingly agitated demands for knowledge, tearing himself away from it only when he recognizes the flaws in its cinematography ("the lights faded too soon").

It is at this point, in the throes of anguish over what he describes as a "lost opportunity," but which I will call a failed displacement, that Mark decides to embark upon another lethal photography session. He replaces the projector with the camera, and pins Mrs. Stephens against the screen with the studio lights, in a startling conflation of two sites—the sites of production and consumption—which are traditionally maintained in a state of complete isolation from each other. Mark's sudden felt need to align himself in a single moment with the entire cinematic apparatus attests to a powerful desire for unity and simultaneity, and functions as a protest against the divisions within both cinema and subjectivity, as well as what might be called their "retroactivity." It also speaks to the impossible dream of complete self-mastery. By implicitly equating that dream with the fantasy of total cinematic control, this scene discloses the abyss that separates the male subject from the phallus. Due to the irony of Mrs. Stephens's blindness, Mark is unable even to deploy his mirror, and is thus thrown back upon his own lack.

In the concluding moments of *Peeping Tom*, Mark acknowledges the splits and losses that have structured his subjectivity and directs against himself the whole battery of weapons he has until then reserved for his female victims—camera, mirror, sharpened tripod knife. In a stunning reprise of all the many textual references to light, Mark times numerous flashbulbs to shine on him at half-second intervals as he levels the psychic barrier separating himself from the female subject, and embraces his own castration.

I would argue that it is not so much the film's preoccupation with voyeurism and murder as its refusal to be complicit in a general cultural disavowal of male lack which provoked such hostility from the popular press at the time of its original release. The reviews are revealingly saturated with references to excrement ("The only really satisfactory way to dispose of *Peeping Tom* would be to shovel it up and flush it swiftly down the nearest sewer"; "*Peeping Tom* stinks more than anything else in British Films since *The Stranglers of Bombay*"; "I was shocked to the core to find a director of his standing befouling the screen with such perverted nonsense"),[59] suggesting intense anxiety about the possible leakage back into a "clean" and "proper" space of what has been thrown violently outside it. Ironically, as I have already indicated, *Peeping Tom* makes boundaries and limits an important part of its meta-critical narrative, showing them to be no more than the temporary trace left behind by projections which must be endlessly repeated, and which are by no means irreversible. However, as Ian Christie points out, "What is conspicuously absent from the reviews . . . is any sense of *recognition*" of the film's relation to either classic cinema or orthodox subjectivity.[60]

The critical defense most frequently mounted against *Peeping Tom* at the time of its original release was to relegate it and its admirers to the category of psychic abnormality. Movie audiences were warned that it "displays a nervous fascination with the perversion it illustrates," that it "wallows in the diseased urges of a homicidal pervert," and that "sick minds will be highly stimulated." Only one reviewer, Isobel Quigly, was prepared to acknowledge that the film attempts to engage its viewer on familiar ground, and her response is consequently worth quoting at some length:

> *Peeping Tom* didn't make me want to streak out of the cinema shrieking . . . it gives me the creeps in retrospect, in my heart and mind more than in my eyes. We have had glossy horrors before . . . but never such insinuating, under-the-skin horrors, and never quite such a bland effort to make it look as if this isn't for nuts but for normal homely filmgoers like you and me.[61]

What is immediately surprising about this passage is its preoccupation with spectatorship. Instead of disavowing her own relation to the film, as the other reviewers were so quick to do, Quigly focuses upon the ways in which *Peeping Tom* destabilized her by triggering a responsive tremor within her own subjectivity. She stresses not only its "under-the-skin horrors," but its capacity for generating "creeps in retrospect." Both of these phrases have a curious resonance, which reverberates once again in her admission that the film takes as its point of address "normal homely filmgoers like you and me." If the emphasis upon interiority and delayed effectivity are not enough to alert the reader to the uncanny nature of Quigly's viewing experience, the adjective *homely* dispels all doubt. The juxtaposition of this adjective with "creeps in retrospect" and "under-the-skin horrors" suggests that if *Peeping Tom* traumatizes and unsettles the viewer, that is because it forces a confrontation with "that class of the frightening which leads back to what is known of old and long familiar."

I have discussed some of the ways in which classic cinema organizes its flow of images so as to protect the male subject against precisely this sort of unpleasurable self-encounter, but so far I have referred only in the most cursory fashion to the ways in which classic cinema organizes its vocal/auditory regime for the same ends. The moment has finally come to pose that question to which this book comes as a partial answer. What about the voice (and ear)? How does classic cinema engender sound?

In the immediately following chapters, I will attempt to demonstrate that Hollywood requires the female voice to assume similar responsibilities to those it confers upon the female body. The former, like the latter, functions as a fetish within dominant cinema, filling in for and covering over what is unspeakable within male subjectivity. In her vocal, as in her corporeal, capacity, woman-as-fetish may be asked to represent that phenomenal plenitude which is lost to the male subject with his entry into language. However, the female voice, like the female body, is more frequently obliged to display than to conceal lack—to protect the male subject from knowledge of his own castration by absorbing his losses as well as those that structure female subjectivity.

The female voice is made the recipient of this double burden of lack through defensive measures similar to those which install woman so firmly on the side of visibility. Here, as there, the difficulty which must somehow be resolved is the male subject's discursive impotence—his exclusion from the point of textual origin. And here, as there, the solution turns upon displacement and reenactment: upon the transfer of enunciative power and authority from the site of production to a fictional male voice, and upon a hyperdramatization of woman's symbolic castration. Otherwise stated, the male subject is protected from unpleasurable self-knowledge through a fictional redrawing of the diegetic boundaries, a redrawing which situates him in a position of apparent proximity to the cinematic apparatus, while firmly reiterating the isolation of the female voice from all productivity. This opposition expresses itself through the close identification of the female voice with spectacle and the body, and a certain aspiration of the male voice to invisibility and anonymity. At its most crudely dichotomous, Hollywood pits the disembodied male voice againts the synchronized female voice.

Since *Peeping Tom* elevates spectacle to the place of reflexive primacy, it seems at first glance to have little to say about sound. Indeed, a Nagra is not even among the pieces of movie equipment Mark obsessively manipulates. It would consequently seem a curious example with which to conclude this chapter. In fact, however, *Peeping Tom* levels as sustained if not as direct an attack upon classic cinema's acoustic regime as it does upon classic cinema's visual regime, showing it to be based upon the same phallic pathology. What makes this critique the more remarkable of the two is that it never replicates its object. Because Mark's "documentary" consists exclusively of an image track, Hollywood's sound regime is present in it only as a structuring absence. This fact is emphasized rather than concealed by the extradiegetic music which accompanies the documentary each time it is screened, because that music evokes a silent-movie-house piano. At the same time, Mark's images of terrified and dying women seem calculated to produce precisely that sound which, as I will attempt to demonstrate in a subsequent chapter, Hollywood is at the greatest pains to extract from the female voice, i.e., the cry. (One thinks here of *Psycho*, released only a year before *Peeping Tom*, which enshrines a musically simulated version of that sound, or of the more recent *Blow-Out* [1981], which turns upon the search for a "realistic" female scream.) Because Mark's "documentary" fails to give us the usual sound analogue to the images it shows, it obliges us to look elsewhere for it. We are consequently directed back to Dr. Lewis's film, and through it to the scene of male subjectivity. Once again, Powell's film suggests that dominant cinema is a mirror with a delayed reflection—only this time the mirror is acoustic.

Although Dr. Lewis's "documentary" is also projected without sound, it has an audio track of sorts. His "files" on the instinct of fear include a large number of tapes, the record of an elaborate surveillance system which enabled him to tune in whenever he wanted to any room in the house. We learn about the existence of these tapes only at the very end of the film, when Mark plays a recording of screams from his childhood to Helen. However, we are alerted to the fact that something is being withheld from us as early as the first screening of Dr. Lewis's documentary, when a paternal voice abruptly intrudes with the words: "That will do, Mark. Dry your eyes and stop being a silly boy." By drawing our attention in this way to the limits of the image track, which is insufficient by itself to account for the reprimand, that voice makes us aware of a sound we are prevented from hearing.

Mark's censorship of these tapes is puzzling, given the alacrity with which he shows the corresponding footage. The fact that he produces them only after he abandons all defenses against his own symbolic castration suggests that they represent an even more psychically intolerable memory than the images, and that they have been the object of a powerful repression. This repression suggests that the voice is capable of manifesting an even greater vulnerability than the body.

At first the admonitory male voice seems to come from Dr. Lewis, and to represent him as pure phallus—disembodied, unlocalized, omniscient, and omnipotent. However, not only is it denaturalized through microphone reverberation, but it is clearly shown to initiate from outside the "documentary," since the latter has been projected without sound. We are therefore given no alternative but to read it as an auditory hallucination, and in so doing to entertain the possibility that this exemplary paternal inscription may never be more than a fantasmatic construction put in place as a defense against the involuntary male cry. That construction collapses like a deck of cards at the end of the film, when Mark not only turns his lights and camera on himself, but adds a sound track to his "documentary" by synchronizing his death with the tapes of his childhood screams.

Because *Peeping Tom* evacuates woman from the center of Mark's horror film, it permits the female viewer to see what her voice and image have been made to conceal, and so to adopt a different position in front of the cinematic "mirror" from that prescribed for her by Hollywood. Helen and her mother dramatize two of the possible discursive relationships which are thus opened up for the female spectator. Mrs. Stephens's response falls under the category of refusal; having grasped the pathological bases of Mark's cinema, she turns away from both it and him, urging him to get "help." Helen, on the other hand, is possessed by the desire to understand the ways in which male subjectivity has been organized. She continues going to the cinema, because she knows the symptoms she is looking for are there, and in the darkened theater she never removes her eyes from the images. However, she talks to herself incessantly during the screenings, interrogating, interjecting, interrupting, until the familiar grows strange, and the strange familiar. She finds herself inside and outside Mark's cinema at the same time, recognizing that she is a part of that cinema, but speaking all the same from elsewhere, with her mother's diagnostic tongue. Perhaps, although I am not certain of this, she believes that her own history—past, present, and future—cannot be separated from that of the male subject. Finally, for all of these reasons, she decides to write a book about the apparatus.

I am, of course, talking here about myself as much as about Helen—like her book, mine is motivated by the desire to look beyond the sounds and images that have constructed my subjectivity to what those sounds and images serve to conceal: male castration. Thus, although on one level this book is a study of the female voice in cinema, on another it is an investigation of the verbal and auditory defenses by means of which Hollywood fortifies the male subject against his own losses.

To approach woman as a symptom, as I will do in the next two chapters, is not to suggest that she is no more than the afterimage of male subjectivity. She may be, as Foucault has said of man, an invention of recent date, but that invention will be far more difficult to erase than "a face drawn in sand at the edge of the sea."[62] Woman is inscribed not only on celluloid and on the surfaces of the male subject's imaginary register, but in the psychic, material, and social conditions of the female subject's daily existence.

[2]

BODY TALK

THE SOUNDTRACK has had a curious theoretical history. Notoriously passed over in favor of the image, it has nonetheless consistently figured as what Marianne Moore would call the "real toad" in cinema's imaginary garden, somehow conjuring belief long after the visual *vraisemblable* has curled and faded. Over and over, film theory has assured us that there is no difference between recorded and prerecorded sounds—that the apparatus is miraculously capable of capturing and retransmitting the profilmic event in all its auditory plenitude, without diminution or distortion. Thus, Béla Balázs writes that "there is no difference in dimension and reality between the original sound and the recorded and reproduced sound as there is between real objects and photographic images,"[1] Metz argues that "auditory aspects, providing that the recording is well done, undergo no appreciable loss in relation to the corresponding sound in the real world,"[2] and Baudry asserts that "in cinema—as in all talking pictures—one doesn't hear an image of the sounds but the sounds themselves."[3] And with each new testimonial to the authenticity of recorded sound, cinema seems once again capable of restoring all phenomenal losses.

Of course, the theoretical conflation of recorded with prerecorded sounds has not gone unchallenged. Recently, Alan Williams and Tom Levin have both argued that since every acoustic event is inseparable from the space within which it occurs, it is difficult for any two sounds ever to be exactly the same, and impossible when a microphone mediates access to one of those sounds.[4] Williams suggests that cinema provides us at best with only a "sample" or "reading" of the profilmic auditory event, and that the act of listening to a film is consequently as fully structured as the act of viewing a film:

In sound recording, as in image recording, the apparatus performs a significant perceptual work *for us*—isolating, intensifying, *analyzing* sonic and
visual material. It gives an implied physical perspective on image or sound
source, though not the full, material content of everyday vision or hearing,
but *the signs* of such a physical situation. We do not hear, we are heard.
More than that: we accept the machine as organism, and its "attitudes" as
our own.[5]

However, it is not so much sound in general as the voice in particular which would seem to command faith in cinema's veracity. The
notion that cinema is able to deliver "real" sounds is an extension of
that powerful Western episteme, extending from Plato to Hélène
Cixous, which identifies the voice with proximity and the here and
now—of a metaphysical tradition which defines speech as the very
essence of presence. Charles Affron situates himself comfortably within
this tradition in a recent book on sentiment, where he writes: "Sound
. . . guarantees immediacy and presence in the system of absence that is
cinema. Images that constantly remind us of the distance in time and
space between their making and their viewing are charged, through
voice, with the presence both that uttered words require for their
transmission and that they lend to our viewing of the art."[6] When he
adds a few pages later that "our belief in fiction is promoted by the
presence of the speaker's voice" (p. 115), he unwittingly points to the
fetishistic value which a surprising number of film theoreticians have
conferred upon the voice—to the key role it has been asked to play in
the larger project of disavowing cinema's lack.

More is at issue here than the recovery of the object. When the voice
is identified in this way with presence, it is given the imaginary power to
place not only sounds but meaning in the here and now. In other words,
it is understood as closing the gap between signifier and signified. Even
more important, at least within the context of this discussion, Western
metaphysics has fostered the illusion that speech is able to express the
speaker's inner essence, that it is "part" of him or her. It locates the
subject of speech in the same ontological space as the speaking subject,
so that the former seems a natural outgrowth of the latter. The fiction of
the authenticity of cinematic sounds thus promotes belief not only in
presence but in self-presence.

It would seem almost obligatory to marshal the forces of deconstruction at this point,[7] but the point I wish to make has been more
precisely anticipated by Lacan, who remarks in "The Function and Field
of Speech and Language in Psychoanalysis" that "I identify myself in
language, but only by losing myself in it like an object."[8] Lacan emphasizes here that speech produces absence, not presence. He also reminds
us that the discoursing voice is the agent of symbolic castration—that at

the moment the subject enters language, he or she also undergoes a phenomenal "fading" or "aphanisis." Finally, he indicates that language preexists and coerces speech—that it can never be anything but "Other."

The voice is the site of perhaps the most radical of all subjective divisions—the division between meaning and materiality. As Denis Vasse observes, it is situated "in the partition of the organic and organization, in the partition between the biological body and the body of language, or, if one prefers, the social body."[9] The sounds the voice makes always exceed signification to some degree, both before the entry into language and after. The voice is never completely standardized, forever retaining an individual flavor or texture—what Barthes calls its "grain."[10] Because we hear before we see, the voice is also closely identified with the infantile scene.[11] On the other hand, because (as I stressed a moment ago) it is through the voice that the subject normally accedes to language, and thereby sacrifices its life, it is associated as well with phenomenal loss, the birth of desire, and the aspiration toward discursive mastery.

This concentration of contradictory values and functions within a single organ would seem almost to encourage conceptual slippage from one "side" to another—from the voice-as-being to the voice-as-discursive-agent. This is precisely what has repeatedly happened in film theory. The voice has been identified with presence by appealing to its pre- or extralinguistic properties—by exploiting its status as "pure" sound. However, as Comolli points out, it is primarily in its discursive capacity that the voice has been called upon to make good the absence upon which cinema is founded:

> As soon as [Speech and the speaking Subject] are produced, sound and speech are plebiscited as *the "truth" which was lacking* in the silent film. . . . The decisive supplement, the "ballast of reality" (Bazin) constituted by sound and speech intervenes straightaway, therefore, as *perfectionment and redefinition of the impression of reality.*[12]

The fetishistic operations of film theory turn not upon actual sounds but upon a "sonic *vraisemblable*," and the voice-as-carrier-of-meaning has a dominant place within that *vraisemblable*.[13] In other words, what is at stake within cinema's acoustic organization, as within its visual organization, is not the real, but an "impression of reality." Cinema creates this "impression of reality" by participating in the production and maintenance of its culture's "dominant fiction," i.e., in "the privileged mode of representation by which the image of the social consensus is offered to the members of a social formation and within which they are asked to identify themselves."[14]

As other writers have noted, Hollywood's sonic *vraisemblable* stresses unity and anthropomorphism.[15] It subordinates the auditory to the visual track, nonhuman sounds to the human voice, and "noise" to speech. It also contains the human voice within the fiction or diegesis. Dominant cinema smoothly effects all four of these ideal projects through synchronization, which anchors sounds to an immediately visible source, and which focuses attention upon the human voice and its discursive capabilities. This emphasis upon diegetic speech acts helps to suture the viewer/listener into what Heath calls the "safe place of the story," and so to conceal the site of cinematic production.[16] It is thus the sound analogue of the shot/reverse shot formation.

However, it has gone largely unnoticed that like the visual *vraisemblable*, the sonic *vraisemblable* is sexually differentiated, working to identify even the *embodied* male voice with the attributes of the cinematic apparatus, but always situating the female voice within a hyperbolically diegetic context. This chapter will attempt to show that Hollywood's soundtrack is engendered through a complex system of displacements which locate the male voice at the point of apparent textual origin, while establishing the diegetic containment of the female voice. It will also suggest that interiority has a very different status in classic cinema from the one that it enjoys in the literary and philo-sophical tradition which Derrida critiques. Far from being a privileged condition, synonymous with soul, spirit, or consciousness, interiority in Hollywood films implies linguistic constraint and physical confine-ment—confinement to the body, to claustral spaces, and to inner narra-tives. Finally, this chapter will argue that Hollywood borrows not only from the Freudian model of female sexuality, but from the Jonesian model, as well, and that its female subject is consequently organized around *both* castration and concentricity.

"You're a beautiful woman; audiences think you have a voice to match," explains a publicist to silent-screen star Lina Lamont in *Singin' in the Rain* (1952) when she wonders why she's not allowed to answer the questions directed to her by fans and reporters. Lina (Jean Hagen) violates this expectation of smooth complementarity whenever she opens her mouth; she speaks shrilly and ungrammatically, with a heavy Bronx accent. The studio for which she works, Monumental Pictures, attempts to conceal the seeming heterogeneity of her voice to her body by having others speak for her.

Singin' in the Rain suggests that synchronization is synonymous with a more general compatibility of voice to body—that a voice which seems to "belong" to the body from which it issues will be easily recorded, but that one which does not will resist assimilation into sound cinema. Since Lina's voice "contradicts" her polished appearance, it stubbornly refuses to be recorded. When the studio attempts to do so, it discovers that Lina can remember to speak into the microphone only if it is attached to her body, but this solution poses other problems: the sounds of her heartbeat and rattling pearls drown out her voice, which, moreover, comes through only intermittently because of the movements of her head. In addition, since the sound wiring has to be inserted beneath her clothing, she falls over every time someone pulls or trips on it. Synchronization is finally effected, but only through the supreme artifice of postdubbing another voice over the image of Lina moving her lips—the voice of Kathy Seldon (Debbie Reynolds).

Early in the film, a demonstration talking picture is shown at a studio party. It consists of an extended close-up of a middle-aged man enunciating with exaggerated clarity the words: "This is a picture and I'm talking. Look how my lips have sounds coming from them, synchronized in perfect unity." Not one of the female characters in *Singin' in the Rain* could echo this claim with absolute credibility. Not only must Lina rely upon Kathy for her singing and speaking voice, but at a climactic moment in the diegesis, the voice of Cosmo (Donald O'Connor) is superimposed over her moving lips. Furthermore, although Reynolds's voice is in fact used for most of the songs, it is replaced by that of Betty Noyes for the number "Would You," which is sung in *The Dancing Cavalier*. Thus, whereas Lina seems to sing the song in the film-within-the-film, and Kathy within the diegesis proper, a third voice, outside both fictions, actually generates the melody. Most baroque of all, in the scenes where Kathy is depicted as postdubbing Lina's dialogue for her, what we in fact hear is the normal speaking voice of Jean Hagen, the actress playing Lina—a voice which contrasts dramatically with the one Hagen employs whenever Lina speaks *in propria persona*.[17]

The bewildering array of female voices marshaled at both the diegetic and extradiegetic levels for the purpose of creating direct sound suggests, even more forcefully than the difficulties Lina encounters in attempting to articulate and record her lines, that the rule of synchronization simultaneously holds more fully and necessitates more coercion with the female than with the male voice—suggests, in other words, that very high stakes are involved in the alignment of the female voice with the female image. I would like to conduct a brief examination of the codified deviations from the rule of synchronization in order to arrive at a clearer understanding of why that rule should be imposed so much more firmly upon female characters than upon their male counterparts.

One of Hollywood's most established deviations from synchronized sound is, of course, postdubbing, which juxtaposes voices with images after the latter have been produced and (usually) edited, so bringing momentarily together in the studio the shadow play of celluloid and the actual voices of flesh-and-blood actors. The latter speak the lines assigned to them while closely observing the lip movements represented on screen, and their voices are recorded as they do so. These actors may be the same or different from those whose images they conform to vocally, but in both cases the aim is usually the complete illusion of "perfect unity." This is the effect for which Monumental Pictures strives when it joins Kathy's voice to Lina's body, just as it is the motivating hope behind MGM's own intricate sound mix of *Singin' in the Rain*.

Like synchronization, postdubbing performs a supervisory role with respect to sexual difference, enforcing the general dictum that female voices should proceed from female bodies, and male voices from male bodies. Violations of this dictum are marked as "comic," and are never more than temporary. Once again, *Singin' in the Rain* offers a convenient example—this time one taken from the very end of the film. After the premiere of *The Dancing Cavalier*, the audience asks Lina to sing them a song. Backstage, Kathy is persuaded to lend her voice to Lina once more, and a microphone is set up behind the curtain. The ploy works until midway through the song, when Don, Cosmo, and the producer pull the curtain to reveal the source of the singing voice. When Kathy runs from the stage, Cosmo replaces her at the microphone, breaking into song as the unwitting Lina continues to move her lips. However, although the unity of a fictional character is thus broken, the larger diegesis of *Singin' in the Rain* is at no point challenged, nor does its representational system falter for a moment. In effect, a "false" narrative structure gives way to the "true" one; the voice is returned to its rightful "owner," who is finally delivered up to the audience of *The Dancing Cavalier*. "This is the girl whose voice you heard tonight," calls Don to the crowd. The specter of sexual heterogeneity is thus raised only so that it can be exorcised, and the female voice "remarried" to the female body. One would have to look beyond Hollywood to find a film in which postdubbing subverts sexual difference—to an experimental text such as Patricia Gruben's *Sifted Evidence* (1980), which is discussed in the final chapter of this book.

A second codified deviation from the rule of synchronization is the voice-off, so designated because its ostensible source is not visible at the moment of emission. The voice-off exceeds the limits of the frame, but not the limits of the diegesis; its "owner" occupies a potentially recoverable space—one, indeed, which is almost always brought within the field of vision at some point or other. Moreover, although the voice-off seems to challenge the primacy of vision by introducing the threat of absence, it generally contributes to the unity of the classic cinematic text by carving out a space beyond the frame of one shot for the next to recover.[18] Sometimes this recuperation is postponed for so long that the invisible source of the voice-off becomes a structuring absence at the level of the narrative, as well as at that of the shot. In Hitchcock's *Psycho* (1960), for instance, "Mrs. Bates" can frequently be heard quarreling with her son in a location beyond the camera's range, each time intensifying the mystery that surrounds "her," and hence the viewer's desire for proairetic resolution. However, even when the voice-off is not employed in either of these ways, it generally extends the boundaries of the fiction beyond what can be seen to what can be heard,[19] and so contributes to the diegetic illusion. As a result, the voice-off is sexually differentiated in much the same way that a synchronized voice is. (I will have more to say about the voice-off later, when I discuss its use in *Kiss Me Deadly*.)

The voice-over, on the other hand, is coded as occupying a different order from the main diegesis. That difference often seems more quantitative than qualitative, merely a slight temporal and/or spatial dislocation. The voice-over of Walter/Fred MacMurray in Billy Wilder's *Double Indemnity* (1944), for example, speaks from a position so closely adjacent to the events represented in the image track that the two eventually converge. On other occasions, as in many traditional documentaries, the voice-over seems separated from the fiction by an absolute partition. To the degree that the voice-over preserves its integrity, it inverts the usual sound/image hierarchy; it becomes a "voice on high," like that of the angel Joseph in Capra's *It's a Wonderful Life* (1947), a voice which speaks from a position of superior knowledge, and which superimposes itself "on top" of the diegesis.

To the degree that the voice-over preserves its integrity, it also becomes an exclusively male voice. The only disembodied female voice-over that I have been able to find in the history of Hollywood film is that which narrates Joseph Manckiewicz's *Letter to Three Wives (1949)*, and even it differs sharply from its male counterpart. Although it "hovers" above the image track, in an invisible spatial register, it occupies the same temporal register as the other characters, and often comments upon events as they occur. Moreover, although its "owner" escapes the viewer's gaze, her appearance is a frequent topic of conversation. At one point, two of the other characters even look at her photograph, obliquely angled so as to resist and tantalize our vision. The disembodied voice-over in *Letter to Three Wives* is thus curiously both corporealized and diegeticized.[20]

There is a general theoretical consensus that the theological status of the disembodied voice-over is the effect of maintaining its source in a place apart from the camera, inaccessible to the gaze of either the cinematic apparatus or the viewing subject—of violating the rule of synchronization so absolutely that the voice is left without an identifiable locus. In other words, the voice-over is privileged to the degree that *it transcends the body*. Conversely, it loses power and authority with every corporeal encroachment, from a regional accent or idiosyncratic "grain" to definitive localization in the image. Synchronization marks the final moment in any such localization, the point of full and complete "embodiment."

Pascal Bonitzer describes the embodiment of the voice in terms of aging and death, remarking that as soon as its source is revealed, it becomes "decrepit" and "mortal," vulnerable to stray bullets.[21] The metaphor is suggestive, but it fails to address the issue which is immediately broached within classic cinema by any reference to the body—the issue, that is, of gender. Much more pertinent here is a recent book by Michel Chion, *La voix au cinéma,* which relies heavily upon the categories of the "masculine" and the "feminine" when articulating the relation of filmic voice to filmic image. Unfortunately, Chion's sorties into the domain of sexual difference seem motivated primarily by the search for poetic props, and so remain for the most part both uncritical and devoid of self-consciousness. Indeed, so determinedly does *La voix au cinéma* circumscribe its discussion of the voice within existing gender demarcations that it assumes much of the symptomatic value of a Hollywood film, and will be correspondingly utilized here.

Chion's argument converges most dramatically with dominant cinema whenever it comments upon the contrasting values traditionally assigned to the embodied voice, on the one hand, and the disembodied voice, on the other. On these occasions, sexual difference almost invariably functions as a major point of reference, the metaphoric terrain upon which the opposition is mapped. In one particularly striking passage, which warrants close scrutiny, *La voix au cinéma* compares the

localization of a previously unlocalized voice to the performance of a
striptease:

> In much the same way that the feminine sex is the ultimate point in the
> deshabille (the point after which it is no longer possible to deny the absence
> of the penis), there is an ultimate point in the embodiment of the voice, and
> that is the *mouth* from which the voice issues. . . . As long as the face and
> mouth have not been revealed, and the eye of the spectator has not
> "verified" the coincidence of the voice with the mouth. . . . the vocal
> embodiment is incomplete, and the voice conserves an aura of invulner-
> ability and of magic power.[22]

Castration is clearly "in the air" here, but it's difficult at first to
locate the bleeding wound, particularly since the terms of the analogy
are quite puzzling. A striptease, after all, turns upon removal, whereas
the localization of the voice involves the addition or supplementation of
the body. However, the equation comes into focus with the reference to
yet another scene within which loss is anchored to female anatomy—
with the reference to that mythical moment when gender is first displayed and apprehended. Chion is in effect comparing the close-up
which discloses the moving lips of an invisible speaker with two situations in which a woman's genitals are exposed to a male gaze: the
climactic moment in a stripper's performance, when she removes her
G-string, and the moment within the Freudian scenario when the young
boy is obliged, if only momentarily, to acknowledge the genital difference of his sexual other.

The ostensible reasons for this complex analogy are several. First,
each term in the equation incorporates a scenario of vision. Second, in
each case the drama is played out at the level of the body. Finally, in
each instance the gaze "discovers" an absence or lack—a lack which is
presumed to be anatomical within the contexts of both the striptease
and the "revelation" of sexual difference, but which in the context of
cinema can be read only as the loss of those symbolic attributes which
accompany the unlocalized voice (authoritative vision and speech, superior knowledge, and a radical alterity with respect to the diegesis).

However, the "common" denominators that link all three scenes
push the analogy definitively in the direction of sexual difference, making the female body the site not only of anatomical but of discursive
lack. By comparing the close-up that installs a filmic voice within a
filmic body to the unveiling of woman's genitals, the passage quoted
above suggests that to embody a voice is to feminize it. It thereby
situates the female subject firmly on the side of spectacle, castration, and
synchronization, while aligning her male counterpart with the gaze, the
phallus, and what exceeds synchronization.[23]

As I have already suggested, dominant cinema also holds the female subject much more fully than the male subject to the unity of sound and image, and consequently to the representation of lack. This is not to say that the male voice consistently occupies the privileged position of the disembodied voice-over within that cinema. On the contrary, the male voice-over actually appears relatively infrequently in Hollywood films, at least in comparison with the synchronized voice, and on those occasions when it does have a part to play, it is usually associated with a diegetic figure. Nevertheless, in his most exemplary guise, classic cinema's male subject sees without being seen, and speaks from an inaccessible vantage point. These qualities can be most efficiently designated through the disembodied voice-over, but they are also recoverable from the much more terrestrial uses to which Hollywood generally puts the male voice.

Insofar as the voice-over asserts its independence from the visual track, it presents itself as enunciator. It seems, in other words, to be a metafictional voice, the point of discursive origin. This impression is sometimes augmented by the disembodied voice's extratextual familiarity—by vocal characteristics that evoke a well-known "personality," such as Mark Hellinger in Jules Dassin's *The Naked City* (1948),[24] or even the director himself. Orson Welles makes the most of the last possibility in *The Magnificent Ambersons* (1942), a film in which he not only functions as a behind-the-scenes narrator, but deliberately conflates that role with his authorial persona through an extraordinary verbal signature in the credit sequence. (At the end of that sequence, we hear the voice to which we have intermittently listened during the past 88 minutes say these words over the image of a microphone: "I wrote and directed [this film]; my name is Orson Welles.")

However, whether or not the voice-over is reinforced in this way, it can never be more than a fictional inscription of a productive activity which is itself situated outside the film, and dispersed over a wide range of technological and human agencies (the apparatuses of sound recording, sound mixing, postdubbing, and projection, as well as the scriptwriter, voice coach, sound crew, actors, and director, to name only the sound agencies). The authority of the disembodied voice-over is thus the effect of both a displacement and a condensation.

Despite its efficiency, this paternal representation is not easily assimilated by the classic fiction film. As Bonitzer points out, it too openly and aggressively proclaims its superior knowledge, a knowledge over which it claims exclusive rights;[25] it is "undemocratic," pulling rank not only on the characters within the diegesis, but on the viewer, as well. Moreover, by insisting so forcefully upon its own detachment

from the events it describes, or upon which it comments, the noncor-
porealized voice-over constantly pulls away from the narrative order to
its own, and so at times inhibits secondary identification. (In Stanley
Kubrick's *The Killing* [1956], for instance, it functions as a kind of court
recorder, coldly and punctiliously establishing the time and place of
each event leading up to the climax, thereby distancing the viewer/
listener from the guilty characters.) It is presumably for these reasons
that it is so rarely utilized by Hollywood, and that when it is, as in such
typical examples as Jean Negulesco's *Johnny Belinda* (1948), Don
Siegel's *Riot in Cell Block 11* (1954), or Billy Wilder's *The Seven Year Itch*
(1955), it is often confined to the beginning and/or conclusion, and so
functions as either a prologue or an epilogue.[26]

The embodied or diegetically anchored male voice-over might seem
the logical alternative to its disembodied or diegetically unanchored
counterpart, but it has not been generally adopted for that purpose. It is
a striking fact that, apart from contemporary movie and television
revivals of film noir, this voice is largely confined to a brief historical
period, stretching from the forties to the early fifties.[27] The instances that
come most quickly to mind, moreover, suggest that the embodied male
voice is likely to speak "over" the image track only because of drastic
circumstances, when it is (or recently has been) *in extremis*. The voice
that narrates Billy Wilder's *Double Indemnity* (1944), for example, "belongs" to a dying man, who received his mortal injury at the hands of a
woman. The voice-over in Rudolph Mate's *D.O.A.* originates from a
man who has been fatally poisoned. The voice that narrates Otto Preminger's *Laura* derives from a character who is shot to death during the
course of the film, and whose virility is in doubt from the very outset.
The narrator of another Wilder film, *Sunset Boulevard* (1950), is even
more dislocated from phallic orthodoxy; not only is he a creatively,
morally, and financially bankrupt writer who permits himself to be
supported and dominated by an aging actress, but (as we learn at the
end of the film) he is dead. His voice thus speaks less from the "heights"
than from the "depths." The male voice-overs in Welles's *Lady from
Shanghai* (1947), Jacques Tourneur's *Out of the Past* (1947), Raoul
Walsh's *Pursued* (1947), and Delmer Daves's *Pride of the Marines* (1945)
are similarly associated with characters who have been scarred by a
major trauma, psychological in the first three cases, and physical in the
third.

In each of these films, the voice-over is autobiographical and self-
revealing. To borrow a phrase from Doane, it turns the body "inside
out," displaying what is "inaccessible to the image, what exceeds the
visible."[28] That display takes the form of a temporal regression, a move-

ment back to a prior moment in the speaker's life which accounts for his present condition. The fact that the voice-over is accompanied in this way by an extended flashback, which translates what it says into images, and so anchors it to the order of the spectacle and the gaze, suggests that its regressive journey carries it to the heart of the diegesis, rather than to the latter's outer edges.

Further attesting to the secondary status of the embodied voice-over, at least in four of the examples cited above, is the compulsion out of which it speaks. The narrative voices in *Out of the Past, Lady from Shanghai, Pride of the Marines,* and *Pursued* are governed by the need to master an intolerable past through linguistic repetition—to "bind" that past by retelling it. This sense of compulsion is even more pronounced in *Double Indemnity;* Walter refers to his story as a "confession," and he produces it for a figure who is not only his elder, but his moral and professional superior (i.e., for a paternal representative).

Involuntary or constrained speech is a general characteristic of the embodied voice-over, as is vividly dramatized by that variant which seems most fully to turn the body "inside out"—the internal mono-logue. The voice in question functions almost like a searchlight suddenly turned upon a character's thoughts; it makes audible what is ostensibly inaudible, transforming the private into the public. It is through this device that we learn about the sexual desires of the women who inhabit the female seminary in Don Siegel's *The Beguiled* (1971), and that we enter Cecile/Jean Seberg's memories in Otto Preminger's *Bonjour Tristesse* (1958).[29]

On these occasions the discursive mode is direct rather than in-direct. No distance separates teller from tale; instead, the voice-over is stripped of temporal protection and thrust into diegetic immediacy. Thus deprived of enunciatory pretense, it is no longer in a position to masquerade as the point of textual origin. Moreover, since this voice-over derives from an interior rather than an exterior register (in other words, since it represents thought rather than speech), the listener's access to it is unlicensed by the character from whom it derives, and so clearly constitutes a form of auditory mastery.

All this is another way of saying that the embodied voice-over designates not only psychological but diegetic interiority—that it ema-nates from the center of the story, rather than from some radically other time and place. Its status is thus quite distinct from that of the dis-embodied voice-over, and it is by no means a satisfactory alternative to it. Indeed, as I indicated earlier, the embodied voice-over is a precarious hook on which to hang the phallus. Hollywood dictates that the closer a voice is to the "inside" of the narrative, the more remote it is from the "outside," i.e., from that space fictionally inscribed by the disembodied voice-over, but which is in fact synonymous with the cinematic apparatus. In other words, it equates diegetic interiority with discursive impotence and lack of control, thereby rendering that situation culturally unacceptable for the "normal" male subject.

However, even as it issues and reissues this sexually differentiating edict, dominant cinema works against it, holding its male as well as its female characters to the imperative of visibility, and securing both within the limits of the story. Hollywood thus erects male subjectivity over a fault line, at the site of a major contradiction. In order both to conceal this contradiction and to sustain the male viewer/listener in an impossible identification with the phallus, classic cinema has elaborated a number of strategies for displacing the privileged attributes of the disembodied voice-over onto the *synchronized* male voice—mechanisms for reinscribing the opposition between the diegetic and the extradiegetic within the fiction itself. As a result of these mechanisms, interiority and exteriority are redefined as areas within the narrative rather than as indicators of the great divide separating the diegesis from the enunciation. "Inside" comes to designate a recessed space within the story, while "outside" refers to those elements of the story which seem in one way or another to frame that recessed space. Woman is confined to the former, and man to the latter. It is thus only through an endless series of *trompes l'oeil* that classic cinema's male viewing subject sustains what is a fundamentally impossible identification with authoritative vision, speech, and hearing.

Before examining the procedures whereby female characters are incorporated within an exaggeratedly diegetic locus, and male characters assigned a seemingly extradiegetic position, I would like to observe that cinematic sound is organized in relation to representations of hearing as well as representations of the voice. Authoritative speech, for instance, often implies or is implied by a heightened faculty of audition—the capacity, as it were, to "over-hear." This is literally the case with the angels at the beginning of It's a Wonderful Life, as well as with the exceptional female voice-over in Letter to Three Wives (1949), who comments ironically on the diegetic flow of sounds and images. It is an implied attribute of the doctor in Irving Rapper's Now, Voyager (1942), to whom the female protagonist confesses everything without quite knowing why. In other films, hearing is played off against the voice, so that the two are defined in terms of antagonism rather than complementarity. This is very much the case with Welles's *Touch of Evil* (1958), an example with which I would like to remain for a moment.

Quinlan (Orson Welles), the corrupt police commissioner in *Touch of Evil*, controls the territory over which he has jurisdiction almost entirely through his voice. He establishes the guilt of others through simple pronouncement, often constructing the necessary evidence in a similar manner. When Vargas (Charlton Heston), a Mexican official, decides to expose Quinlan's corruption, he tapes a conversation between Quinlan and a colleague in which the former is coerced into saying a number of self-incriminating things, and so obtains a legal hold over his American adversary. In short, Vargas uses Quinlan's voice against him.

The sequence where this power struggle takes place occurs at the end of the film, when Menzies (Joseph Calleia), wearing a hidden microphone, calls Quinlan out of a bar and interrogates him about a number of suspiciously solved crimes as the two of them walk across a bridge. Meanwhile, Vargas moves back and forth on the surrounding oil derricks and beneath the bridge, recording the exchange. The camera cross-cuts between the two scenes, so that the space occupied by each functions alternately as "on" and "off."

Vargas does not speak during this sequence; he is "pure" ear, his own hearing supplemented by the apparatus, and closely identified with it. Even when the other two men are out of his line of vision, he is able to follow what goes on between them through the machine he holds— he is in control, that is, of off-screen space. Quinlan, on the contrary, neither sees nor hears Vargas. He continues his conversation with Menzies unconcernedly until he hears his own voice echoed back to him by the tape recorder. He is thus defeated by his inability to master off-screen space.

This auditory failure is represented as the loss of discursive potency. Significantly, it completely neutralizes the authority previously exercised by Quinlan's voice, leaving him mortal and vulnerable. It would thus seem that in certain cinematic situations, the faculty of hearing is privileged over that of speech—that at times it may indicate a position of superiority to and control over the one who talks. The basis for the ear's occasional priority would seem to be its claim to be outside the drama within which the voice is contained. That exteriority is formally figured through the cross-cutting which isolates Vargas from Quinlan and Menzies in the bridge sequence. Vargas's association with the apparatus further emphasizes the exteriority of his position by equating it with the site of cinematic production.

The opposition of "outside" to "inside" is here elaborated through two male characters. However, "interior" rhymes with "inferior" to such a degree in classic cinema that sexual difference is the usual vehicle for its articulation. So imperative is that convention that *Touch of Evil* goes to considerable lengths to establish that although Vargas's hearing is external to Quinlan's speech, woman nonetheless occupies the innermost point of the diegesis. The central female character, Suzy (Janet Leigh), is confined within increasingly restricted spaces over the course of the film until she finally arrives at a jail cell. That interiorization also involves her increasing auditory and verbal incapacity—an incapacity so extreme as to assure Quinlan's discursive superiority over her even at the nadir of his powers.

Early in the film, Suzy is taken at her request to an American motel where she thinks she will be safe while her husband, Vargas, investigates a border murder. A number of subsequent shots show her lying on the bed in her room, half-drugged with fatigue, but prevented from falling asleep by an enormous ear-shaped speaker attached to one of the walls. The music comes from a radio in the motel office, where a group of thugs await the appropriate moment to assault her. Suzy is unable to respond with anything but frustration and panic to the music, baffled by all sounds whose source remains beyond her field of vision. The thugs, on the other hand, are able to control what they cannot see through a flick of the dial or a knock on the wall. They also manage to keep any familiar sounds from reaching her by intercepting her phone calls. This auditory incompetence is linked to a verbal incompetence, which is most pointedly evident in the cry Suzy later utters from the balcony of Grande's hotel—a cry which is swallowed up in the noise of the traffic below, unable to make itself heard by a single diegetic ear.

The interiority/exteriority antithesis, which in classic cinema serves to define the opposition between the levels of fiction and enunciation, is reinscribed into the narrative primarily through three large operations. Each of these operations exploits that ambiguity in the concept of interiority which permits it to designate both a psychic and a diegetic condition, and which makes it possible for the former condition to signify the latter. As a group, they are more or less synonymous with sexual difference in the dominant narrative film.

The first of these operations folds the female voice into what is overtly indicated as an inner textual space, such as a painting, a song-and-dance performance, or a film-within-a-film. Through it the female voice is doubly diegeticized, overheard not only by the cinema audience, but by a fictional eavesdropper or group of eavesdroppers. Male subjectivity is then defined in relation to that seemingly transcendental auditory position, and so aligned with the apparatus.

This operation is staged with unusual literalness in the already cited sequence from *Singin' in the Rain,* where Cosmo and Don pull the curtain to disclose Kathy at the microphone. With that gesture she is transferred from off-stage to on-stage—from outside the spectacle to inside the spectacle. The shift is emphasized by the immense movie screen which is revealed when the curtain is drawn, which frames both Kathy and Lina. When Kathy tries to break out of the frame by running off-stage, she is forcibly prevented from doing so by the audience, to whom Don appeals to "stop that girl." When he adds, "That's the girl whose voice you heard tonight," he summons her not only back onto the stage, but into the diegesis of *The Dancing Cavalier.*

I have already commented on some of the implications of this transaction. The earlier substitution of Kathy's for Lina's voice licensed the former to stray from its legitimate locus, a license which is intolerable to the classic system. It is now revoked with a vengeance, and the female voice resubmitted to the law of synchronization. At the same time, authority is reinvested in the male voice, which is shown to orchestrate the fictional drama from behind the scenes—from the very place, that is, from which Kathy has just been excluded. Even when the male characters finally come out on the stage, they manage to escape the frame that secures Lina and Kathy; Cosmo shatters the illusion of the performance when he grabs the microphone, as does Don when he addresses the audience directly.

Max Ophuls's *Lola Montes* (1955), most "writerly" of woman's films, and more a film about classic cinema than a participant in it, subdivides its diegesis in similar ways by confining its female protagonist (Martine Carol) to a circus ring, and obliging her to offer prewritten answers to the questions posed to her by the ringmaster. Like Cosmo and Don at the end of *Singin' in the Rain,* the ringmaster (Peter Ustinov) is represented as being outside the spectacle, in a position of discursive control. Because he remains to one side of the drama, and because his voice at times speaks "over" the image of Lola, he seems less diegetically anchored, and hence closer to the point of textual origin. Indeed, during Lola's pantomime repetition of her earlier rise to fame and fortune, he maintains a running off-screen commentary, much like a disembodied voice-over.

Another Ophuls film, *Letter from an Unknown Woman* (1948), situates the female voice at the interior of the narrative by contextualizing it within a written rather than a performance text. That film is structured as a letter from the protagonist, Lisa (Joan Fontaine), to the object of her desire, Stefan (Louis Jourdan). Stefan receives it the night before he is scheduled to fight a duel with Lisa's husband; he sits down to read it, and Lisa springs to life as an (almost immediately) embodied voice-over. However, since the letter opens with the statement, "By the time you read this letter I may be dead," and since the convent notation at the conclusion of the letter confirms that this is indeed the case, her voice exists only in and through Stefan's consciousness. Closed up in the sealed envelope handed to his mute servant, it is given a hearing only through his act of reading, permitted to expand only within the receptacle of his imagination. This enclosure is thematized by the contents of Lisa's letter, which assert over and over again her complete subordination to Stefan's wishes ("All I wanted was to see you again, to throw myself at your feet. Nothing else mattered . . ."; "I've had no will but [yours] ever . . ."; "Somewhere out there were your eyes, and I knew I couldn't escape them . . ."; "My life can be measured by the moments I've been with you and our son . . .").[30]

John Schlesinger's *Darling* (1965) offers another version of what might be called the "written" female voice-over, used once again for purposes of containment. The film opens with the shot of a poster being replaced by another on a London billboard. The new poster, which is superimposed over one calling for relief of hunger in the Third World, features a close-up of the protagonist, Diana (Julie Christie), with the logo: "My Story. Ideal Woman." On the soundtrack, a disembodied male voice-over invites Diana to recount her autobiography "in your own words." Diana immediately embarks upon that narrative, also in voice-over. However, whereas the male voice is anonymous, Diana's has already been embodied through the opening shot.

The poster sequence gives way to an extended, episodic flashback, which continues until the end of the film. Diana's voice-over also continues, albeit intermittently, with numerous ellipses. However, the two are not only out of synchronization, but out of narrative alignment, with the diegesis frequently contradicting Diana's verbal reminiscences. Ultimately, her voice is transferred from this seemingly extradiegetic (albeit far from privileged) position to one emphatically inside the diegesis. Although for most of the film it gives the impression of being part of a "live" interview, at the conclusion it is shown to emanate almost like a sound hallucination from an article published in a women's magazine. The magazine, whose cover displays a reduction of the same glamor photograph earlier displayed by the poster, is on sale in massive quantities in a London newsstand, as if to suggest that Diana's voice can be purchased even more cheaply than her body.

Psychoanalysis provides classic cinema with a second strategy for situating the female voice within an exaggeratedly diegetic space. This strategy, which I will call "the talking cure," anchors woman to a fantasmatic interiority through involuntary utterance; she is obliged to speak, and in speaking to construct, her "own" psychic "reality"—a reality which, we are told, has been there all the time, albeit long repressed and forgotten. The talking cure is negotiated with astonishing frequency and openness in the "woman's film" of the 1940s. Many of the texts which fall into this category, such as Robert Siodmak's *The Spiral Staircase* (1945), Curtis Bernhardt's *Possessed* (1947), Anatole Litvak's *The Snake Pit* (1948), and Mitchell Leisen's *Lady in the Dark* (1944), focus on the interaction between a male doctor and a female patient, and they all manifest an intense fascination with a space assumed to be inside the patient's body. However, in each case the internal order clearly derives from an external source, so that these films dispute the very divisions they are at such pains to establish.

In *Possessed*, for instance, an unconscious woman is injected with a drug which induces her to speak on command. What she is obliged to produce in this way is, of course, her past, which flashes onto the screen as her voice embarks upon its regressive journey. Interiority is thus extracted through an action upon the body: liquid is injected into a woman in order that a cluster of memories can then be projected both onto the doctor's diagnostic "screen" and onto our cinematic screen. The slippage between "inner" and "outer" is reiterated by the doctor when he tells his patient that the drug he is giving her will "help you to tell us what we want," and when he confides to a colleague: "Every time I see the reaction to this treatment I get the same thrill I did the first time"—i.e., when he foregrounds the structuring role his own desires play in the talking cure. Interiority and exteriority also spill over each other in the narrative that ensues, since the patient (Joan Crawford) is shown to suffer from a deafening noise which seems to assail her from without, but which proves to have its origin within—to be, that is, the sound of her own heartbeat.

Lady in the Dark gives a more explicitly ideological inflection to the concept of interiority, suggesting that it is a synonym for social as well as libidinal containment. The central character in that film, Liza Elliott (Ginger Rogers), is the editor-in-chief of a fashion magazine—an untenably potent discursive position for an American woman in 1944, and one which, given its active relationship to scopophilia, situates her on the side of what classic cinema decrees to be male rather than female subjectivity. She is consequently eased out of the job she has successfully performed for a number of years, and redefined first as spectacle, and then as wife.

Lady in the Dark opens with Liza's visit to a medical doctor—a visit which results in the recommendation that she see a psychiatrist. She has been prompted to make that visit by a haunting and mysterious melody, which she feels compelled to hum from time to time without understanding why. That melody not only baffles Liza, but it identifies her with another scene, sharply divided from the one she traditionally occupies; it places her "in the dark," with an equal emphasis on the first and last of those words.

Reluctantly acting upon her physician's advice, Liza goes to the psychiatrist and submits to psychoanalysis. As with the protagonist of *Possessed,* this cure follows a regressive path, leading predictably "back" to the family. The recounting of dreams is the agency of Liza's Oedipal "return." It is also the means by which she is equipped with an inner life which is incompatible with her social and economic position, and which is an obvious cultural imposition, despite the psychiatrist's attempt to deny his own productive role in its creation ("Does it strike you that in your dream you were the exact opposite of your realistic self?" he asks Liza. "You dreamt it, no one else did. Strange as it seems, it came from you.") Liza's voice is thus the point at which she is constantly coerced. Indeed, according to the logic of the film, it is a song sung by her as a child which comes back to command her adult voice, and which obliges her to undergo the talking cure.

Liza's dreams insert her into what is a progressively well-articulated subtext, in relation to which the film's larger diegetic organization functions as a kind of frame. This nesting-box effect is reiterated at more and more microscopic levels within the dreams themselves, which revolve around not only images of containment, but images of containment which contain images of containment. Thus, the chest in the first dream opens to reveal a blue dress, which itself encloses an important childhood memory, and into which Liza places her adult body. In the same dream, Liza's portrait is commissioned so that it can be reproduced in miniature on a new stamp. In the final dream, Liza initially stands outside a circus enclosure, looking in, then abruptly finds herself not merely on the other side but in one of the circus's cages.

These objects and places figure a *mise-en-abîme* interiority to which the melody also beckons, an endlessly receding locus which is simultaneously a psychic terrain and a domestic arena, with the one implying and indeed leading to the other. The enclosure of Liza within this black hole at the center of representation isolates her definitively from the discursive authority to which she lays claim at the beginning of the film, itself a figure for the radically external site of cinematic production. It transforms her from a fashion editor to a model, locating her definitively on the side of spectacle. Each of the dream receptacles is the cause or scene of display, from the blue dress which inspires instant exhibitionism in its wearer ("Look at me," Liza appeals over and over to various male characters as soon as she has donned it) to the much more elaborate song-and-dance number staged within the circus setting.

The third of the operations through which Hollywood reinscribes the opposition between diegetic interiority and exteriority into the narrative itself is by depositing the female body into the female voice in the guise of accent, speech impediment, timbre, or "grain." This vocal corporealization is to be distinguished from that which gives the sounds emitted by Mae West, Marlene Dietrich, or Lauren Bacall their distinctive quality, since in each of these last instances it is a "male" rather than a "female" body which is deposited in the voice. Otherwise stated, the lowness and huskiness of each of these three voices connote masculinity rather than femininity, so that the voice seems to exceed the gender of the body from which it proceeds. That excess confers upon it a privileged status vis-à-vis both language and sexuality. The contrivance which is my present concern, on the contrary, involves the submersion of the female voice in the female body, and results in linguistic incapacity and a general vulnerability.

The voice of Suzy in *Touch of Evil*, for instance, is dragged along with her into a state of increasing somnolence, culminating in unconscious moaning. Lina Lamont in *Singin' in the Rain* is another case in point, her voice not only scarred by a Bronx accent which renders it incapable of standard American pronunciation, but so easily giving way to the gravitational force of her body that it is drowned out by her heartbeat on tape. The maladroit utterances of Judy Holiday in George Cukor's *Born Yesterday* (1951) serve a similar function, emphasizing the rule of matter over mind, while the voice of the Marilyn Monroe character in Wilder's *Seven Year Itch* (1955) is so closely identified with her body that she uses the latter to authenticate the former. (She offers to prove the veracity of the lines she speaks in a television advertisement—"I had onions for lunch, I had garlic for dinner, but I stay kissing fresh"—with an actual kiss.)

What is at issue in each of these examples (all, curiously, drawn from the fifties, just as the previous set were drawn from the forties) is the identification of the female voice with an intractable materiality, and its consequent alienation from meaning. Like the other two procedures briefly discussed here—the incorporation of the female voice within a recessed area of the diegesis, and the deployment of that voice to create a psychic order to which its "owner" is then confined—the corporealization of the female voice magnifies the effects of synchronization. It emphatically situates the female subject within the diegetic scene, on the side of what can be overseen and overheard, and in so doing draws the curtain on the male subject's discursive insufficiency. By isolating the female subject from the production of meaning, in other words, it permits the male subject to pose as the voice that constrains and orchestrates the feminine "performance" or "striptease," as enunciator rather than as himself an element of the *énoncé*. The identification of the female voice with the female body thus returns us definitively to the scene of castration.

What this castration entails is perhaps nowhere more dramatically rendered than in the opening sequence of Robert Aldrich's *Kiss Me Deadly* (1955), which shows a car speeding down a darkened highway, brought to a perilous halt when a seminaked woman, Christina (Cloris Leachman), steps abruptly in front of it. As the driver admits the woman to the front seat of his car, he ironically comments: "A thumb's not good enough for you. You've got to use your whole body." When the image yields to white credits rolling across a black surface, Christina's voice continues to be heard, breathing heavily from the exertion of what we later learn has been an extended run. In other words, it adopts the technical status of a voice-over—a voice which speaks from a different order from that to which the image belongs.

However, not only is Christina's voice already embedded in the narrative, but we remain in no doubt as to its temporal and/or spatial location during the credit sequence, since it still seems to issue from the front seat of the now-invisible speeding car. It thus clearly derives from a point inside the diegesis, rather than an external vantage. Indeed, since at this juncture the image track contains information about the film's production rather than its fiction (i.e., the names of the actors, director, producer, etc.), it is privileged over the soundtrack, so that Christina's voice seems to breathe "under" rather than "over" the titles. Finally, although that voice is momentarily detached from the spectacle to which it is initially synchronized, it is not even momentarily disembodied. On the contrary, it is what one might call "thick with body," still vibrating with the effort of inhaling after a long run, and resonant with the remark made by the driver of the car to Christina ("You've got to use your whole body").

Much has been made of the sustained voice-off of Dr. Soberin (Alan Dekker), the villain of *Kiss Me Deadly*—of the invulnerability of that voice during the extended period of time when its source remains invisible, and its abruptly actualized mortality the moment its source comes into view. "To maintain [his face] off-frame (one sees only his legs, knows him only by his blue suede shoes) gives to his sententious voice, swollen with mythological comparisons, a greater power of dis-

turbing, an oracular range: sombre prophet of the end of the world,"
writes Bonitzer.

> And, deprived of that, this voice is submitted to the destiny of the body; the
> only institution in the story to whose law it is submitted renders it decrepit,
> mortal. It suffices that the subject of this voice appear in the image (it
> suffices that he can appear), and it is no longer anything but the voice of a
> man, otherwise called that of an imbecile: the proof? A shot, he falls—and
> with him, in ridicule, his discourse with its prophetic accents.[31]

What has not been remarked is just how fully Christina's voice is,
from the very outset, "submitted to the destiny of the body," and how
quickly that destiny catches up with her: five minutes after her voice has
breathed "under" the credits, she is no longer anything but a memory.
Curiously, her death scene situates her mouth—the source of her
voice—out of frame again, the image showing us only her naked legs
dangling in the air, and her raincoat in a heap below. However, this
framing confers no authority upon her, because once again the sounds
she emits are nonlinguistic and involuntary—here a scream, wrung out
of her by the torture inflicted upon her body.

I have attempted to show that Hollywood's sound regime is another
mechanism, analogous to suture, whereby the female subject is obliged
to bear a double burden of lack—to absorb the male subject's castration
as well as her own. It is hardly surprising, given the weight of this
sexually differentiating load, that the female voice should have come to
represent a stress point in the functioning of the entire cinematic apparatus (the stakes, after all, are of phallic proportions). However, castration is not the only trope through which dominant cinema conflates the
female voice with the female body. Hollywood also organizes female
sexuality around the image of what Montrelay calls "the insatiable
organ hole," an image which gives interiority yet another semantic
extension.

The word *interiority* has supported a number of different meanings
in the preceding discussion. I have suggested that within dominant
cinema it primarily designates the "inside" of the narrative, but that this
primary designation is usually obscured through three textual operations which make interiority a synonym for femininity. By confining the
female voice to a recessed area of the diegesis, obliging it to speak a
particular psychic "reality" on command, and imparting to it the texture
of the female body, Hollywood places woman definitively "on stage," at
a dramatic remove from the cinematic apparatus.

The second of these textual operations clearly complements the first; indeed, it would be difficult to think of a cinematic instance in which the "talking cure" does not simultaneously create a story-within-the-story, and in so doing, doubly diegeticize the female voice. The third operation also overlaps with the first at times, since the corporealized female voice emerges with particular frequency within performance situations. The second and third operations are not as overtly compatible; in fact, at first glance they would seem to occupy contrary sides of the traditional mind/body divide.

However, the opposition between these sexually differentiating procedures is only apparent, since there is no real antagonism between the psychic realm brought into existence through the "talking cure," and the material deposit which often deforms woman's speech within classic cinema. The interiority which Hollywood imputes to her has nothing whatever to do with transcendence or Cartesian cogitation. On the contrary, that interiority helps to establish the female body as the absolute limit of female subjectivity. This is because within classic cinema, woman's psyche is only a further extension of her body—its other side, or, to be more precise, its inside.

In an exemplary chapter from *The Interpretation of Dreams*, Freud insists upon the absolute incommensurability of psyche and body, while at the same time dislocating the former of those concepts from the idealist tradition which has defined it:

> I shall carefully avoid the temptation to determine psychical reality in any anatomical fashion. I shall remain upon psychological ground, and I propose simply to follow the suggestion that we should picture the instrument which carries out our mental functions as resembling a compound microscope or a photographic apparatus, or something of the kind. On that basis, psychical locality will correspond to a point within the apparatus at which one of the preliminary stages of an image comes into being.[32]

This passage is of considerable relevance to the present discussion, not only because it deploys a cinematic metaphor, but because it presents a psychical model which Hollywood renders gender-specific. By so consistently identifying the male subject with authoritative vision, speech, and hearing, classic cinema attributes to the male subject the psychical reality which Freud maintains is the norm for both sexes. As in *The Interpretation of Dreams*, his psychic apparatus is closely identified with the cinematic apparatus, and so radically denatured. It is also emphatically exteriorized (which, of course, is not the case in the Freudian model).

Classic cinema decrees a very different state of affairs for the female subject. The "talking cure" films, whose narrative operations pivot upon female interiority, deprivilege that interiority by referring it insistently back to the body. Indeed, the two most frequent varieties of psychic reality identified with woman in this category of films are hysteria and paranoia, both notorious for collapsing the distinctions between inner and outer, mind and body.[33] The curiously corporealized psyche attributed to woman by the talking cure films is thus perfectly compatible with the blurred consciousness attributed to her by the materiality of her discourse. (It is not surprising, for instance, that the pounding noise which afflicts the patient in *Possessed* is ultimately shown to derive from the same source as the noise which drowns out Lina Lamont's voice during the recording of *The Dancing Cavalier*. In both cases the female body imposes its tyrannical rule.)

The "talking cure" films also deprivilege the female psyche by denying to woman any possibility of arriving at self-knowledge except through the intervening agency of a doctor or analyst. In *The Snake Pit, Lady in the Dark,* Henry Levin's *The Guilt of Janet Ames* (1948), and Hitchcock's *Marnie* (1964), it is this paternal figure who induces the female protagonist to articulate desires she never knew she had, and who then interprets them for her. On those occasions when woman's speech is most fully given over to this obligatory self-articulation, as in the concluding sequence of *Marnie,* her voice often seems to circumvent her consciousness altogether. At these times she speaks not so much the language of the unconscious as the language of unconsciousness.

Although it otherwise falls to one side of the "talking cure" films, *Kiss Me Deadly* provides an extreme example of the corporeal form female interiority assumes within classic cinema. It also locates that interiority irremediably beyond its "owner's" consciousness. The relevant sequence is once again the film's opening, which shows Christina mailing a note to Hammer, the driver who picks her up. Since she writes that note immediately before her death, it assumes an analogous status to the missive in *Letter from an Unknown Woman;* it seems, that is, to promise entry into her innermost self. The letter does, in fact, conform to this expectation, but in a surprising way.

As in the "talking cure" films, the words that map out Christina's interiority derive from an external source, albeit one with the same name. Those words—"Remember me"—are taken from a poem by Christina Rossetti, the first lines of which read: "Remember me when I am gone away,/Gone far away into the silent land;/When you can no more hold me by the hand,/Nor I half turn to go yet turning stay." A few lines later, the speaker of Rossetti's poem expresses her hope that "the darkness and corruption" will "leave/A vestige of the thoughts that once I had." This ambiguous remark, which seems to refer simultaneously to the speaker's own thoughts and to those she once occupied in her lover's mind, identifies the pronoun *me* with idea and memory—with what exceeds the body.

The pronoun has a very different meaning when Aldrich's Christina employs it, leading back to rather than away from corporeality. After reading her note, Hammer searches for material evidence rather than turning to his memories. His investigation leads him first to Christina's apartment, where he finds the Rossetti poem, and then to the morgue, where he demands to see her corpse. In its cinematic recontextualization, "me" thus comes to designate not spirit, consciousness, soul, or memory, but the speaker's body. That body is now cold and speechless, but not for these reasons empty of interiority. Indeed, the sight of Christina's corpse arouses in Hammer the powerful desire to take possession of its "contents."

Since the coroner has already performed an autopsy upon Christina's body, and removed the key he found inside, Hammer must violently extract what he seeks from that person's clenched fist, an image which reiterates the theme of containment. Hammer's obsession with the contents of the female body is also figured through a number of other images of enclosure—the cold-storage unit which holds Christina's corpse, the locker which the key opens, and the multilayered box found inside that locker, which contains the object for which he is looking.

Because that object is secured only through the key that is found inside Christina's body, and because it is contained within a closed box, it functions at least in part as a metaphor for female interiority. (This reading is reinforced by the final sequence of the film, in which Lilah—like the mythological Pandora—opens the box, and unleashes its/her horrors upon the earth.) The ironic phrase coined by Hammer's girlfriend, Vera—"the great Whatsit"—consequently refers to female interiority as much as it does to the mysterious atomic substance, and in so doing, depicts that interiority as inimical to language and representation, as literally "inexpressible." However, far from being a remote and untraveled region, well beyond the phallic pale, what is given here as "femininity" is in fact constructed precisely through language and representation—through Vera's phrase, through the Rossetti poem, through the endlessly repeated play between containers and their contexts, and through the explosion with which the film ends.[34]

What passes for the "dark continent" of femininity is a familiar and well-charted territory not only within classic cinema, but within psychoanalysis, where it at times assumes a similarly corporealized form. According to certain seasoned travelers within that latter discourse, there are three points of entry into woman's inner recesses—the mouth, the anus, and the vagina.[35] Ernest Jones, "pathfinder," explains that although the vagina will ultimately be given pride of place, the mouth is the starting point for female sexuality, and places a definitive stamp upon it: "We all agree about the importance of the oral stage, and that the oral stage is the prototype of the later femininity is also a widely accepted tenet. . . . Helen Deutsch in this connection has pointed to the sucking nature of the vaginal function."[36] At least within the tradition extending from Jones to Montrelay, the female drives are thus believed to revolve around a series of "insatiable" and largely equivalent "organ holes," and hence to follow an alimentary logic.[37] As a result, woman is "more concerned with the inside of her body than with the outside."[38] Within this theoretical paradigm, female interiority is basically an extension of the female body, much as it is within classic cinema.

What I am moving toward here is the hypothesis that Hollywood draws not only upon the paradigm of female sexuality advanced by Freud, but upon that championed by Jones—that it conforms the female voice not only to the model of a "stunted and inferior organ," but to that of an "organ hole." Beyond the striptease, with its "nothing to see" (which Hollywood translates into the paradoxical imperative that woman be precisely given over to visibility), and its revelation of the discursive impotence of the female voice, is projected the yawning chasm of a corporeal interiority. In classic cinema, as in the writings of Jones and his followers, there is an implied equation of woman's voice with her vagina, each of which is posited as a major port of entry into her subjectivity, but which is actually, I would argue, the site at which that subjectivity is introduced into her. The voice is, of course, the preferred point of insertion, but in extreme situations the vagina can be substituted.

I will speak in a moment about Jean Negulesco's *Johnny Belinda* (1948), a film in which the equation of the voice with the vagina is particularly pronounced, but first I want to explain my perhaps too easy slippage from Jones's remarks about the female mouth to the conclusions I have just drawn about the female voice in dominant cinema. The prominence of the talking cure within both psychoanalysis and many Hollywood films of the 1940s suggests that the importance of the female mouth finally has less to do with the inaugural role it is assumed to play within female sexuality—its alimentary logic—than with its status as a generator of gender-differentiated and erotically charged sounds. It is, after all, primarily through those sounds that either psychoanalysis or cinema has access to what it takes to be woman's drives, desires, memories, or pleasures. At its most culturally gratifying, the female voice provides the acoustic equivalent of an ejaculation, permitting the outpouring or externalization of what would otherwise remain hidden and unknowable.[39] Thus, as Heath remarks, the key part played by the voice within the pornographic film—"so many bodies and bits of bodies without voices; merely, perhaps, snatches of dialogue, to get things going, and then, imperatively, a whole gamut of pants and cries, to deal with the immense and catastrophic problem . . . of the visibility or not of pleasure, to provide a *vocal image* to guarantee the accomplishment of pleasure, the proper working of the economy."[40] The female voice is consequently, if not for all intents and purposes, then at least as far as woman's interiority is concerned, the projection of the mouth.

Male access to woman's psyche is blocked at its usual port of entry in *Johnny Belinda*, a "talking cure" film with a difference, necessitating the search for an alternate route. The central character of that film, Belinda (Jane Wyman), is a farm girl who has been deaf and mute since birth. Because she is outside language, her family and the other town residents assume she is without the capacity for reason. However, a newly arrived doctor insists that Belinda merely lacks the words to express her thoughts, and attempts to prove his point by teaching her to use sign language.

The results are less than satisfactory. The mute woman does manage to learn a number of significant gestures, but only by identifying each sign with a concrete object, on a one-for-one basis. Because those gestures belong so fully to an exterior register, and because they are devoid of the "presence" which the voice has long been believed to confer, they do not seem capable of revealing Belinda's inner "reality." The doctor finally takes her to an out-of-town specialist, hoping to find a medical treatment for her deafness and muteness, and thereby to gain access to her interiority.

The examination which the specialist subsequently gives Belinda strays far from its expected object. Rather than producing any new information about her vocal and auditory difficulties, it leads to a major discovery about her reproductive system—to the discovery that she is pregnant. In other words, finding the customary (oral) path to the inner regions of female subjectivity impassable, the specialist would seem to have taken the alternative (vaginal) route. The examination thus effects a startling reversal of the displacement Freud describes in the essay on fetishism: instead of directing his attention "upward," away from woman's genitals to her face, the specialist shifts his attention "downward," away from her face to her genitals.

By adopting the vaginal rather than the oral (and aural) path, the specialist follows in the footsteps of the man responsible for Belinda's pregnancy. Although that earlier penetration was a rape, it is shown to have beneficent results. It gives Belinda what psychoanalysis is always quick to propose as the final solution to the problem of female desire, the one thing able both to make good woman's lack and to give her an ideologically recognizable and coherent "content"—a baby. That "supplement" also provides her with a surrogate voice, capable of emitting that most exemplary of female sounds (at least within classic cinema): the cry.

The degree to which Belinda's interiority is henceforth represented as an extension of her maternal function is indicated when the rapist attempts to appropriate her child, and she kills him in the ensuing struggle. Placed on trial for murder, she is acquitted on the grounds that "something in her was stronger than the precept 'Thou shalt not kill' "—that she obeyed "an instinct stronger than the laws of man—the instinct of a mother to protect her child."

The terms of this defense echo Jones's declaration that "femininity develops from the promptings of an instinctual constitution."[41] By attributing Belinda's emotions and actions to her innate impulse to nurture, the legal apparatus of the film anchors her interiority firmly to her drives, making the former an extension of the latter. Thus, what the talking cure is here unable to coax out of the female voice is "spoken" instead through the female body. However, as in *Lady in the Dark* and *Possessed*, what is thereby "discovered" has in fact been introduced into Belinda from outside, via the penis.[42]

By using one as a back-up to the other, classic cinema indicates that the Jonesian and Freudian models of female sexuality may not be as starkly incompatible as they are generally believed to be—at least not at the level of their filmic deployment.[43] I have already commented at some length upon the vocal "striptease"—upon that unveiling of female discursive lack which follows both from the subordination of the female voice to the female body, and from the enclosure of that voice within narrative recesses and closets. This discursive divestiture works by aligning woman with diegetic interiority, and so by isolating her definitively from the site of textual production. The talking cure gives that interiority an added dimension by projecting "into" woman a psychic realm which generally doubles as a narrative within the narrative.

The Jonesian paradigm, with its insistence upon the "natural" body as the basis of female sexuality, and hence of female subjectivity, is always hovering somewhere in the background of classic cinema, working not so much to contradict woman's castration as to reiterate it by embedding both her voice and her interiority in corporeality. That paradigm comes into more prominent play in the last two films I have discussed because female speech is obstructed there—in *Kiss Me Deadly* because there is no possibility of extracting verbal information from Christina's body after she has been tortured to death, and in *Johnny Belinda* because there is no female voice through which to install interiority. In both of these texts, the female body is made to speak in place of the female voice, obliged to yield up its "secrets" to the physician's or coroner's probing hand and gaze. And in each case, those "secrets" turn in some way upon woman's "instinctual constitution"—upon her reproductive faculties or her explosive sexuality.

I would like to conclude both my textual analysis of *Johnny Belinda* and the chapter as a whole by reappropriating from Derrida a signifier which he has appropriated from sexual difference, a signifier with which he has attempted to erase the opposition between "inner" and "outer," and to suggest that what passes for essence always carries the trace of a previous inscription. That term is *invagination,* which Derrida suggestively defines as "the inward refolding of *la gaine* [sheath, girdle], the inverted reapplication of the outer edge to the inside of a form where the outside then opens a pocket."[44]

Ironically, Derrida's deployment of the concept of invagination has tended to obscure rather than to foreground the ways in which texts engender their readers and viewers; as is frequently the case in his work, it is exploited primarily as rhetorical currency, as a "fertile" metaphor through which to theorize writing.[45] This is unfortunate, because the concept has important ramifications for our understanding of sexual difference, particularly in its cinematic manifestations.

Derrida's definition can be applied with great precision to the three operations which have been the chief concern of this chapter, operations which equate the female voice with diegetic, psychic, and corporeal interiority. They, too, crease the text in such as way as to construct a recess or enclosure into which woman can be inserted. And since this recess is always linked by analogy to the image of female sexuality as a bottomless pit, these operations could also be said to fold that sexuality "into" woman, to be one of the mechanisms whereby she comes to be identified with a dark continent.

The notion of invagination thus has the great merit of obliging us to understand that concentricity has no more of a natural claim upon the female subject than does castration—that far from expressing woman's "instinctual constitution," the bottomless pit of female sexuality, like woman's diegetic interiority, is nothing but a textual "pocket." Indeed, I would go so far as to assert that whenever the female voice seems to speak most out of the "reality" of her body, it is in fact most complexly contained within the diegesis, and most paradigmatically a part of Hollywood's sonic *vraisemblable.*

Moreover, since the male subject can align himself with diegetic *exteriority* only to the extent that the female subject is aligned with diegetic *interiority,* the concept of invagination also reminds us that the seemingly transcendental position from which that subject so frequently speaks, listens, and looks in classic cinema is itself a product of the same textual fold. Although Hollywood usually obliges only woman to display the stigmata of diegetic interiority, both the male and the female subjects are inside meaning, and neither can ever be the punctual source of that meaning. At the level of sound, as at that of the image, Hollywood protects the male subject from unpleasurable self-knowledge by requiring woman to stand in for him.

Not surprisingly, what has been thus disowned returns in the guise of paranoid fantasies of enclosure, entrapment, and suffocation. The female voice figures centrally within these fantasies, often functioning as a lure drawing the male subject to destruction, or as a black hole where meaning drains out of the system. In the next chapter I will attempt to delineate the larger cultural fantasy behind these textual variations on the theme of engulfment, a fantasy about the maternal voice.

[3]

THE FANTASY OF THE MATERNAL VOICE:

PARANOIA AND COMPENSATION

IT HAS BECOME something of a theoretical commonplace to characterize the maternal voice as a blanket of sound, extending on all sides of the newborn infant. For Guy Rosolato and Mary Ann Doane, the maternal voice is a "sonorous envelope" which "surrounds, sustains, and cherishes the child."[1] Julia Kristeva conceives of it as a "mobile receptacle" which absorbs the infant's "anaclitic facilitations."[2] Didier Anzieu refers to it as a "bath of sounds," while for Claude Bailblé it is, quite simply, "music."[3] Michel Chion also subscribes to this general definition of the maternal voice, although he gives it a much more sinister inflection; within his account, that voice not only envelops but entraps the newborn infant.[4]

In this chapter, I will attempt to demonstrate that the trope of the maternal voice as sonorous envelope grows out of a powerful cultural fantasy, a fantasy which recent psychoanalytic theory shares with classic cinema. The fantasy in question turns upon the image of infantile containment—upon the image of a child held within the environment or sphere of the mother's voice. I have described this image as neutrally as possible, but in fact its "appearances" are always charged with either intensely positive or intensely negative affect; Rosolato, for instance, regards the "pleasurable milieu" of the maternal voice as "the first model of auditory pleasure," whereas Chion associates it with the terror of an "umbilical night."[5] These contradictory views of the same image point to the profoundly ambivalent nature of the fantasy which is my present concern, an ambivalence which attests to the divided nature of subjectivity, and which underscores the fact that pleasure for one psychic system almost invariably means unpleasure for another psychic system. The fantasy of the maternal-voice-as-sonorous-envelope takes on a different meaning depending upon the psychic "lookout point"; viewed from the site of the unconscious, the image of the infant held within the environment or sphere of the mother's voice is an emblem of infantile plenitude and bliss. Viewed from the site of the preconscious/ conscious system, it is an emblem of impotence and entrapment.

By identifying the sonorous envelope trope as a fantasy, I mean to emphasize that trope's retroactivity rather than its fictiveness—to indicate its status as an after-the-fact construction or reading of a situation which is fundamentally irrecoverable, rather than to posit it as a simple illusion. In other words, I intend to stress the ways in which the fantasy functions as a bridge between two radically disjunctive moments—an infantile moment, which occurs prior to the inception of subjectivity, and which is consequently "too early" with respect to meaning and desire, and a subsequent moment, firmly rooted within both meaning and desire, but consequently "too late" for fulfillment. The first of those moments, which can be imagined but never actually experienced, turns upon the imaginary fusion of mother and infant, and hence upon unity and plenitude. The second moment marks the point at which the subject introjects a preexisting structure, a structure which gives order, shape, and significance to the original ineffable experience. That preexisting structure is what Laplanche would call a "parental fantasy,"[6] or what Deleuze and Guattari would describe as a "group fantasy";[7] it not only anticipates but exceeds the individual subject.

I will begin this chapter with the negative or dystopic version of the maternal voice fantasy, which I will extract in part from Chion's *La voix au cinéma,* and in part from dominant cinema, and which I will read as a symptom of male paranoia and castration. I will then turn to what might be called the "operatic" version of the maternal voice fantasy, both as it has been theoretically articulated by Rosolato in "La voix: entre corps et langage," and as it has been cinematically formulated in texts such as *Citizen Kane, Diva,* and (most complexly) *The Conversation.* Chapter 4 will address a third version of the maternal voice fantasy, and one with profound feminist resonances—that collectively "dreamt" by Kristeva, Robert Altman, Laura Mulvey, and Peter Wollen.

Like myths, [fantasies] claim to provide a representation of, and a solution to, the major enigmas which confront the child. Whatever appears to the subject as something needing an explanation or theory, is dramatized as a moment of emergence, the beginning of a history.

> Fantasies of origins: the primal scene pictures the origin of the in-
> dividual; fantasies of seduction, the origin and upsurge of sexuality; fanta-
> sies of castration, the origin of the difference between the sexes.[8]

No matter how it is conceptualized, the image of the infant contained within the sonorous envelope of the mother's voice is a fantasy of
origins—a fantasy about precultural sexuality, about the entry into
language, and about the inauguration of subjectivity. That preoccupation is particularly marked in Chion's *La voix au cinéma*, which associates the maternal voice not only with early infantile existence, but with
a moment prior to the creation of the world, and the inception of
Christian history. I would like to look rather closely at the passage
which most fully encapsulates this "nightmare" of the maternal voice, in
an attempt to determine the latent content of what is ultimately a group
or cultural fantasy, a fantasy which extends beyond *La voix au cinéma* to
dominant narrative film:

> In the beginning, in the uterine night, was the voice, that of the
> Mother. For the child after birth, the Mother is more an olfactory and vocal
> continuum than an image. One can imagine the voice of the Mother, which
> is woven around the child, and which originates from all points in space as
> her form enters and leaves the visual field, as a matrix of places to which we
> are tempted to give the name "umbilical net." A horrifying expression,
> since it evokes a cobweb—and in fact, this original vocal tie will remain
> ambivalent.[9]

What first commands the reader's attention about this passage is its
vision of complete engulfment, and the panic which that vision generates. However, it is no easy matter to locate the point from which the
panic issues, or the subjectivity under siege. The cast of possible characters is a familiar one, consisting of the father, evoked through the
deliberate misquotation of the famous opening to the fourth Gospel ("In
the beginning was the Word"), but otherwise conspicuously absent; the
mother, whose voice is associated with the "uterine night" of a prenatal
reality; and the infant, trapped within the vocal continuum of the
maternal voice. It is ostensibly this last site from which the family
romance is described, and from which the sense of crisis issues. However, the phrases "one can imagine" and "we are tempted to give" show
the speaking position to be elsewhere altogether, and point to one of
those "deferred" readings so central to the organization of gender.

These qualifiers suggest, in other words, that the familial drama
outlined by Chion finds its only performance within an altogether
different psychic scene from that inhabited by the child—that it is a
construction superimposed upon infancy from a subsequent temporal
and spatial vantage. The relation of the newborn child to the maternal

voice poses a threat to the one who occupies this subsequent temporal and spatial vantage; in short, to a fully constituted subject. But fresh questions arise: Who is this subject, and why should the relation of the infant to the maternal voice represent such a stress point?

Through the intentional miscitation from John I, Chion opposes the maternal voice to the paternal word, and so identifies the mother with sound and the father with meaning. He also situates the maternal voice in an anterior position to the paternal word, conferring upon it an original (if not originating) status. However, since the maternal voice is associated with the darkness and formlessness of the infant's earliest experiences, rather than with the form-giving illumination of the *logos*, this anteriority implies primitiveness rather than privilege. Indeed, since "in the beginning" is a reference to Genesis as well as to John, the passage under discussion seems to suggest that the maternal voice could be justly compared to the chaos upon which the divine word imposed its order and illumination at the moment of creation.

The opposition of the maternal voice to the paternal word attests to a quite remarkable sleight of hand, although one which has been so frequently effected within recent theory as to have become almost transparent. It attests, that is, to the displacement onto the mother of qualities which more properly characterize the newborn child. The conceptualization of the maternal voice as a "uterine night" of nonmeaning effects a similar displacement; once again the infant's perceptual and semiotic underdevelopment are transferred onto the mother.

An astonishing amount of negative affect accumulates around the maternal voice in the passage quoted above, concentrating primarily around three images of enclosure: the images of a woven enclosure, an umbilical net, and a cobweb. It is through these analogical terms, I would suggest, that we can best grasp both the identity of the fully constituted subject for whom the maternal voice poses a potential crisis, and the motive behind the displacement of the infant's verbal and auditory impotence onto the mother. All three tropes figure enclosure as entrapment and/or danger, and so represent interiority as an undesirable condition. In each case, that interiority is synonymous with the infantile condition. Trapped within the suffocating confinement of the mother's voice, the newborn child resembles a prisoner or prey.

Within the theoretical narrative formulated by Chion, interiority is also identified with discursive impotence, and exteriority (at least by implication) with discursive potency. The child hears, but is not yet able to understand, and emits sounds, but is not yet able to make them meaningful. It is wrapped "inside" the sonorous envelope of the mother's voice, but is still on the far side of signification. Access to the symbolic would seem to turn upon the transfer of the child from the "inside" to the "outside" of that envelope. (I must stress once again that this metaphoric drama unfolds from a time and place other than those occupied by the child—that it is riven through and through with retrospection.)

What is repressed within this narrative, but can be exhumed from a group of symptomatic details, is that since exteriority can be defined only through opposition to interiority, the child's shift to the "outside" of the "umbilical net" requires that the maternal voice be resituated "inside"—that the "container" become the "contained." We can see this inversion in the rhetorical slippage noted above, where the voice of the mother somehow comes to absorb the perceptual and semiotic immaturity which more properly characterizes the infant's condition.

This inversion becomes ideologically explicable as soon as we introduce into the analysis a number of the functions frequently performed by the maternal voice during the first years of childhood—the functions of language teacher, expositor, and storyteller. Psychoanalysis tells us that the mother's voice is usually the first to be isolated by the infant from other noises, and that it is by imitating the sounds she makes that it produces its own initial articulations.[10] Hers is the voice (at least within a traditional familial scheme) that first charts space, delimits objects, explains and defines the external world; as Jacques Hassoun remarks, it is also the voice that first introduces the infant subject to the Other.[11]

Last, but by no means least, within Western culture the mother is the most frequent narrator of nursery rhymes and bedtime stories. Because her voice is identified by the child long before her body is, it remains unlocalized during a number of the most formative moments of subjectivity. The maternal voice would thus seem to be the original prototype for the disembodied voice-over in cinema, as Chion himself acknowledges at one point in his book:

> The first to display images is the Mother, whose voice, before the (eventual) learning of written signs, makes things become detached in a living and symbolic temporality. In the fiction of the fabulator and teller of stories as in the traditional [voice-over] of the commentary, something always remains of this original function.[12]

It is astonishing that a cinematic device which thus carries within it the symbolic "trace" of the mother should have become the exclusive prerogative of the male voice within Hollywood film, while the female voice not only is confined to the "inside" of the narrative, but is forced again and again into diegetic "closets" and "crevices." I would like to suggest that this system of vocal conventions, like the theoretical formulation advanced by Chion, functions to reverse an imagined primordial situation in which the male child was wrapped in the sonorous blanket of the mother's voice, and was as yet unable either to distinguish or to produce meaningful sounds. In both the cinematic and theoretical paradigms, the discursive potency of the male voice is established by stripping the female voice of all claim to verbal authority. And in both instances that divestiture most pointedly negates the mother's earlier role as language teacher, commentator, and narrator. (I refer to the primordial situation as an "imagined" one because the drama of interiority and exteriority upon which it turns is obviously a deferred reading of the infantile scenario from a position fully within the symbolic—a position already structured by lack. The displacement I have just described transfers that lack onto its culturally sanctioned site, the female subject.)

The moment at which it becomes most evident that both the cinematic and theoretical formulations hinge upon the substitution of the mother for the child within the fantasmatic tableau is also the point at which their symmetry is most marked. The moment in question occurs during an astonishing passage from *La voix au cinéma*, a passage where Chion describes cinema as "a machine made in order to deliver a cry from the female voice":

> The *point of the cry* in a cinematographic fiction . . . is defined . . . as something which gushes forth, generally from the mouth of a woman, something which is not, moreover, inevitably heard, but which above all must fall at *a named point*, explode at a precise moment, at the cross-roads of convergent lines, at the conclusion of an often alembic and disproportionate path—but calculated to give to this point its maximum impact: the film functions, then, like those big animating machines, full of gears and connecting rods, of chains of actions and reactions, here a machine made in order to deliver a cry. . . . The point of the cry is an unthinkable point at the interior of thought, an inexpressible [point] at the interior of the enunciation, an unrepresentable point at the interior of representation. . . . This cry incarnates a fantasm of absolute sonorousness. . . .[13]

Again the high drama, the metaphoric excess, the sense of extravagant investment in the female voice. But now, at last, the agenda is out in the open: What is demanded from woman—what the cinematic apparatus and a formidable branch of the theoretical apparatus will extract from her by whatever means are required—is involuntary sound, sound that escapes her own understanding, testifying only to the artistry of a superior force. The female voice must be sequestered (if necessary through a *mise-en-abîme* of framing devices) within the heart of the diegesis, so far from the site of enunciation as to be beyond articulation or meaning. It must occupy an "unthinkable point at the interior of thought," an "inexpressible [point] at the interior of the enunciation," an "unrepresentable [point] at the interior of representation." There is, of course, only one group of sounds capable of conforming precisely to these requirements—those emitted by a newborn baby. This, then, is the vocal position which the female subject is called upon to occupy whenever (in film or in theory) she is identified with noise, babble, or the cry.

The last of these sounds is regularly wrung from the female voice in films of the recent horror, stalker, and slasher varieties, but the textual example I would like to cite at this juncture falls slightly to one side of those generic (or subgeneric) categories. The film, Anatole Litvak's *Sorry, Wrong Number* (1948), dramatizes one evening in the life of a woman who has been confined to her bed with a "cardiac neurosis"— an evening which ends with her murder.[14] That woman, Leona (Barbara Stanwyck), gains access to the outside world only through her bedside telephone, which she employs constantly until her death. The remainder of the film consists of flashbacks which are activated in one way or another by the telephone calls. These flashbacks offer a very different view of Leona from that provided by the diegetic present; they show her proposing to a man who does not love her, coercing him into marriage, engineering their honeymoon, rifling through the contents of his wallets, and destroying the photograph of another woman she finds there, forcing him to move with her into her father's house, and— finally—insisting that he adopt a purely titular position in her father's business. The male character in question, Henry (Burt Lancaster), compares himself at one point to a "pet dog."

Leona's usurpation of functions which the film insists are a male prerogative is most dramatically rendered by an accelerated montage of her wedding and honeymoon, the parts of which are held together by her voice-over repetition of the words: "I, Leona, take thee Henry. . . ." Although this voice-over is not disembodied, it exerts enunciative authority over the images, not only organizing them, but in a sense "causing" them. Since marriage vows belong to the category of what J. L. Austin calls "performative" utterances[15]—utterances which effect or perform what they state—Leona could be said actually to assume possession of Henry with the words "I . . . thee take," and so to generate the subsequent honeymoon celebration. Despite its brevity, this montage sequence enacts a major transgression in the vocal/auditory system of classic cinema, returning to the mother the symbolic mastery she exercises within the infantile situation.

This transgression does not go unpunished. Confined to her bed, and made dependent for all her physical and psychic needs upon the disembodied voices which speak to her through the telephone, Leona is reduced through helplessness and anxiety to a condition of verbal and aural incompetence. At the beginning of the film, a faulty connection permits her to overhear a telephone conversation about her own murder, but she is unable to grasp that she herself is the intended victim. Leona responds to this overheard conversation with a series of hysterical calls to the operator, her husband's secretary, and the police, not one of which exerts the slightest influence over impending events. A number of subsequent incoming calls emphasize her inability to get even a simple message straight.

Leona is thus placed in an analogous position to the fantasmatic infant. Sunk in "motor incapacity" and "nursling dependence,"[16] she inhabits an envelope of sounds which remain largely indecipherable to her, unable to exercise linguistic control over her environment. Indeed, the telephone system which determines all of her interpersonal exchanges in the diegetic present is described by titles at the opening of the film in terms which are strikingly suggestive of an "umbilical net":

> In the tangled network of a great city the telephone is the unseen link between a million lives. . . . It is the servant of our common needs, the confidant of our inmost secrets . . . life and happiness wait upon its ring . . . and horror . . . and loneliness . . . and death.

Ultimately, Leona is asked to establish an even more intimate identification with the vocal status of a newborn child. Overcome with remorse at the last minute, her husband telephones her about her imminent murder, and urges her to run to the window and scream. Her hysterical "refusal" to do so leaves her completely vulnerable to the strangler, who a moment later extracts the requisite cry from Leona by wrapping the telephone cord around her neck.

Reversals of the sort I have been examining here would seem to be facilitated by the double organization of the vocal/auditory system, which permits a speaker to function at the same time as listener, his or her voice returning as sound in the process of utterance. The simultaneity of these two actions makes it difficult to situate the voice, to know whether it is "outside" or "inside." The boundary separating exteriority from interiority is blurred by this aural undecidability—by the replication within the former arena of something which seems to have its inception within the latter. Rosolato refers to this replication as an

"acoustic mirror," and he hints at its potentially destabilizing consequences for subjectivity:

> The voice [has the property] of being at the same time emitted and heard,
> sent and received, and by the subject himself, as if, in comparison with the
> look, an "acoustic" mirror were always in effect. Thus the images of entry
> and departure relative to the body are narrowly articulated. They can come
> to be confounded, inverted, to prevail one over the other.[17]

What Rosolato suggests is that since the voice is capable of being
internalized at the same time as it is externalized, it can spill over from
subject to object and object to subject, violating the bodily limits upon
which classic subjectivity depends, and so smoothing the way for projection and introjection. Paranoia—the attribution of material density to
hallucinated sounds—is only one possible permutation of this slippage.

The notion of an "acoustic mirror" can be applied with remarkable
precision to the function which the female voice is called upon to
perform for the male subject. Within the traditional familial paradigm,
the maternal voice introduces the child to its mirror reflection, "lubricat-
ing," as it were, the "fit." The child also learns to speak by imitating the
sounds made by the mother, fashioning its voice after hers. However,
even before the mirror stage and the entry into language, the maternal
voice plays a major role in the infant's perceptual development. It is
generally the first object not only to be isolated, but to be introjected:

> The child, blind at birth, [is] capable of distinguishing the voice of the
> mother in a selective manner from the age of [only] *ten weeks*. . . . [whereas]
> it is [only] at 5–6 weeks that the look becomes the sense director for the
> exterior delimitation of the object that is always introjected in the first six
> weeks, according to non-visual schemes. . . . One must then recognize the
> importance of auditory introjections and precocious vocalizations; because
> it is only in a second time that the organization of visual space assures the
> perception of the object as *exterior*.[18]

The situation just described is one where the object has as yet no
externality, since it is no sooner identified than it is assimilated by the
child. Nor, since the subject lacks boundaries, does it as yet have
anything approximating an interiority. However, the foundations for
what will later function as identity are marked out by these primitive
encounters with the outer world, encounters which occur along the axis
of the mother's voice. Since the child's economy is organized around
incorporation, and since what is incorporated is the auditory field articulated by the maternal voice, the child could be said to hear itself
initially through that voice—to first "recognize" itself in the vocal "mirror" supplied by the mother.

I would argue that the male subject later hears the maternal voice through himself—that it comes to resonate for him with all that he transcends through language. In other words, through a symmetrical gesture to that whereby the child "finds" its "own" voice by introjecting the mother's voice, the male subject subsequently "refines" his "own" voice by projecting onto the mother's voice all that is unassimilable to the paternal position. As I have attempted to demonstrate in the first chapter of this book, the boundaries of male subjectivity must be constantly redrawn through the externalizing displacement onto the female subject of what Kristeva would call the "abject."[19] In this case, what must be thus jettisoned is the vocal and auditory "afterbirth" which threatens to contaminate the order and system of "proper" speech. Thus, whereas the mother's voice initially functions as the acoustic mirror in which the child discovers its identity and voice, it later functions as the acoustic mirror in which the male subject hears all the repudiated elements of his infantile babble.

However, the very reversibility which facilitates these introjections and projections also threatens to undermine them—to reappropriate from the male subject what he has incorporated, or to return to him what he has thrown away. Alan Pakula's *Klute* (1971) dramatizes the instability of the vocal/auditory system, and the crisis that instability can generate in male subjectivity. It suggests, moreover, that the female voice can become a dumping ground for disowned desires, as well as for the remnants of verbal incompetence.

The film's premise is central to the concerns of this chapter: A prostitute's voice has been taped without her knowledge by one of her customers, who plays it over and over to himself in private. This voice is heard by us repeatedly when detached from the body of the prostitute, Bree Daniels (Jane Fonda), although it is always fully contained within the diegesis. This dislocation creates a kind of ripple effect in the text, which relies to an unusual degree upon voice-off and embodied voice-over.

The words Bree speaks are almost a parody of Freudian discourse. She urges the john, Peter Cable (Charles Cioffi), to suspend all self-censorship, and to give complete expression to his darkest desires ("You should never be ashamed . . . nothing is wrong . . . let it all hang out and fuck it"). Later she tells him, "I'm just trying to figure you out . . . I'll [succeed] before the evening's over," suggesting that prostitution, like psychoanalysis, has as its final goal the penetration of another's psyche. The comparison becomes even more explicit later in the film, when Cable accuses Bree of forcing upon him an unwanted self-knowledge:

There are little corners in everyone which were better left alone—little
sicknesses, weaknesses, which should never be exposed. But that's your
stock and trade, isn't it? . . . I was never fully aware of mine until you
brought them out.

Through this accusation, Cable implicitly acknowledges that he
hears Bree's voice as if it were his own voice—that her voice functions
as an acoustic mirror in which he hears an unwanted part of himself, an
element of himself which escapes "social rationality, that logical order
upon which a social aggregate is based."[20] Cable's imaginary relation to
Bree's voice is further emphasized by the recurrent image of him listening to the tape in his office at the top of a high-rise executive building,
the light from outside casting a sharp reflection of his face and shoulders
on the highly polished surface of his desk. At this moment, he is
unequivocally locked within a narcissistic exchange.

Cable experiences this return of the repressed as a violation—as an
invasion resulting in an unwanted interiority. In other words, he responds to Bree's voice as though it has the power to confine him to
precisely that condition to which cinema habitually confines its female
characters. He reacts by attempting to deflect the aggressivity of Bree's
voice away from himself, and against her. Over and over again, Cable
plays the recorded conversation to Bree over the telephone, forcing her
to play auditress to her own words. He attempts to return her voice to
her by obliging her to hear herself within it, to recognize herself within
the acoustic mirror she earlier held up to him. In other words, Cable
tries to make Bree accept ownership—and so responsibility—for what
she says on the tape.

He also subjects her to a relentless visual surveillance, spying on her
constantly through the skylight of her apartment, and following her
whenever she leaves. When Cable finally vandalizes Bree's apartment,
leaving behind a pool of semen, it becomes clear that all of this scopic
activity is calculated to establish her identification with an unpleasurable (and indeed contaminated) interiority, and his own identification
with a pleasurable and masterful exteriority. Extreme measures are
necessary because these normative identifications have been called into
question by the reversibility of the voice.

The film shows itself to be more than a little complicit with Cable's
project, as eager as he to find ways of containing and regulating Bree's
voice.[21] It installs John Klute (Donald Sutherland) in an apartment
below Bree's, where he is in a position to monitor all her incoming and
outgoing calls. He also compiles a tape dossier of conversations she has
with clients, and manages to extract from others information she has
given them in confidence. However, not even this elaborate system of

auditory surveillance would seem adequate to restrain Bree's voice, since she must additionally be subjected to that most classic of all solutions to discursive deviance in women: the talking cure. A substantial portion of the film takes place in an analyst's office, where Bree pays frequent visits.

The chief obstacle in the way of all these attempts to reanchor Bree's voice to her body is her constant recourse to verbal simulation. Not only is she an aspiring actress who does "interesting" accents, but she approaches prostitution as though it were a form of masquerade. Her favorite client pays her to fabricate stories to him about her erotic encounters in romantic locales, while with the others she feigns pleasure and fakes orgasm (during one session, her seemingly ecstatic cries are completely undercut by a calculated look at her wristwatch). As she tells her analyst:

> For an hour I'm the best actress in the world . . . [I] just lead them by the nose where they think they want to go . . . [I] call the shots . . . and I always feel just great afterwards. . . .

For Bree, control turns upon enunciative authority—upon the capacity to effect through discourse. However, the importance which she attributes to play-acting suggests that enunciative authority can come to be invested only in a voice which refuses to be subordinated to and judged by the body—a voice that resists the norm of synchronization. That she in fact aspires to the condition of a disembodied voice (-over) is indicated not only by her verbal masquerade, with its nonmatch of body and voice, exteriority and interiority, actions and feelings, but by a remark she makes to her analyst: "What I'd really like is to be faceless and bodiless and to be left alone."

Pakula's film asserts the impossibility of Bree's desire within the classic cinematic paradigm—an impossibility which can be seen with particular clarity from the vantage point of male subjectivity. Bree's asynchronous impulses encounter two particularly virulent responses. One of these, which is directed at her through the figure of Cable, takes the form of a demand that she produce "authentic," involuntary sound—i.e., a scream. Managing at last to trap Bree in an empty clothing factory, he obliges her to listen to the tape of the death cries emitted by another of his prostitute victims, and then attempts to extract a similar reaction from her.

The other response to Bree's discursive transgressions is much more insidious, since it does not present itself as a punishment (quite the contrary), and since it is an action on the part of the apparatus rather than on the part of a fictional character. At two key moments in the film, both associated with Bree's emotional surrender to Klute, her voice is quite simply extinguished. The first of these aural "blackouts" occurs when Bree and Klute first make love, and the second when they are shopping for a romantic dinner. The elimination of vocal sound is more conspicuous in the second instance, since lips are seen to move, and since other noises fade in near the end of the sequence. However, the loss of Bree's voice is more significant in the first instance, since it places her fully on the side of the spectacle. This sequence represents a systematic repudiation of the tripartite desire Bree expresses to her analyst—the desire to be faceless, bodiless, and alone. It is hardly surprising that when Bree's voice is returned to her, she should coldly deny that she has experienced any pleasure. Of course, the film uses both her silence and her denial to state the contrary.

As *Klute* so powerfully demonstrates, the reversibility of the vocal/auditory system not only makes possible the systematic projection of all that is culturally debased and devalued onto the female voice, it also poses the constant possibility of the leakage of those same attributes back onto the male voice. The incessant realignment of female characters with diegetic interiority, and male characters with diegetic exteriority, is consequently more than the inversion of an imagined infantile situation in which the child is wrapped in the sonorous envelope of the mother's voice, and more than a mechanism for aligning the male subject with discursive authority while situating the female voice definitively inside the fiction. It must also be understood as a defensive reaction against the migratory potential of the voice—as an attempt to restrain it within established boundaries, and so to prevent its uncontrolled circulation.

Rosolato offers a much more theoretically sophisticated as well as a far more utopian account of the maternal voice than that provided by Chion. He, too, conceptualizes the mother's voice as a sonorous envelope enclosing the newborn infant. However, like Kristeva, but in distinct opposition to Chion, he associates that enclosure with plenitude and bliss, and reads it as an emblem of the idyllic unity of mother and child. Rosolato also argues that this primordial listening experience is the prototype for all subsequent auditory pleasure, especially the pleasure that derives from music:

> The maternal voice helps to constitute for the infant the pleasurable milieu which surrounds, sustains and cherishes him. . . . One could argue that it is the first model of auditory pleasure and that music finds its roots and its

nostalgia in [this] original atmosphere, which might be called a sonorous womb, a murmuring house—or *music of the spheres.*[22]

Thus, whereas Chion's maternal voice traps the newborn infant in an "umbilical net," and plunges it into a "uterine night" of nonmeaning, Rosolato's maternal voice not only wraps the child in a soothing and protective blanket, but bathes it in a celestial melody whose closest terrestrial equivalent is opera.

Rosolato's fantasy of the maternal voice also revolves around a second sonorous image: the image of the child harmonizing with the mother, and making its emissions "adequate" to hers. However, he is quick to point out that sounds can be placed in unison only after they have been differentiated from each other, and he makes that observation the basis for a simultaneous reading of musical, psychic, and corporeal separation and restoration. Rosolato stresses that the dream of recovering the mother's voice can only be born out of the experience of division and loss, and that it consequently testifies to nothing so much as lack:

> Harmonic and polyphonic display can be understood as a succession of tensions and of releases, of the union and the divergence of elements that are . . . opposed in their accords, in order then to be resolved in their most simple unity. It is then the whole drama of separated bodies and their reunion which supports harmony. (P. 82)

Rosolato also indicates that the image of the maternal voice as a sonorous envelope derives from a moment well beyond infancy, on the other side of subjectivity and symbolic castration ("The reawakening of *the* voice always presupposes a break, an irreversible distance from the lost object").[23] He explains that this image is superimposed upon infancy only by means of the backward movement *(la démarche régrédiente)* of fantasy.

Rosolato thus characterizes the maternal voice as a "lost object." This characterization helps to remind us that Lacan includes the maternal voice in the category of the *"objet (a)."* That category, which also includes the feces, the mother's breast, and the mother's gaze, designates those objects which are first to be distinguished from the subject's own self, and whose "otherness" is never very strongly marked. Because the *objet (a)* is "a small part of the self which detaches itself from [the subject] while still remaining his, still retained," its loss assumes the proportions of an amputation.[24] Once gone, it comes to represent what can alone make good the subject's lack. The status of the maternal voice as an *objet (a)* helps to explain why it should be the focus of such a powerful fantasy of phenomenal recovery as that dreamt by Rosolato, Kristeva, Anzieu, Bailblé, and Doane.

However, it must not be forgotten that the maternal voice is also what first ruptures plenitude and introduces difference, at least within the paradigmatic Western family—the voice which first charts out and names the world for the infant subject, and which itself provides the first axis of Otherness. This is a point upon which Denis Vasse strongly insists in *L'ombilic et la voix*, a book which attributes to the maternal voice the role of "constantly reopening the opening which the imaginary object tends to fill."[25] It is in this capacity that the maternal voice functions as the first voice-over, and the first voice-off—as the generator of sounds that proceed from beyond the child's range of vision, or that precede its ability to see.

As I indicated earlier in this chapter, and as I will have occasion to demonstrate further in my discussion of Kristeva, the sonorous envelope fantasy often forecloses upon this aspect of the maternal voice. It usually works either to reverse the respective positions of mother and infant by situating the former inside the umbilical net, on the far side of significa-tion, or to join mother to infant inside the *choric* enclosure. Rosolato is alone in confronting the lack which fuels the fantasy, and in acknowl-edging that what is really at issue is not the mother's exclusion from the symbolic, but the subject's own, irreducible castration—a subject who is male in Chion's account, female in Kristeva's.

This castration has, of course, nothing to do with anatomy, although our culture constantly asserts the contrary. As I indicated in chapter 1, it refers in part to the differentiation of subject from object, and hence to the loss of imaginary plenitude—a loss which is writ large in the drama of the *objet petit autre*. Castration also refers to the fact that the symbolic order precedes and anticipates the subject, providing it with ready-made desires and meanings. Finally, it is a way of designat-ing the cleavage that separates the speaking subject from the subject of its speech—a cleavage which is nowhere in greater evidence than at the site of the voice itself, vehicle of both the cry and the word. In its fantasmatic guise as "pure" sonorousness, the maternal voice oscillates between two poles; it is either cherished as an *objet (a)*—as what can make good all lacks—or despised and jettisoned as what is most abject, most culturally intolerable—as the forced representative of everything within male subjectivity which is incompatible with the phallic func-tion, and which threatens to expose discursive mastery as an impos-sible ideal.

The first of these scenarios is the fundamental drama behind Orson Welles's *Citizen Kane* (1941).[26] Kane not only accumulates the riches of the world in a vain attempt to compensate for the divisions and sepa-rations upon which subjectivity is based, but he builds an opera house to enclose a voice within whose enveloping sonorousness he hopes to be enclosed in turn, and thereby reunited with his lost mother. (It would indeed be difficult to imagine a film which more closely conforms to Rosolato's account of music, or to his particular version of the maternal voice fantasy.)

The fantasy of the maternal voice as an operatic and utopian enclosure also invades Jean-Jacques Beineix's *Diva* (1981), which opens with the illicit taping of an opera singer's voice by one of her fans—illicit because the singer refuses to let her performance be recorded in any way.[27] In thus resisting reproduction, the diva's voice assumes the status of a completely inaccessible object, of an object which not only remains unobtainable itself, but for which there can be no substitute. The singer's young admirer attempts to bring it within symbolic exchange by surreptitiously recording it (as if to reinforce this point, the film shows him immediately struggling for possession of the tape with a group of Japanese entrepreneurs). That character, Jules, also produces a surrogate object, capable of filling in for the absent and impossible object. In so doing, he disavows not the diva's but his own castration.

That disavowal takes the form of an imaginary return to infantile plenitude, or, to be more precise, of an imaginary return to the sonorous envelope of what is clearly (given the generational gap between Jules and the diva) the maternal voice. Near the beginning of the film, Jules returns home from the opera "supplemented" not only with the illicit tape, but with the singer's satin dress, which we watch him appropriate after her performance. He sinks into a chair, embracing the luxurious garment, turns on the tape, and surrounds himself with the rapture-inducing sounds of the diva's (reproduced) voice. The effect is surely as close as cinema has come to an evocation of *jouissance*.

However, the film which attests more powerfully than any other to the ways in which the female voice becomes the receptacle of that which the male subject both throws away and draws back toward himself, functioning by turns as abject and *objet (a)*, is Francis Ford Coppola's *The Conversation* (1974). The central character of that film, Harry Caul (Gene Hackman), is dominated by two contrary impulses, both of which hinge upon his relation to voices. On the one hand, he is obsessed by the desire to establish his complete control over the sounds emitted by others—to over-hear, much like the disembodied voice can be said to over-speak. On the other hand, he is strongly and irrationally attracted by the female voice, which activates in him the desire to be folded in a blanket of sound.

Harry's technological authority is strenuously maintained by the opening sequence of *The Conversation*—so much so that he becomes closely identified not only with the instruments of his own surveillance activities, but with the cinematic apparatus itself.[28] The scene is a crowded Union Square in San Francisco, and the occasion the surreptitious taping of a private conversation between a young woman, Ann (Cindy Williams), and her apparent boyfriend, Paul (Michael Higgens). Everything we hear throughout this sequence conspicuously comes to us through one of the three microphones and tape recorders Harry has placed strategically around the Square (not only do we see the inside of the surveillance van and one of the tape recorders, but we hear electronic static, and miss parts of the conversation when heads are turned away from microphones).

Harry seems similarly responsible for what we *see*. The sequence begins with a slow roof-top zoom in on the Square, a point of view which is associated a moment later with a cameraman on top of the old City of Paris building, another part of the surveillance "net" Harry has thrown over the Square. Although the rest of the sequence does not proceed by means of a rigorous shot/reverse shot logic, a number of subsequent shots are "signed" by the cross hairs of the camera's view finder.

Exteriority is shown to be the necessary guarantee of Harry's identification with the apparatus. That exteriority is perhaps most strongly marked in the opening zoom, which at no point aspires to anything like intimacy with its subjects. It remains determinedly outside the scene it records, stopping its descent as soon as it has a clear view of each figure in the Square, and then moving among the various groups and individuals from an extreme overhead position. However, the issue of exteriority remains a central one both throughout the remainder of this sequence and throughout the rest of the film.

When the targeted couple notice the earphone worn by one of Harry's men, and become suspicious of his proximity to them, he is obliged to return to the surveillance van and surrender his equipment; he has entered the conversation, become part of the profilmic event, and he can no longer lay claim to discursive authority. Harry feels himself vulnerable to a similar divestiture when, upon returning to his apartment, he discovers that the landlady has managed to penetrate the lock and alarm system designed to prevent uninvited visitors, and to leave behind a birthday present. This "invasion" threatens to transform him from what the film would call a "bugger" to what it would call a "buggee"—to shift him from behind the scenes to center stage.

Harry's fear of being overheard is as intense as his compulsion to eavesdrop on others. His preferred position is "outside the door," a metaphor his girlfriend, Amy (Teri Garr), literalizes when she describes

him as always standing in the hall and listening through her door before
he enters her apartment. However, Harry is never able to exteriorize
himself sufficiently. Amy learns to identify the sounds he makes when
he stands outside her door, so that she is able to overhear him trying to
overhear her. Moreover, Harry is haunted by the thought of a heavenly
surveillance system which might at any moment be turned against him.
Since "to use the name of the Lord in vain" would be to incriminate
himself with the operator of that system, he not only avoids swearing
himself, but demands the same from his colleagues.

Harry's desire to remain at all times on the side of the apparatus is
also undermined from another direction—from the direction of the
maternal voice. Ironically, that threat is activated by the very tape which
seems definitively to establish Harry as "the best bugger on the West
Coast"—i.e., by the conversation he records in the opening sequence
and which he obsessively plays and replays throughout the remainder of
the film. That conversation has two nodal points, one of which evokes
the imaginary mother/child dyad, and the other of which warns of the
intervention of a hostile third term.

The first of these nodal points leads like an umbilical cord "back" to
the "uterine night" of nondifferentiation. It occurs in the middle of the
conversation, when the young woman, Ann, notices a drunk asleep on
a park bench in Union Square. Her reaction is heard through Harry's
apparatus, at the time that it ostensibly takes place, and on four subsequent occasions via the recording. She says:

> Oh look! That's terrible. . . . Oh God. Everytime I see one of those guys I
> always think the same thing. I always think he was once somebody's baby
> boy. He was once somebody's baby boy, and he had a mother and father
> who loved him . . . and now there he is half-dead on a park bench. And
> now where are his mother and father and all his uncles? Anyway, that's
> what I always think.

This speech intersects with two other details from the conversation,
which also resonate with maternal affect, and which are similarly privileged by Harry. One of those details is the sound of Ann's voice singing
snatches from the child's song, "When the red, red robin comes bob,
bob, bobbin' along." The other is the image of her solicitously removing
a speck from her companion's eye.

The basis for Harry's investment in these moments in the conversation is not entirely clear until the night of a surveillance convention,
when he invites some colleagues back to his office for a party. One of the
women in the group, Meredith (Elizabeth MacRae), stays behind after
the others leave, and puts Harry to bed on a mattress in his office. He
turns on the Union Square tape, and we hear Ann talking once again

about the lost comfort and security of childhood as the camera zooms in
slowly on his prostrate form, stretched out on the mattress in a visual
reprise of the bum on the park bench. As the sonorous web of Ann's
voice tightens around him, Harry enters the pronominal center of the
tape, and then beyond language, to "an unthinkable point at the interior
of thought."

This entry into the pronominal center of the tape occurs when Harry
anticipates that line which represents the second nodal point of the
conversation—the line "He'd kill us if he had the chance." This is the
most fantasmatic element in the entire conversation, both because it is
initially obscured by other sounds, and must be doctored to the point
where it is virtually constructed by Harry, and because every time it is
heard, the emphasis shifts and the meaning changes. Spoken by Paul, it
initially seems to refer only to the murderous intentions the Director,
Ann's husband (Robert Duvall), harbors against the young couple
("He'd *kill* us if he had the chance"). However, when Harry mentally
rehearses the line at the end of the film, it seems more an extenuation of
the young couple's murderous intentions toward the Director ("*He'd* kill
us if *he* had the chance"). When he utters it on the evening of the
surveillance convention, it has yet another function—the function of
identifying Harry and Meredith with Paul and Ann. This condensation is
effected through the pronoun *us,* which permits Harry to insert himself
into the sentence.

But beyond this fleeting suture—beyond all linguistic identification—Harry is the baby boy about whom Ann speaks, and to whom she
sings, the baby boy wrapped in the warm blanket of his mother's voice.
Meredith seems to contribute to the weaving of that blanket when she
wipes away Harry's tears, murmuring: "Angel, it's going to be all right."
The words on the tape become more and more indistinguishable, approximating pure sonorousness, as Harry retreats from signification and
symbolic differentiation. In the final shot of this sequence, the camera
pulls up and away from the bed on which Meredith now lies with Harry,
enclosed within the security wire cage of his inner office. The cage
throws a weblike shadow on the sleeping forms, a shadow which is the
visual equivalent of the "umbilical net" cast by Ann's voice.

This shot, which inverts the movement of the opening shot of the
film, gives way to a dream sequence, which further clarifies Harry's
relation both to the maternal voice and to the father, or symbolic third
term. In that sequence he calls to Ann from the bottom of a hill, while
she moves remotely above, shrouded in mist. What he says is startling,
since it is an appeal to her to hear his most submerged and private
memories—to hear him in ways which situate her in a position of

superior exteriority (here emblematized by her spatial elevation and abstractness), and himself in a position of subordinate inferiority:

> Listen! Listen! My name is Harry Caul. Can you hear me? You don't know who I am, but I know you. There isn't much to say about myself. . . . I was very sick when I was a boy. I was paralyzed in my left arm and leg. I couldn't walk for six months. One doctor said I'd never walk again. My mother used to lower me in hot baths as therapy. One time the door bell rang and she went down to answer it. I started sliding down. I could feel the water—it started coming up to my chin and nose. When I woke up my body was all greasy from the holy water she put on my body. I remember being disappointed I didn't die.
>
> When I was five my father introduced me to a friend of his and for no reason at all I hit him with all my might in the stomach. He died a year later. He'll kill you if he has the chance. . . . I'm not afraid of death. I am afraid of murder.

Harry's dream attests once again to his desire to retreat from discursive mastery. That retreat is figured through his "recollection" of the warm baths given to him by his mother when he was a child, with their domestic evocation of oceanic intimacies. However, the fact that the baths were a treatment for paralysis marks this "memory" as a fantasy— as a retrospective view of infantile plenitude, motivated by the crisis of symbolic castration.

At the same time that Harry's "reminiscences" testify to his desire to have all wounds healed and all losses recovered, they also acknowledge the impossibility of that desire. The unity of mother and child is interrupted by the intrusion of a third term—of that very term whose trace Harry carries on his body in the guise of a paralyzed arm and leg, forfeit pounds of flesh. His mother is called away by someone "outside the door," i.e., by someone occupying the position to which he himself aspires in his capacity as surveillance expert. That someone is thus clearly another inscription of Harry, or at least of the paternal legacy to which he lays claim in his waking life.

The first of the dream inscriptions of Harry, which can perhaps best be characterized by the phrase "baby boy," implies his identification with the mother—an identification which has the effect of inducing him to accept as his own that burden of lack which is conventionally displaced from the male to the female subject. That identification can be discerned in the logic of male castration, suffering, and masochism which informs the dream at every point, a logic which expresses itself with particular clarity when Harry says, "I remember being disappointed I didn't die," but which also manifests itself in the progression from "I was very sick" to "I couldn't walk for six months," "One doctor said I would never walk again," and "I started sliding down." The second of the dream inscriptions of Harry—the one which is compatible with his surveillance work—implies an identification with the father, and necessitates the return of lack to its customary female site.

The degree to which the two inscriptions function to negate each other is indicated by what happens in Harry's dream when the doorbell rings. Not only does his mother leave the bathroom, thereby disrupting his imaginary plenitude, but Harry-as-baby-boy almost drowns. The negation works in the other direction in the second part of the dream, where it is the father in himself that Harry attempts to disown. That repudiation takes the form of a generalized aggression against the paternal function, here represented by Harry's actual father, by a friend of his father, and by the Director, among whom the male pronoun circulates indiscriminately ("When I was five my father introduced me to a friend of his and for no reason at all I hit him with all my might. He died a year later. He'll kill you if he gets the chance"). Of course, since Harry's aggression takes such a familiar Oedipal path, it attests to the very identification it attempts to deny.

Harry ends his confession by reiterating his moral and psychic distance from the sadistic father, and his moral and psychic identification with the suffering mother ("I'm not afraid of death. I am afraid of murder"). However, that confession is followed by five "dream" shots which situate him once again "outside the door"—in this case the door of room 773 of the Jack Tar Hotel, the place specified for a rendez-vous in the Union Square conversation. The first of those shots shows Harry standing in front of the door. The next shot locates us inside the room, facing the door as Harry slowly opens it. The last three shots depict in a fragmentary and confused way the murder Harry thinks will occur in room 773—first a long shot of Ann standing against the pebbled glass doors leading to the balcony, opening her mouth in a noiseless scream as the Director moves threateningly toward her, then a reverse shot through the gauze curtain, smeared with blood, of the ensuing struggle, and finally a shot through the bathroom door of the toilet, blood streaking the walls.

Several days after the dream, Harry actually goes to the Jack Tar Hotel with the vague hope of somehow preventing the murder of the young couple. He checks into the room next to 773, and after a brief examination of the premises goes into the bathroom, and there, at the empty site of what figured within his dream as the staging place for infantile plenitude, reasserts his auditory mastery. He drills a hole in the wall, flushing the toilet to drown out the noise, and inserts a microphone. What Harry "hears" during this reenactment of the primal scene is almost entirely fantasmatic. Excerpts from the Union Square tape are the only sounds that come through with any distinctness, and they are clearly marked as originating from that tape. Indeed, at the climactic moment in this eavesdropping episode, we hear the tape being rewound to a particular point, followed by the words: "I love you."

The status of those three words is extremely complex at this juncture. For Harry, they seem to issue from the other side of the wall, whereas for the viewer they clearly issue from the tape, and beyond that, from the Union Square conversation. In fact, however, they are elicited only through Harry's desire to hear them. Ann's voice, like that of her companion, is actually a voice "inside" Harry, which he has projected outward as sound. The inclusion of the rewind noise reminds us that the voices of Ann and her friend have been produced by Harry all along—that we have never heard them except through either his technological or psychic "apparatus," and that there may consequently be a much closer connection between those two systems than at first appears.

As I will attempt to demonstrate in a moment, Harry's psychic apparatus, like classic cinema's sound apparatus, is in part a machine made to extract a cry from the female voice. After all, Harry has been drawn to the Jack Tar Hotel as much to hear the mother's scream as he has been to prevent her murder. However, it is his desire for the sonorous envelope of the maternal voice rather than his need to be in discursive control which manifests itself through Ann's "I love you"—a sound which impels Harry to rip off the earphones and run into the other room, horrified lest he be obliged to listen to that scream which only a moment before he was struggling to hear. He sits down on a chair in the bedroom and stares intently at the first of the four infantile inscriptions which punctuate this sequence—the baby-blue waves of an oceanic painting.

Shortly thereafter, Harry goes out onto the balcony and looks toward room 773. As he does so, he "sees" something whose fantasmatic dimensions are as pronounced as those of the sounds he "hears" in the bathroom—another view, as it were, of the murder he earlier "sees" in his sleep. That view consists of a brief image through pebbled glass of a bloody hand reaching out toward someone standing in front of the glass, back toward the camera. The form is vaguely recognizable as Ann, wearing the same dark dress she earlier wears in Harry's dream. On the soundtrack can be heard a sound which is conspicuously absent from the earlier version of the same events—conspicuously because it is implied by Ann's open mouth. That sound begins as a human cry, but is quickly transformed into an electronic scream.

As with the fragments of the Union Square conversation Harry "hears" in the bathroom, the scream clearly issues from his psychic apparatus. Like classic cinema, that apparatus is full of "gears and connecting rods, of chains of actions and reactions," all calculated to "deliver a cry" from the female voice. And as in classic cinema, the sought-after cry "incarnates a fantasm of pure sonorousness." It is, in other words, a mechanism for disavowing the male subject's early history, and for displacing onto woman all traces of corporeal excess and discursive impotence. However, the electronic scream activates what it is intended to neutralize, sending Harry back into the bedroom, and into a fetal position under the bedcovers. He turns on the television at full volume to drown out the intolerable cry, which continues to assail him as an external sound.

When Harry opens his eyes after an indeterminable interval, a cartoon is playing on television, and the voice of Fred Flintstone can be heard talking loudly about taking his wife to the hospital to have a baby. Regression is inscribed here both through the return of the by now ubiquitous infant, and through the reversion to the Stone Age. Of course, the supreme irony of this double inscription is that the Flintstone family is pure simulation—that the "innocent" world of cartoons is in no way anchored to a profilmic referent, and is without any grounding in actors, material objects, or even three-dimensional space. It is a textual form, moreover, where the voice can make no claim to derive from the body—where the voice is openly superimposed upon the body, much like the sounds from which Harry flees.

As usual, Harry is unable to sustain his retreat from auditory mastery, and a moment later he has resumed his characteristic position "outside the door." After checking out of his own room, he listens for a moment outside 773, then picks the lock, lets himself in, and embarks upon a careful inspection of the place. Once again it is the bathroom, fantasmatic site of both infantile plenitude and his own near-death, which preoccupies him. After tearing aside the shower curtain from the bathtub (an item whose semitransparent plastic is reminiscent of his own habitually worn raincoat), he begins a painstaking search for traces of what was an intolerable thought just moments before—for traces, that is, of the mother's death.

Harry focuses most of his attention on the two openings through which waste materials are eliminated: the bathtub drain and the toilet bowl. In other words, he solicits what has been thrown away, and is thus unassimilable to male subjectivity, in a grim reprise of the *fort/da* game. He beckons to the abject, and with a flush of the toilet it returns to him, contaminating the room and his own subjective boundaries. Even before Harry reaches for the flushing mechanism, an electronic scream analogous to the one heard on the balcony starts to well up, reaching a crescendo as blood and tissue spew out of the toilet.

Unlike the earlier scream, this one is electronic from start to finish, and so no longer identifiable in any way with the voice. Instead, it bears Harry's "signature"—his technological, but also his psychic, signature. The blood and tissue spilling out of the toilet are similarly dissociated from the female body. Harry is ostensibly looking for an "afterdeath," but there is nothing to distinguish what he sees from his own "after-birth"—from the sonorous web or membrane from which he must establish his separation in order to maintain a position of discursive mastery. ("Afterbirth" also refers, significantly, to a child who is not covered by the father's will, and who thus falls outside the parental word.)

The meaning of Harry's last name comes fully into play here. "Caul" designates "the amnion or inner membrane enclosing the foetus before birth" *(OED)*—i.e., the sheath that protectively encloses infantile pleni-tude. However, the amnion is the same membrane which subsequently becomes the afterbirth. Harry's name thus conveys both his desire to be restored to the "uterine night" of a presymbolic wholeness—to be enclosed once again in an envelope of pure sonorousness—and his desire to hold back that night by establishing his control over (and exteriority to) sound. Depending upon which definition is activated at any given moment, the female voice assumes the status of an *objet (a)* (of a beloved part of himself which Harry seeks to reincorporate), or of the abject (of that which defiles, and which must consequently be jetti-soned). Through a constant oscillation between these two contradictory relationships to the female voice, Harry attempts, on the one hand, to make good his symbolic castration—to recover the lost pound of flesh—and, on the other, to demonstrate his discursive potency; in short, to disavow the two lacks which afflict him.

In the sequence which follows, where Harry learns that it is the father rather than the mother who has been killed, he rewrites history. He mentally replays the Union Square conversation once again, and reopens the door to room 773. What he now "hears" has a totally different meaning from that of what he heard before, and that meaning produces a fresh set of images. The wifely solicitude with which Ann had seemed to remark, "I don't know what to get him for Christmas. He already has everything," is now dissipated by the portentous im-plications of Paul's response: "He doesn't need anything *anymore*." As Harry "listens" to this part of the tape, he "sees" the Director's corpse lying on the hotel bed, wrapped in a plastic bag (the third item in the series that includes the raincoat and the shower curtain, a series that reiterates Harry's guilt). That image appears again, a moment later, after a fragmentary reenactment of the bloody struggle already imagined by Harry twice before. This time, however, all the violence is aimed at the Director. As Harry "looks" for the second time at the Director's corpse, Paul's voice repeats for the last time the pivotal line, now brought into a new and chilling focus: *"He'd kill us if he had the chance."*

This sequence exposes as an utter fiction Harry's claim to auditory control. Far from being in a position of secure exteriority to the sounds he manipulates, his subjectivity is complexly imbricated with them—so much so that it is often impossible to determine which originate from "outside" of him, and which from "inside." Moreover, that very distinction is radically called into question both by the reversibility of the voice (a reversibility which *The Conversation* is at pains to dramatize), and by Harry's obvious libidinal implication in everything he hears. Finally, the conspicuous part played by cameramen and sound technicians in this scene only underscores Harry's isolation from the apparatus (he is standing all this time in a crowd of people looking on as the press fire questions at Ann about her husband's death).

Significantly, this time when Harry "listens" to the tape, he censors all those portions where Ann's voice approximates the maternal voice. The latter has suddenly assumed an altogether different status, and no longer represents a protective sheath. Instead, Harry now seeks shelter within another figuration of corporeal unity—within the sonorous envelope of his own music. *The Conversation* cuts away from the Director's corpse to a shot of Harry sitting on a chair in his apartment, improvising on his saxophone to a jazz record.

Music performs an important diegetic role throughout the film, where it is usually associated with infantile pleasure. During the Union Square sequence, an off-screen band can be heard playing "When the red, red robin comes bob, bob, bobbin' along," phrases of which Ann subsequently sings, and are "captured" on tape. Shortly after that sequence, Harry listens to a jazz record at home, and accompanies it on his saxophone, just as he does in the final sequence. Much later, on the night of the party, the background music forms a sonorous enclosure within which he feels secure enough to confide in Meredith. Finally, when he wakes up in his room in the Jack Tar Hotel, a jazz saxophone is superimposed over the sounds of "The Flintstones." All of this seems in strong support of Rosolato's contention that music images the fusion of child and mother—that it returns us to the "primordial experience of corporeal harmony." (Interestingly, Rosolato also notes that wind instruments, such as the saxophone, function as an extension or "giant prosthesis" of the voice.)[29]

As in the childhood memory recounted by Harry in his dream, the harmony he produces by improvising with the record at the end of the film is interrupted by a call from the symbolic. Here that interruption takes the form of a ring on the telephone rather than on the doorbell—of a call from the Director's office which begins by playing back to Harry a tape of his own music, and ends with the warning: "We'll be listening to you." This intrusion is the secular realization of his theological anxieties about being overheard by someone whose powers of audition exceed his own. His initial relation to the apparatus has been completely reversed: instead of exercising control over the sounds emitted by others, the sounds he himself makes now fall within the reach of a superior ear. He has been displaced from the position of "bugger" to that of "buggee."

Harry dismantles his apartment in an attempt to locate the hidden microphone and so to establish his superiority to the anonymous eavesdropper. In the middle of his search, he comes across a bookshelf of bric-a-brac and sweeps everything into the trash but a small Madonna, dressed in a baby-blue robe. The mother is still so closely identified with infantile plenitude that it is inconceivable to Harry that she could be complicit in his discursive castration. Later, however, he returns to the Madonna, and in a fury of violence smashes open its body and turns the hollow form inside out. The icon is empty, brilliantly demystifying the notion of interiority, and suggesting that the faculty of a superior and mastering audition can no more be localized in the maternal body than can the cry.

The degree to which the maternal voice nonetheless continues to exercise a fantasmatic hold upon Harry's desire is indicated by his reversion shortly after this act of aggression to that image from the Union Square conversation which seems most fully to sketch the possibility of reintegration with the mother—the image of Ann removing a speck from Paul's eye. The film cuts from there to a shot of Harry playing his saxophone once again, the one object he has overlooked as a possible location for the hidden microphone. This time he plays solo, without the record. However, he is not "alone." He is accompanied (as he has been all along) by the symbolic, evoked here both by an extradiegetic piano and by the final image of the film.

The Conversation concludes with a shot which forcefully reasserts Harry's diegetic interiority—a shot of him sitting in the middle of his ruined apartment, whose overhead angle and back-and-forth panning motion associate it with a surveillance camera. Like the phone call from the Director's office, this shot inverts Harry's earlier relation to the apparatus, transferring him from a position behind the camera and tape recorder to one in front—from a position "outside the door" to one "inside the door." Moreover, whereas in the opening shot of the film we look at and listen to Union Square through Harry's bugging equipment, here we look at and presumably listen to him through someone else's. That someone else remains invisible and unlocalizable, manifesting himself only through the disembodied voice of the telephone call.

In *The Ego and the Id,* Freud shows the ego "wearing" a "cap of hearing" on one side.[30] In the *New Introductory Lectures,* however, he gives the same position to the superego.[31] Otto Isakower draws an interesting conclusion from the substitution of the superego for the cap of hearing, a conclusion which is more than a little relevant to the present discussion. He suggests that the superego is determined primarily by the activity of listening.

Isakower points out (as does Freud) that a word must always be heard before it can be articulated, and that language must consequently be understood as coming to the subject from "outside"—from what he calls an "auditory sphere" or "aura." He argues, in other words, that the acquisition of language proceeds through the internalization of others' voices—most particularly, of course, those of the parents. These voices, which provide a model as well as a source of linguistic information, also form the core of the superego:

> We know that the child is not capable by itself of constructing new words, to say nothing of a language, but that he has to build up his speech from linguistic material which is presented to him ready made. But this very fact sets in motion the process of developing an observing and criticizing institution.
>
> The following formula then suggests itself: just as the nucleus of the ego is the body-ego, so the human auditory sphere, as modified in the direction of language, is to be regarded as the nucleus of the super-ego.[32]

Isakower's equation of the superego with an auditory aura is literalized by one of the patients he cites, who complained of his superego that "I seem to hear everything that has ever been said to me in all my life" (p. 346).

Like the other theoretical models I have examined in this chapter, Isakower's turns upon the dialectic between "inside" and "outside," and upon the image of a sonorous receptacle. Once again interiority implies discursive dependency, and exteriority discursive authority. However, Isakower indicates that interiority is the inevitable effect of subjectivity, rather than a condition that somehow rhymes with femininity—the inevitable effect, that is, of having been inserted into an already existing linguistic structure. His theoretical model also focuses in a way the others do not upon the replication of this inside/outside structure within the psyche itself—upon the setting up of the auditory aura within the subject's own self, in a position of superior exteriority to the ego. Isakower thus shows the subject to be "inside" the symbolic, and "under" the supervision of the superego. He suggests that we can never get "outside the door," in the way that Harry attempts to do.

At the risk of giving Isakower's model too much metacritical weight, I would like to suggest that it is ultimately this auditory aura against which dominant cinema arms the male subject through the textual operations discussed in chapter 2. Hollywood's sexually differentiating drama of interiority and exteriority works to disavow the fact that the male subject, like the female subject, is surrounded by and constructed through voices which he also incorporates as an internal regulatory agency. By folding the female voice into diegetic recesses, submitting it to the "talking cure," and anchoring it to the female body, dominant cinema attempts to move the male subject from a position of linguistic containment and subordination to the one which Freud and Isakower associate with the superego—a position of superior speech and hearing. That position is in turn only a reflection of the symbolic order or auditory aura.

The image of the maternal voice as a sonorous envelope has a similar derivation, although it elicits a wider variety of psychic responses. The paranoid fantasy of entrapment which surfaces both in Hollywood and in Chion's La voix au cinéma is quite clearly a disguised expression of the double interiority which is endemic to subjectivity, but incompatible with the phallic function. The anxiety which that double interiority generates is fantasmatically resolved by reversing the respective positions of the mother and the infant subject, both by stripping the sounds which the mother makes of any linguistic status, and by moving her to the interior of the sonorous envelope. Rosolato, on the other hand, dreams alternately of transforming interiority into *jouissance* by substituting the mother's singing voice for the father's prohibitory voice, and of replacing the hierarchy of ego and superego, subject and symbolic with a "veritable incantation of voices," configured by the lateral vocal interaction of mother and child. Kristeva's *choric* fantasy, as we will see in a few pages, is motivated by the desire to retreat from the superego and the symbolic rather than by the desire to approximate the position of discursive mastery which they represent. By returning to a moment prior to the entry into language and the articulation of subject/ object relationships, it attempts to fuse mother with child, and so to abolish the opposition of inside and outside. However, because that union can take place only within the *choric* enclosure, Kristeva's fantasy still revolves around the image of interiority.

The fact that the maternal voice should provide the focal point for two such powerful fantasies of retreat from the auditory aura as those "dreamed" by Rosolato and Kristeva does not mean that it does not itself figure centrally within that aura. As I have already had frequent occasion to stress, the mother performs a crucial role during the subject's early history. She is traditionally the first language teacher, commentator, and storyteller—the one who first organizes the world linguistically for the child, and first presents it to the Other. The maternal voice also plays a crucial part during the mirror stage, defining and interpreting the reflected image, and "fitting" it to the child. Finally, it provides the acoustic mirror in which the child first hears "itself." The maternal voice is thus complexly bound up in that drama which "decisively projects the formation of the individual into history," and whose "internal thrust is precipitated from insufficiency to anticipation."[33] Indeed, it would seem to be the maternal rather than the paternal voice that initially constitutes the auditory sphere for most children, although it is clearly the latter which comes to predominate within the superego.[34]

The theoretical and cinematic equation of the maternal voice with "pure" sonorousness must therefore be understood not as an extension of its intrinsic nature, or of its acoustic function, but as part of a larger cultural disavowal of the mother's role both as an agent of discourse and as a model for linguistic (as well as visual) identification. The characterization of the mother's voice as babble or noise is also, as I have been at pains to establish, one of the primary mechanisms through which the male subject seeks both to recover an imaginary infantile plenitude, and to extricate himself from the "afterbirth" of perceptual and semiotic insufficiency. Last but not least, that characterization contradicts the notion of exteriority which is implied by the metaphors of enclosure with which it is frequently linked—metaphors such as "envelope," "cobweb," or "bath"—and facilitates the alignment of femininity with an unpleasurable and disempowering interiority.

[4]

THE FANTASY OF THE MATERNAL VOICE:

FEMALE SUBJECTIVITY AND

THE NEGATIVE OEDIPUS COMPLEX

> Fantasy has indeed no other sign, no other way to imagine that the speaker is capable of reaching the Mother, and thus, of unsettling its own limits. And, as long as there is language-symbolism-paternity, there will never be any other way to represent, to objectify, and to explain this unsettling of the symbolic stratum, this nature/culture threshold, this instilling of the subjectless biological program into the very body of a symbolizing subject, this event called motherhood.[1]

IN THE PRECEDING chapter, I commented upon the paranoiac and compensatory forms which the maternal voice at times assumes for the male subject within classic cinema and recent film and psychoanalytic theory. In this chapter, I will be much more concerned with the uses to which female subjectivity has recently put the fantasy of the sonorous envelope. The primary theoretical and cinematic texts I will assemble for that purpose—Kristeva's "Motherhood According to Giovanni Bellini," "Place Names," and "Stabat Mater," on the one hand, and Altman's *Three Women* and Mulvey and Wollen's *Riddles of the Sphinx*, on the other—all derive from the mid-seventies, having been produced within a year or two of each other. These texts mark a distinct historical moment, the moment at which feminism first intersected decisively with alternative cinema, film theory, and psychoanalytic theory. What I will be calling the *"choric* fantasy" may perhaps best be understood as the product of that intersection.

Within Kristeva's writing, the image of the child wrapped in the sonorous envelope of the maternal voice is not only a fantasy about pre-Oedipal existence, the entry into language, and the inauguration of subjectivity; it is also a fantasy about biological "beginnings," intrauterine life, and what she calls the "homosexual-maternal facet." The primary term with which she conceptualizes that fantasy is, of course, the *chora*, a word she borrows from Plato, who uses it to designate "an unnameable, improbable, hybrid [receptacle], anterior to naming, to the One, to the father, and consequently, maternally connoted."[2]

The concept of the *chora* is an expansive one within Kristeva's corpus, functioning at times as a synonym for "semiotic disposition," "*signifiance*," and "geno-text," and at other times as a signifier for a moment prior to the mirror stage and the symbolic. However, a remarkable conflation occurs each time the *chora* is sighted, regularizing what might otherwise remain heterogeneous and disparate "views": the mother is either fused or confused with her infant, and in the process comes both to be and to inhabit the *chora*. Although this fantasy, like Chion's, forces the maternal voice to the inside of the sonorous envelope, its motives are much more mixed. On the one hand, that transaction clearly speaks to the desire to put a maximum distance between the mother and the symbolic order, a desire that is in no way threatening to sexual difference as it is presently constituted. However, the *choric* fantasy is also predicated upon Kristeva's desire to be "shifted, traversed, made negative, and brought to *jouissance*" rather than upon the "symbolic, structuring, regimenting, protective, historicizing thesis"[3] that governs Chion's fantasy. Finally, Kristeva's account of the maternal voice speaks to an erotic desire which is completely unassimilable to heterosexuality, and which functions in some very profound way as the libidinal basis of feminism. I will briefly review what I see as Kristeva's three primary definitions of the *chora* before exploring its status as a fantasy.

In what is perhaps her most familiar formulation of the *chora*, Kristeva associates it both with the mother and with the prehistory of the subject, referring it simultaneously to the primordial role played by the mother's voice, face, and breast, and to the psychic and libidinal conditions of early infantile life. As she explains it, the *chora* refers equally to mother and infant because it is put in place through a creative collaboration, a collaboration which is synonymous with anaclisis: the infant invokes the mother as a source of warmth, nourishment, and bodily care by means of various vocal and muscular spasms, and the mother's answering sounds and gestures weave a provisional enclosure around the child.[4] That enclosure provides the child with its first, inchoate impressions of space, and with its initial glimmerings of otherness, thereby paving the way for the mirror stage and the entry into language.[5] However, the *chora* is more an image of unity than one of archaic differentiation; prior to absence and an economy of the object, it figures the oneness of mother and child.[6]

According to the terms of this particular definition, the infant in-habits the interior of the *chora,* and (as in Chion's account) that interior-ity implies perceptual immaturity and discursive incapacity. However, whereas metaphors of entrapment abound in *La voix au cinéma,*[7] Kris-teva's account of life at the center of the maternal container is at times euphoric, and at other times tempered by anxiety. In "Place Names," she suggests not only that the infant solicits the anaclitic enclosure, but that it finds within that enclosure a "riant (laughing) spaciousness."[8] Here the *chora* clearly functions as a utopian figure for the primordial integration of mother and child. (As I will indicate later in this discus-sion, pregnancy is the ultimate prototype for this figure.) Elsewhere, though, the nondifferentiation of mother and child is seen as a "chaos" which must be "abjected."[9]

Kristeva identifies the *chora* not only with infantile existence and maternal care, but with what she calls the "semiotic disposition" of the drives, a disposition which is the effect of familial and social pressure upon the child's body:

> Discrete quantities of energy move through the body of the subject who is not yet constituted as such and, in the course of his development, they are arranged according to the various constraints imposed on this body—always already involved in a semiotic process—by family and social struc-tures. In this way the drives, which are "energy" charges as well as "psy-chical" marks, articulate what we call a *chora;* a nonexpressive totality formed by the drives and their stases in a motility that is as full of move-ment as it is regulated.[10]

According to the logic of *this* definition, the *chora* is situated *inside* the subject, in the guise of a libidinal economy. However, because the mother's body "mediates the symbolic law organizing social relations," becoming "the ordering principle of the semiotic *chora,*"[11] it would perhaps be more precise to speak of the latter as the subject's inter-nalization of the mother in the guise of a "mobile receptacle" or provi-sional enclosure.

This account of the *chora* thus extends its function well beyond the infantile scene, giving it a longevity equal to the life of the subject. The oral and anal drives assume a privileged place within this durable libidinal economy, making it simultaneously assimilatory and destruc-tive. However, it is ultimately the death drive, most "instinctual" of the drives, that predominates within the semiotic disposition, and which governs it according to a profound negativity.[12] The *chora* is consequent-ly the "place" where the subject is both generated and annihilated, the site where it both assumes a pulsional or rhythmic consistency and is dissolved as a psychic or social coherence.

In attempting to distinguish the Lacanian imaginary from the Kristevian semiotic or *chora,* Jane Gallop suggests that whereas the former is "conservative and comforting, tends toward closure, and is disrupted by the symbolic," the latter is "revolutionary, breaks closure, and disrupts the symbolic."[13] It seems to me that this is correct only up to a point; not only do the labile dualities of the imaginary threaten to undo the stability of the symbolic fully as much as the father or any other third term works to triangulate all imaginary dualities, but (as the preceding discussion indicates) the semiotic has a claustral as well as an interruptive dimension. The *chora* both encloses the newborn infant in the envelope formed by the mother's voice, warmth, and gestures (an envelope which can be "opened" only through the letter knife of castration), and poses a fundamental challenge to representation and signification. It is crucial that we grasp the paradoxical status which Kristeva confers upon what she alternately calls the "semiotic" and the *"chora,"* a paradox which cannot be resolved by parceling out its discrepant functions between those two signifiers.

The confusion clears somewhat when one realizes that Kristeva's theoretical model hinges upon a double temporality, affording a very different "take" on the *chora* depending upon whether it is the pre-Oedipal child or the adult subject who is under discussion. In the first of these instances, the *chora* is itself the condition or regime under siege from the symbolic, the unity which must be ruptured if identity is to be found. In the second it is the force that assails language and meaning, the negativity that threatens to collapse both the *je* and the *moi.* However, the contradictions inherent in Kristeva's account of the *chora* can never be entirely ironed out, since they are the discursive marks of a profound psychic ambivalence.

Kristeva's third definition of the *chora* is offered in the context of a general discussion of place names, a discussion which conceptualizes subjectivity as a spatial series in which each term is superimposed upon the preceding one, much like a palimpsest. That series begins with the *chora,* continues with the child's apprehension of space (presumably at the mirror stage), and his or her initial experiments with demonstrative and localizing utterances, and concludes with the accession to subject-predication. As the child proceeds through this series, s/he not only acquires a clearer and clearer understanding of spatial relations, but increases his or her psychic distance from the *chora.*

So far this summary seems unremarkable. However, Kristeva goes on to draw some rather startling conclusions from it, asserting that *"the entry into syntax constitutes a first victory over the mother,* a still uncertain distancing of the mother, by the simple fact of naming,"[14] and that "naming, always originating in a place . . . is a *replacement* for what the speaker perceives as an archaic mother—a more or less victorious confrontation, never finished, with her" (p. 291). It is understandable, at least from within a Lacanian paradigm, why language would work to separate the child from the mother, or, for that matter, the child from the world of objects. What is less explicable is why Kristeva would have recourse at this juncture to a twice-repeated military metaphor—why she would conceive of the child's linguistic mastery as a "victory" over the mother. The only obvious triumph would seem to be that which the child "wins" over its previous perceptual and discursive incapacity, or, to deploy the terms used by Freud in *Beyond the Pleasure Principle* and invoked by Kristeva in *Revolution in Poetic Language* and elsewhere, over the drives or the semiotic disposition.[15] Are we to understand the mother as somehow representing these vanquished forces, as an agency antipathetic to language and identity? The answer is apparently yes. What occurs here is more than a little reminiscent of what happens to the maternal voice in *La voix au cinéma:* once again the child's discursive exteriority—its emergence from the maternal enclosure—can be established only by placing the mother herself inside that enclosure, by relegating her to the interior of the *chora,* or—what is the same thing— by stripping her of all linguistic capabilities.

(This is perhaps the moment at which to note that Kristeva's writing is characterized by a massive disavowal of the tutelary role the mother classically assumes with respect to the child's linguistic education—of her function as language teacher, commentator, storyteller. This disavowal is quite marked in "Place Names," which discusses the child's entry into language in great detail, but it is even more pronounced in *Histoires d'amour.* In "Freud and Love: Treatment and Its Discontents," a chapter from that later book, Kristeva insists that it is the father's rather than the mother's speech which the child first incorporates, and that sonorous or acoustic identification occurs in relation to the paternal rather than the maternal voice. This negation of the mother's discursive role is part of a larger refusal to assign the female subject a viable place within the symbolic, a point which Ann Rosalind Jones has recently made with considerable force.)[16]

However, what distinguishes Kristeva's formulation from Chion's is that the *chora* and the archaic mother continue to live on within the subject, no matter how linguistically proficient it becomes. The *chora* remains one of the permanent "scenes" of subjectivity, not so much superseded as covered over and denied by succeeding spatial developments. Kristeva is also far more willing to conceive of the subject finding itself once again within the *chora*, and far more divided about what such an eventuality would entail.

It is, I would argue, precisely as an extension of the rhetorical flourish with which Kristeva characterizes the child's linguistic accomplishments as a "victory" over the mother, and thereby relegates her to the interior of the *chora*, that she has consistently associated the semiotic with the maternal, and thereby conflated the latter with whatever muddies the clear waters of rational discourse. Significantly, however, Kristeva has been obliged to look rather far afield in her search for these ostensible "feminine" irruptions, passing over all the varied texts to have ever been inscribed with a female signature in favor of the (male) avant-garde. Thus, we learn that although the symbolic attempts to negate the *chora*, the maternal substratum of subjectivity surfaces in carnivalesque, surrealist, psychotic, and "poetic" language. It is also, according to Kristeva, an inevitable feature of even the most normative speech patterns, manifesting itself through rhythm, intonation, and gesture. However, the *chora* is most fully showcased within infantile language, which permits the adult subject to hear what has not been fully rationalized within its own discourse, and which thereby provides it with a privileged access to the archaic mother.[17] Once again the maternal voice is theoretically conflated with the voice of infancy, but here, at least, there can be no doubt that the sounds for which Kristeva is listening in fact issue from only one of those voices.

Kristeva makes a curious recommendation in "Place Names": she proposes that if we wish to gain access to the *chora*, we should not only listen to infantile language, but do so with a "maternal attentiveness." She adds emphasis to her recommendation by pointing out that recent child psychology has enacted a shift from a "paternal, Freudian attentiveness to a maternal attention," and in so doing she closely identifies the figure of the analyst with that of the mother. However, a remarkable passage follows close upon the heels of this recommendation, contradicting and undercutting it. What makes this passage all the more puzzling is that it comes as an apparent extension of the argument about psychoanalysis and the mother, but drastically alters the terms of the discussion. Because it represents one of the "nodal points" of Kristeva's fantasy of the maternal voice, I will quote from it at length:

> For a woman, the arrival of a child breaks the auto-erotic circle of pregnancy . . . and brings about what, for a woman, is the difficult account of a relationship with an other: with an "object" and with love. Is it not true that. . . . in order . . . to have access to the symbolic-thetic level, which requires castration and object, she must tear herself from the daughter-mother symbiosis, renounce the undifferentiated community of women and recognize the father at the same time as the symbolic? . . . It is precisely the child that, for a *mother* . . . constitutes an *access* (excess) toward the Other. . . . The mother of a son (henceforth the generic "infant" no longer exists) is a *being* confronted with a *being for him.* The mother of a daughter replays in reverse the encounter with her own mother: differentiation or leveling of beings, glimpses of oneness or paranoid primary identification phantasized as primordial substance. . . .
>
> From this point on, for the mother . . . the child is an *analyzer.* He releases the hysteric woman's anguish, often hidden, denied or deferred in its paranoid course, directing it toward others or toward the array of consumer goods. It is an anguish that brings the mother to grips with castration. . . .[18]

Suddenly, without any explanation, the mother has been moved from the position of the analyst to that of the analysand. Her condition, moreover, mimics that of the newborn child; locked in a symbiotic embrace with her own mother as well as with her progeny, she remains stubbornly beyond the structuring reach of castration and difference, oblivious both to the possibility of object relations and to the governing role of the phallus. Even more startling, the infant has been abruptly elevated to the position of the analyst, and is now posited as the only one capable of leading the mother into the individuating light of the symbolic. The two protagonists of the pre-Oedipal drama would seem once again to have traded places; it is the mother who inhabits the *chora,* and the infant who points the way beyond.

I would like to reclaim the position of analyst for the female voice by suggesting that this passage affords several points of hermeneutic entry into the Kristevian fantasy. To begin with, its opening sentence summons one of the organizing images of *Polylogue,* the book from which "Place Names" and "Motherhood According to Giovanni Bellini" derive, and in so doing it makes explicit what I would argue is always the implicit subtext of the *chora.* It summons, that is, the "auto-erotic circle of pregnancy," an image which permits Kristeva to conceptualize the mother both as a receptacle and as the inhabitant of that receptacle—as simultaneously the container and its contents. Moreover, enclosure within that circle is synonymous with nondifferentiation, objectless libido, and meaninglessness, just as it is within the *chora.*

The similarities between Kristeva's account of pregnancy and her account of the *chora* are even more strikingly suggested in a passage from "Motherhood According to Giovanni Bellini." The passage in question turns upon the word *enceinte*, with its double meaning of "a protective wall" and "a pregnant woman," and it once again situates the mother inside an enclosure like the one she herself provides. It thus effects an even more extreme displacement than that enacted elsewhere with respect to the *chora*, locating the mother where the fetus in fact belongs—inside the womb. Having negotiated this transfer, Kristeva manages once again to identify motherhood with a force that resists difference and signification:

> [The mother] is within an "enceinte" separating her from the world of everyone else. Enclosed in this "elsewhere," an "enceinte" woman loses communital meaning, which suddenly appears to her worthless, absurd, or at best, comic—a surface agitation severed from its impossible foundations. Oriental nothingness probably better sums up what, in the eyes of a Westerner, can only be regression.[19]

Kristeva's *choric* fantasy would thus seem to be informed by the desire to return the mother to the *enceinte*. However, the image of the "auto-erotic circle of pregnancy" is obscured by several as yet unanswered questions. Who forms that circle, and who else occupies it? What is the desire behind Kristeva's desire to enclose the mother within the womb?

The passage which I quoted from "Place Names" a few pages ago provides us with a second point of hermeneutic entry into Kristeva's *choric* fantasy when it asserts the primacy of gender over "generic" infancy—when it tells us that "the mother of a son [. . .] is a *being* confronted with a *being for him*," but that "the daughter of a mother replays in reverse the encounter with her own mother." Sexual difference clearly plays an important part here. At first glance, Kristeva's emphasis upon gender works primarily to disenfranchise the daughter—to align the male child with the symbolic order and the paternal legacy, while dooming the daughter to "primordial oneness or paranoid identification phantasized as primordial substance." It also helps to establish the son's exclusive access to the position of analyst, and in so doing it reenacts the discursive gesture whereby Kristeva divests the mother of her psychoanalytic laurels.

However, I would ultimately argue for a rather different reading of this sexual bifurcation. It seems to me that Kristeva's unconscious desires are ultimately as fully engaged by the scenario of regression as they are by that of symbolic progression, and that what seems to be the son's phallic investiture should also be understood as his *exclusion* from the privileged site of the *chora*. The key to such a reading is the phrase "replays in reverse" ("*refait à rebours*"). That phrase aptly summarizes what Kristeva does when she substitutes the mother for the (male) infant in the account she offers of the pre-Oedipal scene, and makes *her* the protagonist of *his* story. It also crystallizes Kristeva's preoccupation with origins, a preoccupation which is at the very heart of the *choric* fantasy. Finally, and most important, "replays in reverse" describes an action which takes place entirely between women. It affords us a fleeting glimpse of an intimate relationship between a mother, her own mother, and her daughter, a relationship predicated upon regression, return, and replication. Kristeva negotiates this privileged (re)union by ejecting the son from the *chora,* and placing the mother inside.

If we penetrate the Kristevian fantasy at a third point of entry, we eventually stumble upon the same homosexual-maternal scene, although the path leading there is strewn with greater obstacles. That point of entry is indicated by the sentence that reads: "[Is it not true that in order] to have access to the symbolic-thetic level, which requires castration and object, [the mother] must tear herself from the daughter-mother symbiosis, renounce the undifferentiated community of women, and recognize the father at the same time as the symbolic?" (*"[N'est-il pas vrai] que pour accéder à cet Un toujours altéré, à l'instance symbolique-thétique qui exige castration et objet, [la mère] doit s'arracher à la symbiose fille-mère, renoncer à la communauté indifférenciée des femmes et reconnaître, en même temps que le symbolique, le père?"*) No answer follows, but as with all rhetorical questions, one is implied.

Let us look at the question more closely. It actually begins in the preceding sentence, with the words: "Is it not true?" These words are (to say the least) ambiguous, susceptible through only slight rearrangement to a completely different reading—to a reading, that is, that flatly denies rather than affirms the validity of what follows. The ambiguity is compounded by the very fact that a sentence as crucial as this one is to any understanding of Kristeva's own relation to the *chora* should be posed as a question admitting of a negative as well as a positive answer. This rhetorical hesitation attests to the psychic division that structures the speaker's relation to what she calls the "semiotic." The words "Is it not true" preface a "reality" to which she cannot entirely accede, although she pays lip service to it: the "reality" of castration, the phallus, and the (existing) symbolic order.

To what end, then, is this "reality" invoked? I will attempt to answer this query in a moment. First, however, I want to note that Kristeva's rhetorical question actually contains two different questions. One of these questions turns upon cause and effect—upon the issue of what woman must do in order to have "access to the symbolic-thetic level." The other question pivots rather upon the issue of compulsion. It reads: "[Is it not true that the mother] must tear herself from the daughter-mother symbiosis, renounce the undifferentiated community of women, and recognize the father at the same time as the symbolic?" It is around this second question, I would maintain, a question which remains hidden within the larger structure of the sentence, that all the ambiguity crystallizes.

What would seem to be at work here is a curious *negation* of the desire to negate—a denial of the desire to repudiate the force of the symbolic imperative, of the "must" that tears daughter from mother, and which subordinates both to the law of the father. *Verneinung* or negation, as Freud tells us, simultaneously acknowledges and disowns what has been repressed.[20] It is a "procedure whereby the subject, while formulating one of his wishes, thoughts or feelings which has been repressed hitherto, contrives, by disowning it, to continue to defend himself against it."[21] This is precisely what happens in the text under discussion, which simultaneously states and conceals that desire which is at the center of the Kristevian fantasy—the desire to fuse the daughter with the mother, and the mother with her own mother. "Is it not true" corrects and covers over the parapraxis which is on the tip of Kristeva's tongue, the parapraxis which would have read: "It is not true." That desire surfaces not only in the insistence with which Kristeva here and elsewhere confines the mother to the *chora,* but in the four elided words with which the sentence begins.

The desire for the corporeal union of mother and daughter is also inscribed into the text of "Motherhood According to Giovanni Bellini," but it wears a different set of disguises there. It reveals itself first in an astonishing description of childbirth, a description which stresses what Kristeva calls the "nonsymbolic, nonpaternal causality" of motherhood:

> The body of [the] mother is always the same Master-Mother of instinctual drive, a ruler over psychosis, a subject of biology, but also, one toward which women aspire all the more passionately simply because it lacks a penis: that body cannot penetrate her as can a man when possessing his wife. By giving birth, the woman enters into contact with her own mother; she becomes, she is her own mother. She thus actualizes the homosexual facet [*le versant homosexuel*] of motherhood, through which a woman is simultaneously closer to her own instinctual memory, more open to her own psychosis, and consequently, more negatory of the social, symbolic bond.[22]

This passage offers another striking example of denial. Although Kristeva goes so far here as to acknowledge the homosexual basis of the union she seeks with the mother, she also repeatedly denies that "homosexual" means "homo*sexual.*" To begin with, she tells us that the daughter rejoins the mother only as a mother herself, and hence through the implied mediation of both a father and an infant. (Moreover, as I will attempt to show in a moment, within the manifest text of "Motherhood According to Giovanni Bellini," that infant is emphatically male.) Second, Kristeva disavows the erotic nature of the mother/daughter union by attributing it to the "eternal return of the life-death biological cycle" (p. 239). Finally, Kristeva splits the mother into two—into the genetrix, who blindly participates in the instinctual experience of procreation, and into the speaking subject, who remains elsewhere altogether. She insists that it is the former rather than the latter who rejoins her own mother.

The eroticism which this passage denies is extravagantly displayed elsewhere in the essay, when Kristeva deals with Bellini. The desire which cannot be openly expressed with regard to the daughter is displaced onto the son, producing this wish-fulfilling summary of a cluster of paintings from the early 1460s:

> The mother's hands remain at the center of the painting[,] bringing its miniature drama to a head. Although still possessive, they now shift toward the child's buttocks (*Madonna and Child*, New Haven; *Madonna and Child*, Correr Museum) or rest on his sexual member (National Gallery, Washington; Brera). (P. 254)

The libidinal bases of Kristeva's analysis become even more evident once one has examined the two paintings with which she illustrates it. As Mary Jacobus points out, there is little in the Correr *Madonna* to account for the sexual drama which Kristeva finds there:

> The Correr Madonna . . . gazes abstractedly away from her child, while her hands half hold, half display his body. Once more the child grips her thumb, but (it seems to me, at any rate) almost casually, as the palm of one hand cradles his buttock. The other hand, spread across the baby's chest, ritualizes the gesture of holding into one of merest indication. Kristeva writes of the mother's hands holding their object tightly; yet the pair—mother and child—could be seen as folded loosely together in a formalized pattern which emphasizes, not her grip, but the interlacing of hands and legs, the repeated folds of sleeve and veil, the crinkles and curls of mother's and child's hair.[23]

There is a similar discordance between the New Haven *Madonna* and the reading Kristeva provides of it.

However, even here the dream of the erotic union of mother and child is shrouded in disavowal. Kristeva emphasizes that Bellini's "real" mother was both lost and dead, and that even her imaginary counterpart is absent from sexuality ("Her characterless gaze fleeting under her downcast eyes, her nonetheless definite pleasure, unshakeable in its intimacy, and her cheeks radiating peace, all constitute a strange modesty"). She also goes to extreme and contradictory lengths to disavow the child's desire for fusion with the mother, attributing the physical

contact between them first to the "symbiotic clinging syndrome," and
then to the mother's predatory gestures, from which the child attempts
to extricate himself ("The climax of this series is the *Madonna and Child*
in Bergamo, a spotlight thrown on a dramatic narrative. Aggressive
hands prod the stomach and penis of the frightened baby, who, alone of
all his peers, frees himself violently, taking his mother's hands along on
his body" [p. 254]).

The reader is no doubt wondering what has become of the maternal
voice, to which there has been no explicit reference for a number of
pages. It is no coincidence that this voice should have thus dropped
from theoretical view, or that its eclipse should have occurred at the
precise moment that I began looking closely at the passage from "Place
Names" which inverts the relative positions of mother and child. By
relegating the mother to the interior of the *chora*/womb, Kristeva re-
duces her to silence. "Place Names" enforces the connection between
motherhood and muteness when it suggests that "to reach the threshold
of repression by means of the identification with motherhood" is "no
longer [to] hear words or meanings; not even sounds" (p. 249). Kristeva's insistence upon the split nature of motherhood leads to much the
same result, since in the final analysis it is always the mother-as-
genetrix rather than the mother-as-speaking-subject who commands
her interest.

Of course, if the mother is mute, she is also irrecoverable (or
recoverable for the daughter only when she herself enters into childbirth); once her voice has been silenced, it can no longer help to weave
the anaclitic enclosure which figures her union with the child. Kristeva's
maternal fantasy is thus grounded in a fundamental impossibility; the
mother cannot simultaneously be and inhabit the *chora,* at least not
once childbirth has taken place. This impossibility can be resolved only
by finding someone else to speak for the mother. It will come as no
surprise to the student of Kristeva that this "someone else" is the artist.
In "Motherhood According to Giovanni Bellini"—as in *Revolution in
Poetic Language, Powers of Horror,* and elsewhere in *Polylogue*—Kristeva
attributes to that figure the faculty of speaking *for* the mother, of providing her with a voice:

> At the intersection of sign and rhythm, of representation and light, of the
> symbolic and the semiotic, the artist speaks from a place where [the
> mother] is not, where she knows not. He delineates what, in her, is a body
> rejoicing. . . . through a symbiosis of meaning and nonmeaning, of repre-

sentation and interplay of differences, the artist lodges into language, and
through his identification with the mother . . . [traverses] both sign and
object. . . . At the place where it obscurely succeeds with the maternal body,
every artist tries his hand, but rarely with equal success. (P. 242)

These are all conspicuously male names, a point that is not without
significance. I would argue that the artist is necessarily male for Kristeva, and that this imperative proceeds at least in part from the same
unconscious "logic" that motivates her to focus her erotic attention
upon the male child in Bellini's paintings. The insistently masculine
identity of the artist permits Kristeva to articulate her desire for the
mother under the cover of heterosexuality, or of a preoccupation with
male homosexuality. However, the insistent return of the figure of the
male artist also speaks to the tremendous anxiety which accompanies
Kristeva's *choric* fantasy, an anxiety which has much to do with her own
status as a speaking subject, and which helps to explain her ambivalent
relationship with feminism.[24]

One cannot fail to remark upon the glaring discrepancy between
Kristeva's description of "femininity" and her own discursive mode—to
notice how little her voice functions as a vehicle for the semiotic, and
how emphatically she speaks from a position of linguistic and epistemological authority, a position she herself identifies with the father. How
are we to account for the distance that separates Kristeva's enunciative
stance from her theoretical preoccupations, her discourse from the
dream that sustains it? Her highly rationalized language must be understood at least in part, it seems to me, as a defense against her desire
for union with the mother, since within the terms of her own analysis
that union would necessarily mean the collapse of her subjectivity and
the loss of her voice. There is clearly a second anxiety at work here, as
well. Despite Kristeva's own assertions to the contrary, she consistently
equates woman with the mother, and the mother with what she calls
the "genetrix." Woman-as-speaking-subject is finally nowhere to be
found in texts such as *Revolution in Poetic Language* or *Polylogue*. For
Kristeva, to speak is thus necessarily to occupy a "male" position; even
the maternal voice can be heard only through the male voice.

Kristeva guards against the first of these threats by approaching the
mother only through the protective agency of the father (or the son, in
the case of Leonardo and Bellini); by substituting "poetic language" for
"biological ciphering." She guards against the second by speaking about
the *chora* or the semiotic only from a position deep within the symbolic.
There is a passage from *Revolution in Poetic Language* in which Kristeva
quite openly musters these defenses, situating herself emphatically on
the side of castration, language, and the thetic, and replacing the *chora*
with "artistic practices":

> The subject must be firmly posited by castration so that the drive attacks
> against the thetic will not give way to fantasy or to psychosis but will
> instead lead to a "second-degree thetic," i.e. a resumption of the function-
> ing characteristic of the semiotic *chora* within the signifying device of
> language. This is precisely what artistic practices, and notably poetic lan-
> guage, demonstrate. (P. 50)

There is, of course, one text in which Kristeva frankly acknowledges
her own maternal yearnings, and which seems to draw attention to the
divisions which structure her authorial subjectivity—"Stabat Mater," or
"Hérethique de l'amour."[25] That text splits the page into two columns of
print, one of which comments upon the Christian cult of the Virgin
Mary, and the need for a new discourse of motherhood, and the other of
which offers a much more informal and apparently stream-of-con-
sciousness record of its author's personal experiences with maternity.
However, although the left-hand column at time approximates that
"whirl of words" which *Polylogue* associates with the *chora*, it moves
increasingly in the direction of grammatical propriety and subject-
predication. It also enacts a drift toward theory, coming more and more
to resemble its symbolic counterpart.

It strikes me with some force, moreover, that while Kristeva speaks
in a very self-implicating way about maternal *jouissance*, what she is
really celebrating is the mother's relationship to a *male* child. As I tried
to demonstrate earlier in this chapter, that relationship is not part of the
choric fantasy. It is characterized in "Stabat Mater," as in "Place Names,"
as an interaction capable of breaking the "auto-erotic circle of pregnancy," and leading the mother into the thetic phase. Unlike the relationship of mother and daughter, that between mother and son is
predicated on separation and loss:

> There is this . . . abyss that opens up between the body and what had been
> its inside: there is the abyss between the mother and the child. What
> connection is there between myself, or even more unassumingly between
> my body and this internal graft and fold, which, once the umbilical cord has
> been severed, is an inaccessible other? My body and . . . him. No connec-
> tion. Nothing to do with it. And this, as early as the first gestures, cries,
> steps, long before *its* personality has become my opponent.[26]

Although Kristeva goes on immediately to insist that her remarks
obtain to the female as well as the male infant ("The child, whether *he*
or *she,* is irremediably an other"), she intimates elsewhere in "Stabat
Mater" that mothers and daughters recognize their mutual differences
only with the greatest difficulty. The passage I have in mind, which is

once again taken from the left column, describes what it calls "the community of women" in terms that are startlingly reminiscent of the *enceinte* or *chora*, that "place" where otherness, language, and identity slip imperceptibly away:

> Women doubtless reproduce among themselves the strange gamut of forgotten body relationships with their mothers. Complicity in the unspoken, connivance of the inexpressible, of a wink, a tone of voice, a gesture, a tinge, a scent. We are in it, set free of our identification papers and names, on an ocean of preciseness, a computerization of the unnameable. No communication between individuals but connections between atoms, molecules, wisps of words, droplets of sentences. The community of women is a community of dolphins. (Pp. 180–81)

Despite the impression it conveys of being the most "confessional" of the three essays Kristeva devotes to motherhood, this text in fact goes to great pains to erase all traces of *choric* desire, and to erect a panoply of symbolic defenses. It even manages to entrust the most manifestly maternal of its two voices with various disclaimers of mother love and love for the mother ("Belief in the mother is rooted in fear, fascinated with a weakness—the weakness of language" [p. 175]; "concerning that stage of my childhood, scented, warm, soft to the touch, I have only a spatial memory. . . . Almost no voice in her placid presence. Except, perhaps, and more belatedly, the echo of quarrels; her exasperation, her being fed up, her hatred" [p. 180]). However, most astonishing of all—at least for those who have taken Kristeva at her (earlier) word—about halfway through "Stabat Mater," the left column gives utterance to a desire that can only be seen to derive from the heart of dominant culture, a desire which runs counter to everything that Kristeva has ever had to say about the operations of *signifiance*, the semiotic, or poetic language:

> The impossibility of being without repeated legitimation (without books, man, family). Impossibility—depressing possibility—of "transgression."
> Either repression in which I hand the other what I want from others.
> Or this squalling of the void, open wound in my heart, which allows me to be only in purgatory.
> I yearn for the Law. (Pp. 174–75)

Filled with incredulity as I read and reread this passage for the first time, I turned to a 1974 interview with Kristeva, looking for a very different passage I seemed to remember. I found what I was seeking:

> If women have a role to play . . . it is only in assuming a *negative* function: reject everything finite, definite, structured, loaded with meaning, in the existing state of society. Such an attitude places women on the side of the explosion of social codes: with revolutionary moments.[27]

However, I also found these two sentences, following close upon the heels of the others: "But women tend to move immediately to the other side—the side of social power. Women can become the most solid guarantee of sociality . . . because they tend to identify with power after having rejected it" (p. 166).

Obviously, neither assertion has any descriptive authority with respect to the female subject. These two very different views of "women" grow, rather, out of that libidinal division that structures all of Kristeva's writings, the division between what she calls the "symbolic" and what she calls the "semiotic," categories which she always conceives as mutually antagonistic. These categories are, it seems to me, the theoretical analogue of the two very different desires that surface in her work, and which in so doing render it sometimes affirmative of phallic dominance, and at other times profoundly antipathetic to it: desire for the father, and desire for the mother.

I will have more to say about this libidinal rift in a moment, but first I want to note that desire for the father seems to be gaining ascendency in Kristeva's recent writing, particularly in "Freud and Love: Treatment and Its Discontents." That essay not only erases all evidence of the *choric* fantasy, it also safeguards against that fantasy's return by completely reconstructing the pre-Oedipal scene. The mother no longer provides the child with its first "potential space" and intimations of otherness by weaving a provisional enclosure of sounds and gestures around it. Instead, she adheres to the child like a "protective wrapping," a "poultice," a "balm," or a "diving suit," analogies which imply a clinging, suffocating action on her part. Kristeva even goes so far as to propose that the maternal space "can only come into being as such, before becoming an object correlative to the Ego's desire, as an *abject*," i.e., only through being excreted or sloughed off.[28]

This adhesion of mother to child completely blocks the latter's access to alterity, which now awaits the intervention of the paternal third term. "Freud and Love" also makes the child's primordial identity dependent upon that intervention; primary narcissism has become an effect of the father/child relationship, rather than, as in earlier texts, that of the mother/child relationship.[29] Kristeva makes it possible to imagine the father performing these new functions by giving him a pre-Oedipal persona.

Although this suddenly all-important figure splits what can perhaps be best described as the mother/child "monad" by inducing the child to abject the mother, he emerges not as an object to be loved but as a model to be incorporated. Pre-Oedipal paternal identification thus proceeds along the lines of oral assimilation, one of the two instinctual processes Kristeva earlier associated with the semiotic disposition and the regime of the mother. This newly reformulated primary narcissism is reminiscent of the *choric* relationship in other ways, as well. For instance, it is based on "archaic *replication*" rather than imitation, much as "Motherhood According to Giovanni Bellini" envisages the homosexual-maternal axis operating. "Freud and Love" also describes the child's psychic intercourse with the pre-Oedipal father as a "primary fusion, communion, unification," a description which would apply equally well to the desire at the center of the *choric* fantasy. The pre-Oedipal father would thus seem to have supplanted the mother altogether. All that remains to the latter within the more recent scheme is to satisfy the child's needs, and to refer it to the paternal third party.

Kristeva maintains that because the child's identification with the imaginary father takes place prior to sexual differentiation, that father is "the same as both parents" (p. 244), by which she seems to mean that unlike secondary identification, primary identification is not en-gendering. However, her account of primary narcissism is itself permeated with sexual difference, and the scenario she outlines conforms closely in certain key respects to Lacan's account of the Oedipus complex. In the former situation, as in the latter, it is incumbent upon the mother to reveal herself as incomplete and lacking, and to direct her desire beyond the child to the father/phallus. The child will then follow the path traced by her desire, and either incorporate the phallus (primary narcissism) or aspire to *have* the phallus (Oedipus complex). In both cases the child thereby comes to exist "within the signifier of the [paternal] Other" (p. 253).

It is thus the mother who is once again obliged to assume the sole responsibility of representing castration, a detail whose sexually differentiating consequences are too familiar to require further elaboration. It is also the father with whom both male and female child must align themselves as the necessary condition of subjectivity. This situation is exactly symmetrical to that whereby the female spectator is asked to identify first and foremost with the generally masculine point of view through which the images, sounds, and narrative events of a film are given as intelligible, and only secondarily with the subject-position designated for her by a female character; or with the linguistic rule which dictates that the noun *man* and the third-person male pronoun be understood as referring to the entire human race, but the noun *woman* and the third-person female pronoun be understood as referring only to the "second sex." In each of these three instances, male subjectivity is established as the norm, and female subjectivity as the deviation, a situation which does much to ensure the perpetuation of a phallocentric symbolic order.

Granted, there *are* certain divergences between Kristeva's reconceived primary narcissism and the classic Oedipus complex. Whereas the latter is regulated according to the difference between having or not having the phallus, a difference which is determined along strictly gender lines, the crucial question in the former is whether one is or is not the phallus, a question whose answer depends upon whether primary identification has taken place, not upon gender (p. 262). Kristeva also insists that primary narcissism, unlike the Oedipus complex, occurs outside either mediation or desire. (I feel impelled to note here that this is a highly contentious claim, since the mother's desire is crucial to the activation of primary identification, and since she could therefore plausibly be said to play a mediating role.) Finally, primary narcissism occurs at a moment prior to the coherent "objectification" of the other, and hence before the child could be said to be a subject.

However, the ostensibly earlier event leads so inexorably into the later one that it would be difficult to establish the point at which one ends and the other begins. Indeed, one of the chief functions of primary narcissism would seem to be the guarantee it places upon proper Oedipalization; Kristeva writes that it entails "the subject's entry into [the] disposition . . . of an ulterior, unavoidable Oedipal destiny" (p. 261). Furthermore, the end result in both cases is to wrest from the mother any claim to primacy, and to install the phallus within the psyche as the absolutely privileged term. These aims could even be said to be better achieved by primary narcissism than by the Oedipus complex, since it makes the father the first love object (p. 252), gives him a privileged position within the imaginary as well as the symbolic, and establishes him as the agency that confirms and shapes identity from the very outset. The mother, on the other hand, is now not only separated from the child at the moment of the latter's entry into language, but jettisoned at the very moment at which the child accedes to its first identification, well before the mirror stage. Irretrievably so, one might add, since her abjection is made the necessary precondition for language, is presented as that which alone creates the gap separating sign from referent, and signifier from signified (p. 242).

Kristeva's new paradigm becomes even more troubling to the feminist reader when she discovers the way in which it dispenses with the maternal voice. Ironically, given its foreclosure upon the mother, "Freud and Love" maps out as central a place for acoustic identifications in the early history of the subject as I have attempted to do in this book. Kristeva argues there that primary narcissism "should not be conceived as simply visual, but as a representation activating various facilitations corresponding to the *sonorous* ones," both because of their "precocious appearance in the domain of neuro-psychological maturation" and because of their "dominant function in speech" (p. 256). Elsewhere in the same essay, Kristeva suggests that primary narcissism may even give the voice priority over the image:

> The ideal identification with the symbolic upheld by the Other . . . activates speech more than image. Doesn't the signifying voice, in the final analysis, shape the visible, hence fantasy? (P. 253)

However, she insists that this founding identification aligns the child with the father rather than with the mother, thereby making the *paternal* voice the acoustic mirror in which it first hears itself. Kristeva is obliged to admit at one juncture that this claim flies in the face not only of previous psychoanalytic theory, but of clinical evidence ("We know that, empirically, the first affections, the first imitations, the first vocalizations as well are directed to the mother" [p. 245]). But she explains away this difficulty by pointing out that all identifications, including the primary one, are symbolic, and therefore (by virtue of the one-to-one relation she has consistently maintained between the father and the symbolic) necessarily paternal. She suggests, that is, that the child only seems to be directing his or her imitations and vocalizations to the mother; they are, in fact, directed to the father through her. Not only is language acquisition now completely under paternal jurisdiction, but Kristeva makes no mention in "Freud and Love" of the semiotic disposition, which seems to have fallen by the wayside.

What a writing out of the maternal! The thoroughness with which Kristeva goes about this discursive erasure can surely be explained only as a defensive mechanism, a way of safeguarding herself against the libidinal hold the mother exercises over much of her earlier writing. I would indeed go so far as to suggest that there is a direct relation between the complexity of the paternal fortification system and the intensity of the desire it gainsays. For Kristeva to have felt the need to double up in this way on the Oedipus complex—to install the father within the pre-Oedipal scene, thereby guaranteeing that everything that happens within the development of subjectivity has a phallic imprimatur—the tug of the maternal must be strong indeed.

The mother who is the object of Kristeva's unconscious desire, and against whom she enlists the protective resources of the father, is not, I hasten to add, the same as the one about whom she speaks in "Place Names," "Motherhood According to Giovanni Bellini," and "Stabat Mater." Those textual citations are what might be called "misrecognitions" of the fantasmatic mother who commands her unconscious desires, who is, I would maintain, none other than the Oedipal mother. In thus compounding what is already a highly unorthodox reading of Kristeva, I am leaning hard on an important passage from *The Ego and the Id,* a passage which suggests that the subject is generally obliged to negotiate his or her way between two versions of the Oedipus complex, one of which is culturally promoted and works to align the subject smoothly with heterosexuality and the dominant values of the symbolic order, and the other of which is culturally disavowed and organizes subjectivity in fundamentally "perverse" and homosexual ways:

> One gets the impression that the simple Oedipus complex is by no means its commonest form, but rather represents a simplification or schematization which, to be sure, is often enough justified for practical purposes. Closer study usually discloses the more complete Oedipus complex, which is twofold, positive and negative, and is due to the bisexuality originally present in children: that is to say, a boy has not merely an ambivalent attitude towards his father and an affectionate object-choice towards his mother, but at the same time he also behaves like a girl and displays an affectionate feminine attitude to his father and a corresponding jealousy and hostility towards his mother.[30]

It is to be regretted that Freud does not immediately spell out the consequences of this extremely interesting theoretical premise for the female subject as he does for her masculine counterpart. One is inclined to account for this elision by assuming it to be another instance of Freud's "indifference," as Luce Irigaray would say. However, when the reader turns for further clarification to "Female Sexuality" and "Femininity," she finds a curious erasure at work. The first of those essays hesitates both at the beginning and at the end between the concept of the negative Oedipus complex and a new category, to which it otherwise gives preference—the category of the "pre-Oedipal." By 1933, when Freud completed "Femininity," the latter had completely supplanted the former, and it has since then passed into general usage as the preferred paradigm by which to account for the little girl's erotic investment in the mother.

I intend nevertheless to hold Freud to his much earlier formulation, and to attempt to demonstrate that "the pre-Oedipal phase" has improperly replaced "the negative Oedipus complex" as the appropriate rubric with which to designate what, in the early history of the female subject, conventionally precedes her desire for the father. Both "Female Sexuality" and "Femininity" alert the careful reader to this impropriety. To begin with, in each of those essays Freud stresses the continuity rather than (as might be expected) the discontinuity between the little girl's love for her mother, and her love for her father. In "Female Sexuality" he notes that "except for the change of her love-object, the subsequent phase [adds scarcely] any new feature to her erotic life,"[31] while in "Femininity" he adds that "almost everything that we find later in her relation to her father [is] already present in this earlier attachment and [is] transferred subsequently on to her father."[32] Second, in the earlier of those essays, Freud remarks upon the extremely lengthy duration of the little girl's erotic attachment to her mother, commenting that in a number of the cases with which he was familiar, it had lasted into the fourth year, and in one case even into the fifth—well into that period normally assumed to coincide with the Oedipus complex (p. 226). Finally (and most crucially), Freud acknowledges uncovering seduction fantasies in which the girl's seducer was the mother rather than the father. However, this admission is no sooner made than qualified, as Freud attempts to ground fantasy in fact: "Here . . . the phantasy touches the ground of reality, for it was really the mother who by her activities over the child's bodily hygiene inevitably stimulated, and perhaps even roused for the first time, pleasurable sensations in her genitals."[33]

It was, of course, precisely through the fantasy of paternal seduction that Freud discovered the positive Oedipus complex. To be more exact, it was through his realization that what many of his female patients remembered as an actual seduction was, in fact, a psychic construction that Freud "stumbled" upon the daughter's desire for the father.[34] Thereafter the fantasy of paternal seduction became a definitive symptom of the positive Oedipus complex. Why this sudden retreat in the last of Freud's essays on female sexuality back into facticity, this abrupt refusal to read the fantasy of maternal seduction as an equally unequivocal signifier of the negative Oedipus complex? Because the stakes, as we will see, are of monumental proportions.

Near the conclusion of "Female Sexuality," Freud cites with surprising approval a 1927 essay by Jeanne Lampl-de Groot which recapitulates everything he himself has said about the girl's pre-Oedipal passion for the mother, but which attributes that passion quite definitively to the negative Oedipus complex. However, Lampl-de Groot's essay makes it clear that more is at issue here than a terminological difference of opinion. To insist upon the Oedipal bases of the little girl's attachment to the mother is to force a complete reconceptualization of the female Oedipus complex, which can now be seen to replicate the male version in its early stages:

> [The little girl], too, takes as her first object-love the mother who feeds and tends her. She, too, retains the same object as she passes through the pregenital phases of libidinal evolution. She, too, enters upon the phallic stage of libido development. . . . We may suppose that in the psychic realm also, children of either sex develop up to this point in an entirely similar

manner; that is to say, that girls as well as boys, when they reach the phallic stage enter into the Oedipus situation, i.e., that which for the girl is negative. She wants to conquer the mother for herself and to get rid of the father.[35]

To resituate the girl's libidinal investment in the mother firmly within the Oedipus complex is also to force a serious reconsideration of the role which is played there by the castration crisis. We recall that Freud presents that crisis as the mechanism by means of which the male subject is made to *exit* from the Oedipus complex, but the female subject to *enter* it. However, once the mother is included within the general equation, the castration crisis becomes the impetus whereby the little girl enters only into the *positive* Oedipus complex, and not the Oedipus complex *tout court*.

However, I do not mean to suggest that castration has no inaugural part to play with respect to the female subject's negative Oedipus complex—or, for that matter, with the male subject's positive one. In both cases, it seems to me, desire for the mother is initiated only through *symbolic castration*, i.e., only through the entry into language. It is, after all, impossible for either subject to enter into desire until linguistic immersion, since it is only through the consolidation of the signifier that the lack necessary to desire's functioning is opened up, and that the object as such both comes into view and slips beyond the subject's reach.

I would also argue that symbolic castration leads not just to desire, but to desire specifically for the mother, at least within the classic familial paradigm. It entails, after all, not merely that "fading" of the subject's "being" so movingly described by Lacan (the loss, as it were, of the subject's very life), but that separation from the mother upon which Kristeva places such emphasis. Those traumas are so complexly imbricated as to be virtually synonymous (it is surely no accident, for instance, that Freud's *fort/da* anecdote has been used as an allegory for both)[36] and to give to the latter, as to the former, all the force of major surgery. What other object than the mother, either for the girl or for the boy, could initially assume the status of that "all" which has been sacrificed to meaning? Or, to put the case in more strictly Lacanian terms, of the one for whom the child wishes to be all-in-all?[37]

What I am in effect suggesting is that accession to language marks not only the eclipse of the real, and the child's division from the mother, but the inception of the Oedipus complex for both boy and girl.[38] The crisis of dismemberment to which Freud so insistently returns thus plays a different role in female subjectivity from the one he attributes to it. It is both a delayed reflection of symbolic castration, as I suggested in chapter 1, and a crucial element within that system of sexual differentiation by means of which woman is made to assume the burden of male lack as well as her own. It accomplishes this end not merely by defining the female body as the site of anatomical insufficiency, and the female voice as the site of discursive impotence, but by propelling the girl into the positive Oedipus complex.

The female subject is thus split, in some profound way, between two irreconcilable desires, desires which persist in her unconscious long after the Oedipus complex has ostensibly run its course. (According to Freud, there is no real terminus to the girl's positive Oedipus complex,[39] and his account of patients who moved all their lives back and forth between love for the father and love for the mother[40] indicates that this holds equally true for the negative version.) I say "irreconcilable" because within the present symbolic order, desire for the mother can never be anything but a contradiction of the daughter's much more normative and normalizing desire for the father. It is not only that within Freud's paradigm these two desires cancel each other out,[41] but that whereas the latter is a libidinal investment in the phallus, and hence in the symbolic order, the former is a libidinal investment in everything which that order disvalues.

My insistence upon the Oedipus complex as the mediating agency between the daughter and her love for the mother may appear at first glance as treacherous a betrayal of feminism as Kristeva's installation of the father within the domain of primary narcissism. Certainly my theoretical paradigm closes off the pre-Oedipal domain both as an arena for resistance to the symbolic and as an erotic refuge. It also brings the homosexual axis of mother and daughter fully within symbolic castration and lack, and so renders it incapable of leading to any full and final satisfaction even if the incest taboo could be surmounted. However, to impute the daughter's erotic investment in the mother to the pre-Oedipal phase is to suggest that female sexuality precedes language and symbolic structuration—to give it, in other words, an essential content. It is also to align woman in an extremely problematic way with categories such as "nature" and "the imaginary," and to render her relation to language highly unstable. Finally, insofar as the relationship of mother and daughter is understood to stand outside signification, it must also be understood to stand outside desire, and so to exercise little influence over psychic life.

To situate the daughter's passion for the mother within the Oedipus complex, on the other hand, as I think we are obliged to do, is to make it an effect of language and loss, and so to contextualize both it and the sexuality it implies firmly within the symbolic. It is also to bring it within desire, and hence psychic "reality." Finally, and most important, it is not to foreclose upon what might be called a "libidinal politics," but to make it possible to speak for the first time about a genuinely oppositional desire—to speak about a desire which challenges dominance from within representation and meaning, rather than from the place of a mutely resistant biology or sexual "essence." Once we have recognized that unconscious desire is far from monolithic—that it is divided between at least two very different fantasmatic scenes—then it becomes possible to think of all sorts of discursive and relational strategies for activating the fantasmatic scene which corresponds to maternal desire, one which the symbolic does its best to cordon off and render inactive by denying it representational support.

The psychic division I have just described is clearly what is responsible for the very palpable tensions that collect around all the maternal categories in Kristeva's work. What figures there as the *"chora,"* the "semiotic," *"signifiance,"* or the "geno-text" is quite simply the textual eruption of the unconscious desire that anchors her to the symbolic or Oedipal mother. The negativity which Kristeva feels impelled to associate with all of these concepts is in the final analysis the negativity of the negative Oedipus complex, not the trace of some more primordial union of mother and child; it is the negativity, in other words, of a desire which is at odds with the phallus and the law of the father. The pre-Oedipal tableau comes into play only as an after-the-fact construction that permits the subject who has already entered into language and desire to dream of maternal unity and phenomenal plenitude. It is a regressive fantasy, that is, through which the female subject pursues both the Oedipal mother and the wholeness lost to her through symbolic castration. As can be seen in texts such as *Revolution of Poetic Language* and *Polylogue,* the homosexual component within this fantasy poses a powerful threat to the father, the phallus, and the operations of dominant meaning, but not, I would argue, to meaning per se.

As I suggested a moment ago, the daughter's unconscious desire for the mother does not enjoy the same kind of broadly based representational support that sustains her unconscious desire for the father. It is perhaps for this reason that Kristeva believes the homosexual-maternal facet of female subjectivity to be beyond representation, and indeed to threaten its very continuation. However, she also tends to literalize the *choric* fantasy, reading it as an accurate account both of the pre-Oedipal period and of the mother who exercises such a hold upon her own libido. As a result, she is simply incapable of imagining that the mother can have any place within the symbolic, or that the daughter can maintain a relation to language while pursuing her unconscious desire for the mother. But these problems are endemic to Kristeva's version of the *choric* fantasy, it seems to me, not to the desire that fuels it, or even the fantasy itself, which is capable of assuming other forms.

Before turning to some films that occupy the same discursive space as "Place Names" and "Motherhood According to Giovanni Bellini," I want to draw a few tentative conclusions about Kristeva's relation to feminism. What seems to me to be the most important thing about that work is the way in which the negativity of the negative Oedipus complex surfaces there, albeit in disguised and misrecognized forms. Feminism can't really manage without the negativity, which is an indispensable weapon not only against the name, meaning, and law of the father, but against the female subject's unconscious investment in those things. Moreover, without it feminism threatens to settle into its own complacencies, and to subscribe to its own fictions of identity.

We may also need the positivity of the *chora*, its promise of a female *enceinte*. It, in fact, represents one of the governing fantasies of feminism, a powerful image both of women's unity and of their at times necessary separatism. I would even go so far as to argue that without activating the homosexual-maternal fantasmatic, feminism would be impossible— that it needs the libidinal resources of the negative Oedipus complex. However, it is imperative that we recognize the unconscious mother for who she is, the Oedipal rather than the pre-Oedipal mother. As Kristeva herself says in "Women's Time," an essay which reads at times like an inadvertent auto-criticism, the utopia of an "archaic, full, total englobing mother with no frustration, no separation, with no break-producing symbolism (with no castration, in other words)," may indeed represent "an unbelievable force for subversion in the modern world! [But], at the same time, what playing with fire!"[42]

Furthermore, because Kristeva's account of the *choric* fantasy excludes both mother and daughter from language, it makes it difficult to imagine them participating in the articulation of new discourses, and so keeps their social disruption from being meaningful, in the strictest sense of that word. It also conceives of the maternal challenge in extremely deterministic ways, and it grounds that determinism in biology. Equally troubling, it conceptualizes the integration of mother and daughter in exclusively regressive terms, as a backward journey. In order for the *choric* fantasy to function as an effective political implement, it must point forward as well as backward—accommodate transformation as well as return.

Finally, it may be as crucial for feminism to come to terms with symbolic castration and division as to find ways of bringing women together—to confront the gap that separates the subject not only from pre-Oedipality and the phenomenal order, but from other subjects, no matter how ostensibly "similar," and—not least—the various manifestations of its "self." Kristeva herself speaks eloquently about this project in "Women's Time," in a passage that quietly and unobtrusively displaces the concept of negativity from the pre-Oedipal register to the symbolic register, thereby bringing it more theoretically in line with the negative Oedipus complex that fuels it. The passage in question calls upon feminism to interiorize *"the founding separation of the socio-symbolic contract"* so as to introduce "its cutting edge into the very interior of every identity[,] whether subjective, sexual, [or] ideological" (p. 210). This is perhaps the point at which to note that Kristeva knows how to read motherhood as an emblem not only of unity, but of its opposite—of the "radical ordeal of the splitting of the subject."[43] She has recourse to the image of motherhood as division in "Women's Time," where she uses it both as a way of anticipating the passage I cited a moment ago, and as a repudiation of the image of motherhood as plenitude. The juxtaposition vividly dramatizes the compensatory role which the latter image is asked to play with respect to the former. It makes clear, in other words, that the *choric* fantasy attests to nothing so much as the entry into language and the negative Oedipus complex:

> Redoubling up of the body, separation and coexistence of the self and of an other, of nature and consciousness, of physiology and speech. This fundamental challenge to identity is then accompanied by a fantasy of totality—narcissistic completeness—a sort of instituted, socialized, natural psychosis. (P. 206)

Robert Altman's *Three Women* and Laura Mulvey and Peter Wollen's *Riddles of the Sphinx,* the first released in 1977 and the second in 1976, inhabit the same fantasmatic space as Kristeva's writings on the *chora,* with which they are roughly contemporaneous (*Polylogue* was also published in 1977, although individual essays appeared somewhat earlier). There is another point of intersection between these texts, which is that each is at least to some degree the product of feminism. This is, of course, manifestly the case with *Riddles of the Sphinx,* which foregrounds its concern with feminism at every turn, and where point of view is always so sharply—and so theoretically—focused. It is perhaps less apparent with *Three Women,* where the "tale" seems to lack a teller—where, in Metz's words, the *discours* is concealed behind the *histoire.*[44] However, although that latter film is certainly not a feminist text, its preoccupation with what Kristeva calls the "homosexual-maternal facet" makes it, too, finally unassimilable to the Hollywood system, which is centered on the father, the phallus, the law, and the male version of the sonorous envelope fantasy. Not surprisingly, both films also deviate from that system's formal paradigm, although once again that deviation is much more marked in the case of *Riddles*.

Three Women reads almost like a dramatization of "Place Names" and "Motherhood According to Giovanni Bellini." It shows the female subject to have a tenuous hold upon identity and social exchange—so much so that she easily slips outside the symbolic altogether. It defines that subject primarily through the three women of the title—Milly (Shelly Duvall), Willy (Janice Rule), and Pinky (Sissy Spacek), each of whom has a troubled relationship to language, and highly permeable subjective boundaries.

Milly talks incessantly, in an unconscious parody of dominant discourse; her speech consists almost entirely of citations from advertising and popular women's magazines. No one but Pinky ever pays the slightest attention to what she says, which increasingly over the course of the film assumes the status of cultural "noise" or babble. Although Milly's verbal patter seems ineffective as an agency of communication, it is shown to serve an important phatic function in the sanitarium where she works. As she slowly moves the elderly patients through the warm water of the therapeutic pools, she wraps them in the sonorous blanket of her voice; indeed, the film establishes a metaphoric connection between Milly's voice and the curative waters. There is also a strongly implied metaphoric connection between the elderly patients and small children. The former, like the latter, are helpless to perform even the most rudimentary actions by themselves, and must be led by the hand when they walk. Speech flows past them, leaving only a ripple of comprehension in its wake. Milly closely approximates Kristeva's "mother-as-speaking-subject"; she is inside language, but only marginally so, and her discursive standing is radically jeopardized by every tug on the umbilical cord.

Willy more closely resembles Kristeva's genetrix. Not only is she hugely pregnant, but she is completely absorbed in her pregnancy; she is the very prototype of the mother enclosed in the *enceinte*, the mother who is simultaneously container and contained. Willy also remains wordless for most of the film. She breaks her silence only on three occasions—once to scream for help when she finds Pinky floating face downward in the swimming pool, once to fashion the obligatory cries of childbirth, and once (at the very end of the film) to remark: "I just had a lovely dream. I wish I could remember it." All three sets of sounds attest to her inability to manipulate language.

Willy performs another important role—one which Kristeva associates with the mother, but which she nevertheless reserves for the male subject. She functions, that is, as an artist, obsessively drawing primitive figures on the floors of swimming pools. These submerged, underwater figures form a kind of genotext to the film's phenotext; half-human, half-animal, frozen in postures of sexual aggression and submission, they pose an archaic and antiperspectival challenge both to "realist" representation and to the civilizing sublimations of the symbolic. They also foreground Willy's privileged relation to the drives.

If Willy and Milly embody aspects of the prototypical mother, Pinky represents the prototypical daughter. She has the clothing, the gestures, and the undefined features of a child. She burps noisily and with enthusiasm after gulping down a glass of beer, blows bubbles through the straw in her milk, and spills shrimp cocktail down the front of her pink smocked dress. Like a very young girl, she derives her only sense of identity from Milly, appropriating her robe, her bed, her name, and her social security number. Pinky also attempts to burrow deep inside Milly's voice; like the geriatric patients, she "bathes" in that voice at the beginning of the film, and is before long echoing its aphorisms and turns of phrase, making it the acoustic mirror in which she hears herself. She spends her evenings furtively delving into Milly's diary, which she ultimately claims as her own. These appropriations and penetrations all attest to a powerful desire to fuse with the mother—the desire which, as I have indicated, is also the motive force behind Kristeva's *choric* fantasy.

When Pinky's dyadic union with Milly is shattered by the entry of Edgar, Willy's philandering husband, her desire finds an even more extreme expression. She dives from a second-story balcony into the apartment swimming pool, aiming both her gaze and her body at the pregnant belly of one of Willy's underwater figures. In so doing, she substitutes the wordless enclosure of Willy's womb for the unwelcoming receptacle of Milly's voice. Significantly, it is Willy who rescues Pinky from the pool, and who in so doing gives life to her once again.

Ultimately, Altman's three women are united in the act of childbirth. When Willy goes into labor, Milly assists, and Pinky watches, transfixed by the spectacle of motherhood. This scene is immediately preceded by the dream in which Pinky's image merges with those of Willy and Milly, a dream which prompts her to seek actual refuge in Milly's bed. It is followed by the concluding scene of the film, which shows Milly, Willy, and Pinky acting out the respective roles of mother, grandmother, and daughter. Childbirth is thus emphatically associated with precisely that three-generational relay described by Kristeva, whereby "the mother of a daughter replays in reverse the encounter with her own mother," and in so doing actualizes the homosexual dimension of motherhood. As in "Place Names" and "Motherhood According to Giovanni Bellini," there is no room within the *choric* enclosure for the male child, who is stillborn. Pinky immediately takes his place, assuming the status anticipated by her name.

The exclusion of the male child from the *enceinte* is part of a larger repudiation of the symbolic. Edgar is dismissed by all three women at the moment that Willy goes into labor, and is never seen again. (There is an oblique reference near the end of the film to his death, presumably at the hands of the women.) The doctor never appears to help Willy deliver her child (he is, indeed, never summoned). The isolated house in which Willy, Milly, and Pinky establish their domestic economy at the film's conclusion emphasizes their distance from the social order, as does the dreamlike quality of their few gestures and words. The final shot of the film, which lingers on a pile of abandoned tires, suggests that in so retreating, the three women have reduced Edgar's phallic regime to the status of trash or waste. In so doing, it reiterates the fantasmatic argument that the homosexual facet of motherhood makes a woman "closer to her instinctual memory, more open to her own psychosis, and consequently, more negatory of the social symbolic bond."

In *Three Women,* as in *Polylogue,* the *choric* fantasy is elaborated in emphatically regressive terms, as a threefold "return": to the grand-mother/mother/child *enceinte* of which Kristeva speaks, which is itself what might be called a "double replay," to the drives, and to an implied matriarchy. Once again that fantasy works to subvert the symbolic, but not to transform it. Moreover, by weakening the relation between the female subject and language, it leaves her without the signifying resources either to imagine or to effect change. Finally, *Three Women* encourages us once again to confuse the Oedipal mother with either the pre-Oedipal mother or the "Master-Mother of instinctual drive," thereby eliding altogether that negative desire from which feminism derives its libidinal resources. The *choric* fantasy assumes much more complexly political forms in the last of my texts, to which I now turn.

Whereas the *choric* fantasy surfaces only in fairly oblique ways in Kristeva's work, and is always met there by a powerful counterforce, it could reasonably be said to be the organizing principle of Laura Mulvey and Peter Wollen's *Riddles of the Sphinx.* That fantasy manifests itself at the level of the film's articulation as well as at the level of its fiction, determining the kinds of shots that are used in the lengthy middle section, the unusual voice-over that accompanies five of those shots, and the overall narrative progression. At issue once again is desire for the mother, a desire which turns in some fundamental way upon the recovery of a lost maternal voice. However, what makes this particular "telling" of the *choric* fantasy so compelling are the displacements to which it subjects its central image. Although the *chora* is initially configured as a sonorous envelope enclosing the infant daughter, it is subsequently moved out of the pre-Oedipal scene, and installed at various sites within the symbolic. *Riddles* also differs from the other texts with which I have grouped it in entrusting the mother with a wide variety of discursive functions, ranging from *"lalangue"* to the language of psychoanalysis.

Like "Motherhood According to Giovanni Bellini" and *Three Women, Riddles* links the maternal voice to an archaic moment in the history of civilization and subjectivity. That linkage occurs primarily through the figure of the Sphinx, to whom the film obsessively returns, and who occupies the position of what is technically a voice-over but is described in the script as a "voice-off." (I will consequently refer to it henceforth by the second of those appellations.) "Laura's" opening commentary associates the Sphinx with "motherhood as mystery," and with "resistance to patriarchy," thereby installing it as a kind of mythic mother. The close identification of the voice with Louise in pans 1 – 3 further consolidates the connection between those two figures.

Before discussing the specific uses to which it is put, I want to emphasize that the voice of the Sphinx/mother enjoys a complex conceptual status. To begin with, it comes as answer to a quite extraordinary solicitation—to a solicitation which takes the form of a series of zooms into and extreme close-ups of the mouth of the Egyptian Sphinx (or, to be more precise, of some found footage of the Egyptian Sphinx), shots which have the quality of a knock on a closed door. Second, "Laura" (as Mulvey is designated within the film) characterizes it as an "imaginary narrator," suggesting that it is an overtly fantasmatic voice. It in fact "belongs" to no character in the main diegesis, and can be traced back only to the most denaturalized of images in the theoretical prologue—to the images, that is, of the Sphinx, which are so many generations away from the original footage that they openly proclaim their status as photographs. The voice of the Sphinx/mother consequently escapes that anatomical destiny to which classic cinema holds its female characters, and upon which Kristeva places such a premium; it is denatured and ultimately disembodied. At the same time, it never assumes the privileged and transcendental qualities of a traditional voice-over, or even the much more limited powers of a traditional voice-off. It is more (as the film itself suggests) a voice "apart," in both senses of that word—a voice which asserts its independence from the classic system, and which is somehow a part of what it narrates.

This voice assumes a distinctly *choric* role during the first three of the thirteen shots that constitute the film's center. It weaves Louise (Dinah Stabb) and her child, Anna (Rhiannon Tise), within a nest of repetitive and incantatory sounds, whose progress is as slow and circular as that of the tightly framed camera ("If only I hadn't minded, I used to say, but I did mind very much, I minded more than I could ever have dared. Mind the door. Mind the glass. Mind the fire. Mind the child. I never minded the warmth. I minded the need. It was needed to have minded, I used to say, but was it needed to have minded more than very much?").[45] In so doing, it seems to speak to Louise's condition as much as to that of her child—to their imaginary confusion and interpenetration, and to the resulting breakdown in subject/object delimitation. (As with the other texts I have grouped together here, *Riddles* reads the pre-Oedipal scene through Louise rather than through her daughter, and in fact tends—at least in the beginning—to project the former into the latter's position. I will have more to say about this below.) Here, as elsewhere in the film, the panning camera provides the visual analogue of the *choric* voice, tracing (as it were) the spatial boundaries of the sonorous envelope.[46]

The voice-off disappears during the next five shots, and the camera breaks free from its domestic moorings, pivoting around a series of increasingly public places—a day-care center, a telephone switchboard office, an institutional cafeteria, a traffic roundabout, an indoor shopping center. The framing becomes much wider, and in shot 7 the camera travels in a circle as well as pans 360 degrees, following an almost unreadable itinerary. These are the formal indications of a psychic opening out, of Louise's and Anna's emergence from what the film characterizes as an imaginary dyad into the world of the symbolic. Significantly, it isn't the father who precipitates this rupture (he is, in fact, powerless to intrude), but the exigencies of work, Louise's practical concerns about day-care, and—most important—her new friendship with Maxine (Merdelle Jordine).

However, the voice of the Sphinx/mother resurfaces in shot 9, where it poses a series of unanswered questions about the politics of motherhood. Its discourse is still circular (the questions it asks form what is described as "a linked ring, each raising the next until they [lead] the argument back to its original departure"). But like the camera framing, that circle has become wider. The *chora* is no longer synonymous with the claustral enclosure of the maternal embrace, but has expanded to include the entirety of women. Moreover, far from

foreclosing upon the social, the maternal voice now establishes motherhood as a point of crucial intersection between politics and subjectivity,
economics and the family, personal history and a collective future. The
questions it asks lead back into memory and "out into society":

> Should women demand special working conditions for mothers? Can a
> child-care campaign attack anything fundamental to women's oppression?
> Should women's struggle be concentrated on economic issues? . . . Could
> there be a social revolution in which women do not play the leading role?
> How does women's struggle relate to class struggle? Is patriarchy the main
> enemy for women? Does the oppression of women work on the uncon-
> scious as well as on the conscious? What would the politics of the uncon-
> scious be like? How necessary is being-a-mother to women, in reality or
> imagination?

What I am trying to suggest is that the *chora* in effect becomes the
subjective, economic, social, and political "space" of feminism; the
enceinte is transformed into an all-inclusive "community of women,"
and (*pace* Kristeva) its inhabitants don't communicate like dolphins.

Shot 10 shows us that community in miniature, while at the same
time indicating the psychic terrain upon which it is based. Louise sits
with Maxine in her mother's garden while Anna and her grandmother
build a bonfire. The cast of characters constitutes the by now familiar
ménage à trois of the homosexual-maternal facet—mother, grandmother,
and child—but Maxine's inclusion complicates the libidinal dynamics.
She introduces otherness into what would otherwise escape difference
and desire. She is the third term that separates Anna from Louise,
thereby making it possible for the former to invest erotically in the latter.
Maxine is also, at least within the terms of this reading, the trace of
Louise's negative Oedipus complex, in much the same way that a
photographic negative might be said to be a trace of its positive—she is
both a black figure in the otherwise white tableau, and the object of
Louise's desire. Finally, Maxine is the crucial (racial) other with respect
to the "establishment" of feminism, the signifier of what it all too easily
forgets and excludes. The maternal voice is both interiorized in this shot
and entrusted to Louise's mother, whose only intermittently audible
monologue swathes the scene in a sonorous haze akin to the smoke of
the bonfire she is building.

In shot 11, the maternal voice undergoes yet another permutation.
Banished from its former (imaginary) narrative position, it nevertheless
returns as a narrator, this time of a film (and tape) within the film. The
camera pans around Chris's editing room as he, Louise, and Maxine
look at a documentary on the *Post Partum Document, ICA 1976*. Mary
Kelly's disembodied voice speaks "over" these assorted images, from a
vantage point which is interior with respect to the shot but exterior with

respect to Chris's film and tape. Its status thus transgresses the binary opposition which serves to distinguish male from female voice within classic cinema, a transgression which is magnified by Kelly's claim to theoretical authority. (Despite its diegetic status, it is the only voice to speak with such authority in the thirteen-shot sequence, and it is rivaled only by "Laura's" voice within *Riddles* as a whole.)

What further distinguishes Kelly's voice-over from other voices in the film, as well as those produced by Hollywood, is that she speaks theoretically about her own experience of motherhood—that her access to maternity is mediated through psychoanalysis, and does not issue directly from the body. This maternal voice, in other words, in no way approximates a "biological ciphering," nor does it issue out of what Mulvey elsewhere describes as "the half light of the imaginary."[47] What is surprising and rather disappointing, however, is Kelly's own tendency to reenact in her account that curious slippage by means of which childhood language somehow comes to be characterized as maternal language, and the mother is projected into the position of the one for whom boundaries are by no means firm:

> The diaries in this document are based on recorded conversations between mother and child (that is, myself and my son) at the crucial moment of his entry into nursery school. The conversations took place at weekly intervals between September 7th and November 26th 1975. They came to a "natural" end with his/my adjustment to school. There also occurs at this moment a kind of "splitting" of the mother/child dyadic unit which is evident in my references in the diaries, to the father's presence and in my son's use of pronouns (significantly "I") in his conversations and of implied diagrams (for example, concentric markings and circles) in his "drawings." The marking process is regulated by the nursery routine, so that almost daily finished "works" are presented by the children to their mothers. Consequently, these markings become the logical terrain on which to map out the "signification" of the *maternal discourse* [my emphasis].

As this passage would indicate, with its invocation of the "mother/child dyadic unity" and its attention to "concentric markings and circles," the *chora* figures centrally in what Kelly has to say about motherhood. Significantly, however, she focuses upon its rupture rather than upon its constitution or maintenance—upon the emergence of the infant subject out of the maternal enclosure, and its transition from imaginary to symbolic. The same could be said of the entire middle section of the film, which moves Louise and Anna very quickly out of the home and into a series of social spaces. The realm of the imaginary is "revisited" in shot 12, but only from a position of fully constituted subjectivity.

Despite superficial appearances to the contrary, *Riddles* does *not* privilege the pre-Oedipal scene. Its concern is rather with forgotten or

censored details within the Oedipal narrative—with semic and proairetic elements which might permit that story to be told rather differently
than it usually is. The detail upon which the film predicates its transformative intervention is, of course, the Sphinx, who not only is left out
of that abbreviated version of the story which circulates most widely
(that version which derives its coherence from psychoanalysis), but who
in Sophocles' account remains emphatically outside the city gates. *Riddles* is thus, as Teresa de Lauretis would say, "an interruption of the
triple track by which narrative, meaning, and pleasure are constructed
from [Oedipus's] point of view"—a film which is "narrative and Oedipal
with a vengeance."[48]

As I have already attempted to show, *Riddles* conflates the Sphinx
with the mother, reading the former's exclusion from Thebes as a
metaphor of the latter's isolation from power and privilege. Similarly,
the frequent excision of the Sphinx from the Oedipal narrative
represents for the film a telling image of all the ways in which the
mother is denied cultural recognition. However, "Laura" goes on in her
opening remarks to suggest that the Sphinx/mother also poses a serious
challenge to the system that seeks to exclude and censor her—that
what the symbolic order defines negatively is capable of returning as
negativity:

> The Sphinx is outside the city gates, she challenges the culture of the city,
> with its order of kinship and its order of knowledge, a culture and a political
> system which assign women a subordinate place.
>   To the patriarchy, the Sphinx as woman is a threat and a riddle. . . .

The question which poses itself with a certain insistence at this point is:
In what guise does the Sphinx/mother return, and in what does her
negativity inhere?

The conclusion of the theoretical prologue restates a point made
only a moment or two earlier in the film, but it does so with a significant difference. Initially, "Laura" says: "The [Oedipus] myth confirms
women's sense of exclusion and suppression." Later she puts it this way:
"We live in a society ruled by the father, in which the place of the
mother is suppressed." She suggests, that is, that it is not merely women
themselves who have been forgotten and denied, but the position the
mother occupies. *Riddles* does not specify here what this position might
be, but I do not think it would be unfaithful to the spirit of the film to
gloss the puzzling sentence in this way: "We live in a society ruled by
the father, in which the *psychic* place of the mother is suppressed," a
suppression which in the case of the female subject entails the repression of her desire for the mother. Certainly the last shot of the middle

section points in the direction of such an explanation, as I will attempt
to show in a moment.

By focusing less on desire than on identification, shot 12 provides
yet another account of what the psychic "place of the mother" might be.
The camera pans around a room full of mirrors, while Maxine applies
make-up to her face, and Louise reads aloud from the transcript of one
of Maxine's dreams. The room is presumably in Maxine and Louise's
apartment, and so reprises the *choric* spaces of the first three shots.
Louise's voice provides the acoustic equivalent, wrapping the two
women in a blanket of largely mystifying sounds. The proliferation of
reflections indicates that we are deep within the imaginary, and draws
our attention to two crucial psychic doublings—that of Louise with
Maxine (at a certain point the dream becomes common property, their
regressive journey a joint one), and that of Maxine and Louise with a
shared mother. Shot 12 thus serves as an important reminder of the
crucial role played by the mother in both the visual and the acoustic
mirror stages (if I may be permitted to coin a phrase) and of the central place of the maternal imago within the constitution of female
subjectivity.

In Maxine's dream, identification with the mother leads to an
immediate disinvestment from the father, and to an eruption of negativity within the symbolic order over which he presides:

> I realized that it was Ash Wednesday and I thought that I must be my
> mother, although I knew she was dead. I had a feeling of jubilation and in a
> very loud voice I ordered that all my father's property should be sold by
> auction. All the women threw away their combs and shouted, "Bravo! Well
> done!" They unstrapped all the sheep and knocked the helmets and mili-
> tary caps off the soldiers. I don't remember much more except that I was
> dancing on the deck of a ship, in front of a sheet of canvas or sailcloth.

But identity is not determined by the imaginary alone. It is imperative
that Maxine and Louise's psychic journey lead forward as well as
backward, and that they not remain stranded in the (reconstructed)
chora. Consequently, at the precise moment that Louise finishes speaking these words, the reflections of the camera and cinematographer are
caught in one of the many mirrors, introducing the critical third term,
and returning the viewer (and, by implication, Maxine and Louise)
definitively to the symbolic. Significantly, though, the cinematographer
is a woman, intimating that the social order to which we return is not
the same as the one we left.

Once again, then, *Riddles* indicates that the third term need not
necessarily be phallic; the female cinematographer reprises the role
earlier played by Maxine, separating mother from daughter without

requiring that the mother assume the status of the abject. In both situations the distance necessary to desire is opened up without the mediation of the father, suggesting *the potential symbolic adequacy of the negative Oedipus complex.* This drama will be enacted yet again, albeit more obliquely, in the final shot of the thirteen-shot sequence. Before turning to that shot, I want to point out that identification with the mother can assume the subversive form it takes in Maxine's dream only if the negative Oedipus complex is activated at the same time, and if the maternal position is thereby rendered desirable. Incorporation of the maternal imago is, after all, an indispensable component of conventional female subjectivity, and it has very different effects there. The crucial distinction which must be made between these two identificatory instances is that in one case the image of the mother is erotically invested, and in the other case it is erotically disinvested. (I will return to this point in the next chapter.)

The last time we hear the maternal voice-off within the middle section of *Riddles* is in shot 13, in which Louise and Anna visit the Egyptian Room of the British Museum. This is the juncture at which the film insists most strenuously upon the fantasmatic nature of the Sphinx's voice, tracing that voice to the interior of a thrice-framed text. It also begins with a statement about the discursive status of memory—a statement which radically qualifies the recollections that follow, making it impossible for us to read them as the simple recovery of earlier events: "She remembered reading somewhere a passage from a book which she could no longer trace, words which had struck her at the time, and which she now tried to reconstruct."

For the listener who hears these words for the first time, the third-person female pronoun seems to refer to Louise, who in the preceding shot is shown reading the transcript of Maxine's dream, and puzzling out its meaning. However, in the same speech the voice-off associates the pronoun *she* with memories which we know to belong more appropriately to Anna, because we have been shown the events from which they seem to derive in a fragmentary and elusive way earlier in the thirteen-shot sequence:

> She remembered how, when she had been very small, her mother had lifted her up to carry her on her hip, and how she had hovered round the cot while she fell asleep. She remembered her feeling of triumph when her father left the house and the sudden presentiment of separation which followed. . . . And she remembered one morning coming into her mother's room and finding her mother's friend sleeping next to her mother, and she suddenly understood something she realized her mother had tried to explain and she felt a surge of panic, as if she'd been left behind and lost. She thought her mother would be angry, but she smiled, and, when she got out of bed, she noticed the shape of the arch of her foot and her heel and the back of her calf.

At this point in the film, then, a quite remarkable temporal and referential shift takes place: the listener is suddenly asked to understand the act of remembering childhood events to which the voice-off refers as taking place not in the present, but rather at an unspecified moment in Anna's future.

The memories which we are thus encouraged to impute to an adult Anna dramatize the entry into the Oedipus complex. They begin with images evocative of pre-Oedipal closeness and boundary confusion (the daughter grafted to the mother's hip, the mother part of the daughter's environment as the latter goes to sleep), and lead on to Anna's recollection of her father's departure, an event which gives her a "presentiment of separation," but which is finally powerless to rupture the *chora*. What does finally manage to tear Anna away from the maternal body is a primal scene of sorts, in which she enters her mother's bedroom and finds her in bed with a friend (presumably Maxine). This event not only severs the pre-Oedipal umbilical cord, it also produces a profound sense of loss, thereby inaugurating desire. (There is also an unspecified linguistic intervention here, the intrusion of the language—and desire— of the mother-as-Other.) Significantly, it is only after this "castration" that the maternal body becomes eroticized, as indicated by the aroused description of Louise's arched foot and calf. What Anna thus recollects at some indeterminate point in the future is a series of images that speak, perhaps fantasmatically, but with no less consequence for her psychic life, to the inception of what I have been theorizing as the negative Oedipus complex. This mnemic cluster is pivotal to what happens in the rest of the shot, as well as to the organization of *Riddles* as a (divided) whole.

The other act of memory to which the maternal voice refers—that involving the passage from an unknown book—also undergoes a revision between the first and subsequent viewings of *Riddles*, becoming something which it is impossible to attribute exclusively to either Louise or Anna, and which is therefore temporally unlocatable; it becomes, in other words, a recollection/construction which is shared across time. This set of memories also intersects with the temporal register represented by the glass-enclosed mummies, whose "enigmatic script" (according to the intertitles) reminds an unspecified "her" of a "forgotten history and the power of a different language"—the history and language of the Sphinx, who, as I have tried to demonstrate, is a metaphor for the Oedipal or symbolic mother. Indeed, pan 13 in its entirety must be understood as a "detour" through a series of Egyptian texts.

The recollections are anchored to the diegetic present, as well, since Anna's memory of her mother's arched foot meshes neatly with the image of Louise moving slowly through the Egyptian Room, her feet and calves conspicuously arched by the high heels she wears throughout the film. The innermost narrative of this shot—that involving the Greek Sphinx—introduces yet another time and place. The pan in its entirety is thus articulated around an almost inconceivably complex network of cultural, spatial, and temporal references.

If shot 13 is a "detour" through the "enigmatic script" of the mummies, the reading memories add several more stops to the semiotic excursion. The voice-off tells the story of Louise/Anna's recollections, recollections which themselves contain—as a text-within-a-text—the story of the anonymous "she." That story encloses in turn yet another text—a box inscribed with the words "Anatomy Is No Longer Destiny." The box opens to reveal the enigmatic figure of the Sphinx (a text in her own right), who produces the final level of textuality—the words *Capital, Delay,* and *Body:*

> "Inscribed on the lid of the box were the words: 'Anatomy Is No Longer Destiny' and inside, when she opened it, she found the figure of the Greek Sphinx with full breasts and feathery wings. She lifted it up out of the box to look at it more closely. As she did so, it seemed to her that its lips moved and it spoke a few phrases in a language which she could not understand, except for three words which were repeated several times: 'Capital,' 'Delay' and 'Body.' She replaced it in the box and closed the lid. She could feel her heart beat. . . . She felt giddy with success, as though, after laboring daily to prevent a relapse into her pristine humanity, she had finally got what she wanted. She shuddered. Suddenly she heard a voice, very quiet, coming from the box, the voice of the Sphinx, growing louder, until she could hear it clearly, compellingly, and she knew that it had never been entirely silent and that she had heard it before, all her life, since she first understood that she was a girl!"

This part of the voice-off narration further destabilizes the pronoun *she,* which is now extended to include not only Louise and Anna, but an anonymous female character. Because of this pronominal slippage, the "she" who reads the inscription on the lid, opens the box, and listens to the Sphinx's words, seems to include the first two characters as well as the third, and so to describe a condition that is somehow a part of female subjectivity rather than an isolated incident. This impression is reinforced when the voice-off reverts to the remembering "she," and her attempts to recollect the details of the forgotten text. What had seemed a textual memory suddenly connects intimately with Anna's infantile memories, and the distinction between the three women completely evaporates ("The rhythm of the sentence was not quite right and she felt sure there was some particular she had forgotten. . . . Could she have known the language which the Sphinx spoke? The more she tried to remember, the more she found her mind wandering, mislaying the thread of logical reconstruction and returning to images from her own childhood").

However, even as it insists upon the commonality of this maternal legacy—a legacy which, I would argue, is precisely the negative Oedipus complex—*Riddles* is careful to stress its cultural basis. There could be no firmer denial of biological determinism than the assertion that "Anatomy Is No Longer Destiny," especially when that assertion is buttressed by images of age-defying mummies. Even the immediately following acrobatic sequence, with its apparent "return" to the body, offers a demonstration not of corporeal laws and limits but of how to violate and exceed them. The acrobats are "bodies at work, expending their labor power upon its own material," rather than upon the task of reproduction. They are also formally denatured, appearing to us first as grainy black-and-white figures, and then as optically printed two-color figures. Finally, they are bodies determined to reverse gravity—to fling themselves through the air. *Riddles* uses the dream of unity at the center of the *choric* fantasy to affirm the possibility of a female collectivity capable of transcending class, ethnic, cultural, geographical, and historical boundaries—a collectivity based not just upon the shared experience of exclusion, and a shared belief in the possibility of both articulating and transforming that experience through new forms of sexual, social, political, and artistic practice, but upon a primary and passionate desire for the mother.

The words the Sphinx utters—"Capital," "Delay," and "Body"— isolate the three terms around which female subjectivity has traditionally been organized. "Capital" designates that system of economic and social exchange which constructs women as consumers, and in which they themselves circulate as commodities and signs;[49] that system which also, in the words of the film, "wants women to work, even needs them to, but denies them facilities and often seems to be punishing them for leaving their proper place." "Delay" is a synonym for the Oedipus complex, with its regime of deferral, displacement, and substitution. The point here is not, it seems to me, to opt for presence and immediacy—qualities which are antipathetic to all forms of desire—but to pit the negative version of the Oedipus complex against the positive and normalizing one. "Body" refers to that destiny to which classic cinema and the existing symbolic order have so insistently held the female subject—to the obligatory representation of male lack and male desire. It is primarily at the second and third of these junctures, as I have indicated, that *Riddles* makes its transformative intervention.

In the British Museum episode, as earlier in Louise's story, the Sphinx functions as what is technically a voice-over, and hence as the most fully exteriorized element within the shot that circumscribes that episode; it is, in other words, that textual component which most fully avoids visual localization and diegetic subordination. However, it is also represented as speaking from the most profoundly interior point of the narrative—from the inside of the small figure contained within the box, which is itself framed both by the passage from the obscure text and by Louise and Anna's recollections. The Sphinx's voice is thus simultaneously "on" and "off," "inside" and "outside," apart from the female subject and a part of her.[50] These seeming paradoxes encourage the viewer/listener to conceptualize text and subject less in terms of closed compartments and privileged look-out points than in terms of a maze or labyrinth through which the voice travels. It is, indeed, precisely with the image of a maze puzzle that the film ends.

Riddles thus accomplishes what neither *Polylogue* nor *Three Women* is able to do: It opens up the *choric* enclosure to accommodate not just mother, daughter, and grandmother, but a community of women as broad and all-inclusive as feminism itself. Its highly evocative dramatization of what I have theorized as the negative Oedipus complex also does much to dispel the confusion which surrounds the homosexual-maternal scene both in Kristeva's writings and in Altman's film. Finally, it gives the maternal voice such a range of discursive functions as to shatter altogether the fiction of the mother's troubled relation to language.

Through its dislocation of voice from body, as well as the more general challenge it poses to Hollywood's sound regime, *Riddles* anticipates a number of the more recent experimental films I will be discussing in the penultimate chapter of this book—films which will enable me both to extend my investigation of the negative Oedipus complex in the direction of narcissism, and to suggest that there may be a close connection between melancholia and the positive Oedipus complex.

[5]

DISEMBODYING THE FEMALE VOICE:

IRIGARAY, EXPERIMENTAL FEMINIST

CINEMA, AND FEMININITY

FOR A SURPRISINGLY large and diverse group of women theorists, feminist speech and writing revolve in some fundamental way around the female body. Annie Leclerc, for instance, has devoted an entire volume to the excretions and ecstasies of her biological body, giving rise in the process to what she calls *"parole de femme."*[1] Hélène Cixous has generated a plethora of essays and books which attempt to incorporate the female body, and thereby to become not so much texts as "sexts."[2] In "This Sex Which Is Not One" and "When Our Lips Speak Together," Luce Irigaray dreams of a language capable of replicating the improper and nonunitary qualities of the female genitalia.[3] Closer to home, Nancy Miller has repeatedly insisted, contra Barthes, that the sexual identity of an author's body does make a critical difference.[4] And in two highly original essays in the same volume of *Yale French Studies*, Gayatri Spivak and Naomi Schor have argued for the primacy of the clitoris within feminist theory, Spivak defining it as the mark of "woman-in-excess,"[5] and Schor characterizing it as the detail par excellence.[6]

Within that variety of feminist film practice which is characterized by a similar theoretical sophistication, on the other hand, the female voice is often shown to coexist with the female body only at the price of its own impoverishment and entrapment. Not surprisingly, therefore, it generally pulls away from any fixed locus within the image track, away from the constraints of synchronization. In Yvonne Rainer's *Film about A Woman Who . . .* and Bette Gordon's *Empty Suitcases*, for instance, the female voice is multiplied in such a way as to make it impossible to tie it down to a specific corporeal anchor. A disembodied female voice speaks "over" the images of Patricia Gruben's *Sifted Evidence*, in relation to which it constantly shifts its position, while Yvonne Rainer's *Journeys from Berlin/71* abounds with female voices that have no bodily correlative. The female voices in Sally Potter's *The Gold Diggers* move in and out of synchronization so fluidly as to blur all distinction between diegetic interiority and exteriority, and to redefine the relationship between spectator and spectacle. In this chapter I want to juxtapose these films with the most sustained and extreme of the arguments that have been made on behalf of an "embodied" speech or writing—that elaborated by Luce Irigaray. I also want to confront the concept of the "feminine," so central to Irigaray and to the films enumerated above, and in so doing both to expand further upon the negative Oedipus complex, and to suggest some of the consequences of the positive Oedipus complex for female subjectivity. This chapter will consequently sustain two simultaneous theoretical arguments, one about the relation of the female voice to the female body, and the other about "femininity."

Irigaray offers a brilliant critique of what might be called "the economy of the phallus" in both *Speculum* and *This Sex Which Is Not One.* What makes this critique so forceful is also what makes the alternative economy elaborated in the second of those texts so problematic—the argument, that is, that the model elaborated by Freud (a model with considerable descriptive value for the present symbolic order) promotes not so much sexual *difference* as sexual *indifference.* This insight provides the motive force behind Irigaray's reactive insistence precisely upon what that model represses—woman's "morphological" difference. The crucial project, it seems to me, is to find a way to maximize the deconstructive potential of the first of these arguments without succumbing irretrievably to the second.

Irigaray painstakingly and compellingly demonstrates that the economy of the phallus is predicated upon the demand for symmetry—that it conceptualizes woman as a "little man" prior to the castration complex, and as a man *manqué* thereafter:

> "Sexual difference" is a derivative of the problematics of sameness, it is, now and forever, determined within the project, the projection, the sphere of representation, of the same. The "differentiation" into two sexes derives from the a priori assumption of the same, since the little man that the little girl is, must become a man minus certain attributes whose paradigm is morphological—attributes capable of determining, of assuring, the reproduction-specularization of the same. A man minus the possibility of (re)presenting oneself as a man = a normal woman.[7]

Thus, the female genitals are defined either through their symmetry with the penis, in which case it is the clitoris—that "small and inconspicuous organ," as Freud would say[8]—which becomes the focus of attention, or through their complementarity to the penis, in which case it is the vagina which becomes the focus of attention. When woman is not held to one of these two representations, she is obliged to function as a stand-in for the male subject's mother, who is the only (heterosexual) object he is ever capable of loving.[9]

Monique Plaza has produced a very trenchant analysis of what is implied by Irigaray's insistence upon an irreducible feminine essence, but she misses the force of the accompanying critique of phallomorphism. She objects in particular to the concept of sexual indifference, maintaining that it is based upon a misunderstanding of the way in which difference works culturally:

> It is curious that Luce Irigaray in calling this movement the "a priori of the Same," distinguishes it from the step of differentiation. For the "a priori of the Same," far from being an autonomous construction is, on the contrary, *the logical complementary concept of the Difference:* the Difference refers the Other (woman) to the One (man) placed in the dominant position. The other is always the negative of the One, the Same. . . . It consists of a double movement: it accords primacy to one term that it erects as a norm and casts the Other into the negative, the monstrous.[10]

Now, Irigaray is obviously familiar with this line of reasoning, which passed into feminist theory early on, via Simone de Beauvoir.[11] If she seems to forget it throughout *Speculum* and *This Sex Which Is Not One,* that is because she wants to emphasize that at some fundamental level, normative male desire has nothing whatever to do with women—that it is solipsistic and self-referential. In two important essays from the second of those texts, "Women on the Market" and "Commodities among Themselves," she even goes so far as to argue that the economy of the phallus is based upon repressed homosexuality, a point to which I will return at the end of this chapter, in my discussion of *The Gold Diggers.* If Irigaray seems to lose sight of how binary opposition classically works, that is also because, as I have already suggested, she wants to posit another kind of difference, one not contained within its relational logic.

Irigaray claims this nonrelational difference both for woman's sexuality and for her discourse. Her corporeal model privileges the two lips of the vulva over those elements of the female anatomy foregrounded by Freudian psychoanalysis—the clitoris and the vagina. However, she doesn't exclude the latter two elements from female sexuality. On the contrary, she casts a wide net, including not only the vulva, the clitoris, and the vagina, but the breasts, the wall of the uterus, and indeed the whole female body within her erotic inventory.[12] One of the crucial points which Irigaray seeks to make about the "morphology" of that body is that it does not have a *single* sexual organ, but at the very least *two*. The other point to which she returns emphatically is that female sexuality is fundamentally continuous and auto-erotic; the vulval lips are "always joined in an embrace."[13] In her determination to tear female sexuality free from the economy of the phallus, she even characterizes the insertion of the penis into the vagina as an interruption of woman's natural pleasure, an unwelcome intrusion into her erotic domain.[14]

Irigaray extrapolates what she calls a "feminine language" from this corporeal model, attributing to the former the same qualities of plurality, contiguity, and simultaneity that she attributes to the latter. In a by now infamous passage from *This Sex Which Is Not One,* she also maintains that unless woman has been coopted by the symbolic order, her speech will always start from and return to the body:

> "She" sets off in all directions, leaving "him" unable to discern the coherence of any meaning. Hers are contradictory words, somewhat mad from the standpoint of reason, inaudible for whoever listens to them with ready-made grids, with a fully elaborated code in hand. For in what she says, too, at least when she dares, woman is constantly touching herself. She steps ever so slightly aside from herself with a murmur, an exclamation, a whisper, a sentence left unfinished. . . . When she returns, it is to set off again from elsewhere. . . . For if "she" says something, it is not, it is already no longer, identical with what she means. What she says is never identical with anything, moreover; rather it is contiguous. *It touches upon.* And when it strays too far from that proximity, she breaks off and starts again at "zero": her body-sex.[15]

What Irigaray advances here and elsewhere in *This Sex Which Is Not One,* as well as in "Woman's Exile," is the notion of a language which would be "adequate for the [female] body,"[16] a language capable of coexisting with that body as closely as the two lips of the vulva coexist. This is the obverse of the linguistic model proposed by Lacan, which stresses the incommensurability of signifier and body, the loss of the latter constituting the price which must be paid for access to the former. It is also, to my way of thinking, an impossible paradigm, one which attempts to deny the fundamentally arbitrary relation of language to the referent.[17]

(Once again, it is not that Irigaray doesn't understand the discordant relation of existing language to the body; it is, rather, that she imagines it possible to elaborate a new language which would have a different relation to the body. In *Le corps-à-corps avec la mère,* she writes, "We have also to find, to invent, to discover, the words which speak the relation which is at the same time the most archaic and the most actual to the mother's body, to our body, the phrases which translate the bond between her body, our own, [and] those of our daughters. A language which does not substitute for the tussle of bodies [*le corps-à-corps*], as paternal language does, but which accompanies it, words which do not bar the corporeal but which speak corporeally.")[18]

Irigaray thus dreams of forging an existential or indexical relation between words and the female body, a dream which she translates into the present tense. She also celebrates, as though it were an accomplished fact, the isomorphic or iconic relation of feminine language to the female body—a symmetry precisely of the sort to which she objects so strenuously in dominant Western discourse. Nowhere is this symmetry more marked than in the repeated pun on the word *lips,* with its double reference to the mouth that speaks and the vulva that *"jouirs."* Irigaray could thus be said to mimic what she complains that phallic language has done for centuries. ("It can be shown that all Western discourse presents a certain isomorphism with the masculine sex," she writes in "Woman's Exile," "the privilege of unity, form of the self, of the visible, of the specularisable, of the erection" [p. 64]). And although Irigaray presents mimicry as a potentially subversive strategy in *This Sex Which Is Not One,*[19] this particular instance of mimicry does not conform to the definition she offers of it there. Rather than resubmitting herself to " 'ideas,' in particular to ideas about herself, that are elaborated in/by a masculine logic, but so as to 'make visible,' by an effect of playful repetition, what was supposed to remain invisible: the cover-up of a possible operation of the feminine in language" (p. 76), Irigaray models "the feminine in language" upon what might be called "the masculine in language," at least within the terms of her own analysis.

This is not the only way in which the author of *Speculum* falls back upon analogy, or in which she could be said to be "indifferent." Because she believes that feminine language is capable both of relating indexically to the female body and of being isomorphic with it, she fails to distinguish adequately between the real body and the discursive body. I would like to read her account of female corporeality "optatively," as Carolyn Burke has recommended that we do,[20] or to see it as one possible model for what a radically reconstructed female body might look (or should I say "feel") like. However, Irigaray herself insists that what she has described as "woman" has an extradiscursive reality, and comes into existence without any cultural interference or mediating representation. She also speaks about woman so insistently in the present tense that it is difficult not to assume that she means her words to have some referential value:

> Without any interference or special manipulation, you are a woman already.[21]

How can I say it? That we are women from the start. That we don't have to be turned into women by them, labeled by them, made holy and profaned by them.[22]

Prior to any representation, we are two. . . .[23]

Of course, I do not mean to suggest that there is no basis for confusing real and discursive bodies. Although meaning inhabits one order, and the biological body another, the former mediates and indeed determines our relation to the latter. I am prepared to state the case even more forcefully: not only is the subject's relation to his or her body lived out through the mediation of discourse, but that body is itself coerced and molded by both representation and signification. Discursive bodies lean upon and mold real bodies in complex and manifold ways, of which gender is only one consequence.[24] Even if we could manage to strip away the discursive veil that separates the subject from his or her "actual" body, that body would itself bear the unmistakable stamp of culture. There is consequently no possibility of ever recovering an "authentic" female body, either inside or outside language.

Nor do I mean to suggest that we should not attempt to "(re)write" the body. On the contrary, I think that this is a crucial part of the feminist project. However, the aim of that undertaking should be the transformation of the discursive conditions under which women live their corporeality, rather than the liberation of a prediscursive sexuality. I also think that it is crucial for feminist theory to recognize that it will be no easy matter to disengage ourselves from the bodies which we presently inhabit, and that those bodies have been zoned and inscribed in ways which have profound implications for female subjectivity.

Irigaray's tendency to conflate the body which she constructs in *This Sex Which Is Not One* with the "actual" female body also works to close down the psychic, physical, social, economic, and political differences between women, fashioning them all according to a logic of the "same." Ann Rosalind Jones enumerates some of these differences in an early essay on *l'écriture féminine*:

> What is the meaning of "two lips" to heterosexual women who want men to recognize their clitoral pleasure—or to African or Middle Eastern women who, as a result of pharaonic clitoridectomies, have neither lips nor clitoris through which to *jouir?* . . . And it is hard to see how the situations of old women, consigned to sexual inactivity because of their age or, if they are widowed, to unpaid work in others' families or to isolated poverty, can be understood or changed through a concept of *jouissance.*[25]

This is very much the same critique which Spivak levels not just against Irigaray, but against French feminism in general.[26] (What is particularly

instructive about this latter analysis is that it manages to chart a theoretical pathway to difference *across the female body*, that site where
analogy most prevails within the Irigarayan paradigm.)

Irigaray fails, in addition, to distinguish between sexuality and the
body, treating the former as if it were absolutely coterminous with the
latter. Sexuality cannot be read directly off the body in the way she
attempts to do both in "Woman's Exile" and in *This Sex Which Is Not
One*, where she repeatedly invokes the image of woman "touching
herself in and of herself without any need for mediation."[27] Even if, as I
have suggested elsewhere, the psyche is in certain respects nothing more
than a projection inward from the surface of the (constructed) body,[28]
nevertheless it is a category without which there can be no sexuality.
Sexuality requires the internalization and fantasmatization of both the
subject and the object—the installation of both as *corporeal images* within
the psyche.

Sexuality also obliges the subject to occupy a particular position
within a psychic *mise-en-scène*. The female patients whom Freud discusses in "A Child Is Being Beaten," for instance, derived (unconscious)
erotic gratification from putting themselves in "fact" or fantasy into a
masochistic subject-position.[29] The psychic *mise-en-scène*, moreover, is
itself the product at least in part of reminiscence and deferred action.[30]
Thus, if the body is the place where pleasure is finally experienced, that
pleasure is made possible only through what happens elsewhere, in
memory, fantasy, and history. I cannot believe that this holds any less
true for the female subject than for her masculine counterpart, nor do I
feel that feminism has anything to gain from buying into a myth of
sexual immediacy.

Finally, Irigaray relies heavily upon binary opposition, itself a powerful form of symmetry. At one point in *Speculum*, she invokes a wonderful sentence from Proust's *Within a Budding Grove* to illustrate the
"*a-contrario* representation" of the boy through which Freud defines the
girl.[31] That sentence reads: "They are, these women, a product of our
temperament, an image inversely projected, a negative of our sensibil-
ity." This is, indeed, a penetrating gloss on Freud's binary reasoning,
and on his implicit "indifference." Unfortunately, it provides an equally
apt commentary on Irigaray's own account of the female body and
feminine language. Having established that male sexuality and discourse are teleological in organization, Irigaray argues that their feminine equivalents rely instead upon simultaneity.[32] She goes on to associate the former with identity, unity, and vision,[33] a sense which (as
Metz stresses)[34] relies upon distance, and to equate the latter with

nonidentity, plurality, and tactility,[35] a sense which depends upon proximity.

Needless to say, I do not mean to hold Irigaray to the task of disclosing woman's absolute "otherness" with respect to man. This undertaking can only lead back to binary oppositions of the most predictable sort. (It is not surprising, for instance, that many of Irigaray's formulations of "the feminine" are completely congruent with traditional derogations of woman, such as the claim that she is irrational, speaks incoherently, can't concentrate on one thing at a time, lacks visual authority, is closer to her body, or is more oriented toward pleasure than man.)

At the same time, I am more than a little reluctant to jettison the concept of femininity in favor of the much more currently fashionable notion of a subject capable of occupying multiple and even contradictory positions, without necessary reference to biological identity. While the subject's history may not be narrowly *determined* by his or her biological identity, there is scarcely a moment within that history which is uninflected by it. Although it cannot always be assigned with absolute certainty, it usually has considerable bearing on how one is culturally "recognized," and hence on the social positions to which one has access, even when one's identifications run completely counter to that "recognition." The subject's pattern of identification, moreover, assumes its meaning and political value in relation to his or her socially assigned gender. (It is not the same thing, for instance, for the daughter to align herself psychically with the father as it is for the son to do so, since whereas the latter case constitutes a successful Oedipal interpellation, the former constitutes an Oedipal irregularity—a refusal to become "a little woman.")

What I am trying to suggest is that there is some cultural specificity, or, to state it somewhat differently, some commonality of experience, behind the categories of "man" and "woman." If what generally passes in this country as "French feminism" tends to ground that commonality of experience in the body, and to view it positively, many more overtly political feminists in both Europe and North America tend to equate it with the exclusion and oppression of women, and to view it negatively. In the first case, then, femininity is an inherent condition, whereas in the second it is a set of learned responses and attitudes for coping with the *réel politique*. My own desire to salvage the concept of femininity is based upon a very different set of assumptions about how that concept should be articulated. I want to lay out those assumptions in some detail before returning to Irigaray.

To begin with, femininity turns upon the obligatory acknowledgment of three things which are fundamental to all subjectivity, but whose disavowal and projection serve in large part to define masculinity: castration, subordination to the gaze of the cultural Other, and what I have been calling "discursive interiority" (i.e., insertion into a preexisting symbolic order). Classic cinema, as I have attempted to demonstrate in chapters 1, 2, and 3, is one of the cultural institutions which insist most firmly upon woman's lack, specularity, and (diegetic) containment, while associating man with potency, vision, and (diegetic) exteriority. However, since no one assumes identity except by being separated from the mother, losing access to the real, and entering into a field of preexisting meaning, and since no identity can be sustained in the absence of the gaze of the Other (about which I will have much more to say when I return to Irigaray), what passes for "femininity" is actually an inevitable part of all subjectivity. Women have nothing to gain from denying this legacy. On the contrary, what is needed here is not so much a "masculinization" of the female subject as a "feminization" of the male subject—a much more generalized acknowledgment, in other words, of the necessary terms of cultural identity.

There is also another dimension of femininity which I think needs to be maximized, one which has for the most part been confined to the unconscious, but whose transformative potential is enormous. I realize that in introducing it in this way I am flying in the face of Foucault's important critique of the "repressive hypothesis,"[36] but I don't think that feminist theory can manage without the concept of repression. I am also echoing Irigaray when she suggests that there is "in what has been historically constituted as the 'unconscious', some censored, repressed element of the feminine."[37] However, rather than equating this censored femininity with "certain functional criteria . . . like non-contradiction, contiguity, etc.,"[38] or with the female body, I would like to associate it with the girl's negative Oedipus complex, i.e., with her desire for the mother. I would also like to extend that psychic paradigm in the direction toward which I gestured in the preceding chapter by suggesting that it turns upon not only desire for the mother, but identification with her.

This formulation differs sharply from the one which is most consistently maintained in "Female Sexuality" and "Femininity," in both of which Freud characterizes the period during which the little girl cathects erotically with her mother as a "phallic phase." During that period, he writes, the daughter "[lives] in a masculine way," able "to get pleasure by the excitation of her clitoris."[39] It is only with the castration complex and the subsequent desire to get a child from the father, we learn, that she becomes "a little woman." Prior to that moment, she is for all intents and purposes "a little man."

In proposing that desire and identification may be strung along a single thread in the female version of the negative Oedipus complex, I am also taking issue with the general assumption, at least within that psychoanalysis which operates under Freud's name, that desire for one parent presupposes identification with the other. Freud's account of the Oedipus complex—positive and negative—is predicated upon this assumption, as is his reading of Dora's homosexuality.[40] The notion that the little girl goes through a phallic phase also implies a bifurcation of object-choice and identification; her activity, in other words, is interpreted as the trace of her imaginary alignment with the father, and of her wish to take his place with the mother.

Irigaray has given us an acute analysis of the sexual "indifference" that informs this part of Freud's argument, making it impossible for him to conceive of female homosexuality as anything but an identification with the father. "Doesn't he thereby miss the singularity of the relationship of the female child to her mother and to maternity, just as, though in a quite other way, he scotomizes elsewhere the originality of a desire among women? Doesn't he reduce all of these specific modalities of libido to the desire the man feels for the woman-mother or that the man . . . feels for the phallus (represented here by the phallic mother)?"[41] she asks in *Speculum*.

I would answer both questions in the affirmative, although for slightly different reasons from those which prompt Irigaray to do so. It is not, I would argue, that the phallic model fails to account for what is "morphologically" different about female sexuality, but that it fails to take into account the crucial role that the mother plays in the early history of subjectivity. Not only is her face the visual mirror in which the child first sees itself, but her voice is the acoustic mirror in which it first hears itself. The child gropes its way toward identity by incorporating the mother's facial expressions, sounds, and movements, not just before that mythical moment at which it first catches sight of its own reflection, but afterwards, as it begins to assimilate the system of language. It would thus be more correct to suggest that the little boy is "feminine" until his castration crisis than to suggest that the little girl is "masculine" until hers, although both concepts come into play only retroactively, after sexual differentiation. There may even be a period of time after the beginning of the positive Oedipus complex when the male child simultaneously desires and identifies with the mother, thereby approximating the female version of the negative Oedipus complex. It is, at any rate, this conjunction of identification and eroticism which I would describe as the "censored, repressed element of the feminine," and which I believe to have a vital relation to feminism.

My seeming deviation from Freud on the pivotal issue of the little girl's identity during the so-called "phallic phase" is authorized in part by an important passage from "The Psychogenesis of a Case of Homosexuality in a Woman," where Freud speaks about homosexual patients in whom a feminine identification did not give rise to the usual masculine object-choice, or in whom a masculine identification failed to dictate the expected feminine object-choice, but in whom desire and identification might be said to converge around either "femininity" or "masculinity":

> The literature of homosexuality usually fails to distinguish clearly enough between the questions of the choice of object on the one hand, and of the sexual characteristics and sexual attitude of the subject on the other, as though the answer to the former necessarily involved the answers to the latter. Experience, however, proves the contrary: a man with predominantly male characteristics and also masculine in his erotic life may still be inverted in respect to his object, loving only men instead of women. A man in whose character feminine attributes obviously predominate, who may, indeed, behave in love like a woman, might be expected, from this feminine attitude, to choose a man for his love-object; but he may nevertheless be heterosexual, and show no more inversion in respect to his object than an average normal man. The same is true of women; here also mental sexual character and object-choice do not necessarily coincide. The mystery of homosexuality is therefore by no means so simple as it is commonly depicted in popular expositions. . . .[42]

This is not the only occasion on which Freud argues against the necessary divergence of identification and desire. Surprisingly, given his emphasis in both "Female Sexuality" and "Femininity" upon the little girl's masculine positioning during the phallic phase of her sexuality—during the phase, that is, in which she takes the mother as her love-object—similar statements can be uncovered there. Indeed, in a long-overlooked passage from the later of those two essays, Freud goes even further than he does in "The Psychogenesis of a Case of Homosexuality in a Woman," this time in the direction of what he at times refers to as the pre-Oedipal period, and at other times as the negative Oedipus complex, but which, as I attempted to demonstrate in the preceding chapter, is properly indicated only by the second of those appellations. Within the normative version of the female Oedipus complex, Freud observes, desire for the father has as its logical correlative identification with the mother (or, to be more precise, with the *place* of the mother), but in the earlier formation the mother functions as both love-object and point of identification:

A woman's identification with her mother allows us to distinguish two strata: the pre-Oedipus one which rests on her affectionate attachment to her mother and takes her as a model, and the later one from the Oedipus complex which seeks to get rid of her mother and take her place with her father. (P. 134)

Freud anticipates this distinction in "Female Sexuality," where he also emphasizes the girl's early identification with her adored mother. He cites as evidence of this imaginary axis the games little girls play with their dolls, games in which they mimic the mother's behavior to themselves. What is remarkable about this example is that it prompts Freud to offer an account of the female child's activity which radically disengages it from any masculine identification, thereby giving the lie to both the nomenclature and the assumptions of a phallic phase. In the passage to which I allude, Freud explains that children always seek to translate their passive experiences into active ones through repetition and play, and that in so doing they imitate the mother:

The first sexual and sexually colored experiences which a child has in relation to its mother are naturally of a passive character. It is suckled, fed, cleaned and dressed by her, and taught to perform all its functions. . . . In the first place, being suckled at the breast gives place to active sucking. As regards other experiences the child contents itself either with becoming self-sufficient—that is, with itself successfully carrying out what had hitherto been done for it—or with repeating its passive experiences in an active form of play; or else it actually makes its mother into the object and behaves as the active subject toward her. (P. 236)

The first of Freud's examples are ones in which the child does not as yet necessarily distinguish between itself and the mother, and may properly belong to the domain of the pre-Oedipal. However, by the time Freud arrives at his final example, subject/object demarcations are manifestly in place, even at the level of his own language, and they would seem to be implicit as well within the child's capacity to effect symbolic equivalence through play. (One of the things implied by the notion of entry into the symbolic, it seems to me, is precisely that capacity, which moves Freud's exemplary female subject, for instance, to displace her desire from penis to baby to father.)

What this passage from "Femininity" encourages us to conceptualize is a period after the little girl's separation from the mother—after pre-Oedipality—but before the onset of the positive Oedipus complex, during which her identity is formed through the incorporation of the mother's imago. This identification would seem to coincide in a very exact way with what Freud mistakenly, in my view, describes as the phallic phase, and indeed to be responsible for the girl's aspiration toward activity. In fact, Freud himself comes perilously close to saying just that in "Female Sexuality," when he adds that what finds expression in play is "the *active* side of femininity," and that "the little girl's preference for dolls is probably evidence of the *exclusiveness of her attachment to the mother, with complete neglect of her father object*" (p. 237 [my emphasis]). I want to underscore not only the second of these assertions, but the first, upon which I have not until now placed the same emphasis: Identification with the mother during the negative Oedipus complex is at least in part an identification with activity. The equation of femininity and passivity is a consequence only of the positive Oedipus complex, and the cultural discourses and institutions which support it.

Significantly, the symptoms which Freud adduces as proof of the girl's love for the mother slip almost imperceptibly into the symptoms of her imaginary investment in that figure. As he puts it in "Femininity," "what is most clearly expressed is a wish to get the mother with child and the corresponding wish to bear her a child" (p. 120). In effect, the girl aspires both to possess and to be possessed by the mother, or, to state it in more classically Oedipal terms, both to seduce the mother and to be seduced by her. Of course, what is *not* classically Oedipal about this situation is that the girl's aspiration to occupy the place of the mother does not imply the latter's exclusion from her erotic economy, but the endless reversibility of their relative positions. Moreover, although there *is* a third term, and it is—as usual—the father, he figures as the object neither of desire nor of identification. He is "only a troublesome rival," as Freud insists in both "Female Sexuality" and "Femininity."[43] Finally, I cannot help but wonder whether there is not another, more important third term here, one which plays a far more central place within the daughter's early libidinal economy than does the father. I refer, of course, to the child whom she both wishes to give to the mother and to receive from her. We noted the centrality of this particular configuration to the operations of negative Oedipal desire more than once in the previous chapter; the *choric* fantasy as it is formulated by Kristeva, Altman, Mulvey, and Wollen invariably projects a three-generational community of women.

This convergence of object-choice and identification speaks to nothing so much as narcissistic love, as does the reversibility implicit within the wish both to possess and to be the mother. It seems to me, indeed, that Freud's essay on narcissism can be read as a virtual gloss upon the female version of the negative Oedipus complex. In that text he remarks on the close coincidence of narcissism and object-choice in infantile life, and elaborates upon certain later forms of object-choice which are predicated in some way upon identification. He characterizes these forms of object-choice as "narcissistic," and he breaks them down into four categories. A person can love, Freud explains,

(a) What he is himself (actually himself).

(b) What he once was.

(c) What he would like to be.

(d) Someone who was once part of himself.[44]

Are not (b), (c), and (d) all modalities of the desire which binds the little girl to the mother with whom she once confused herself, prior to differentiation, and whom she aspires to become, after the division of subject from object? And is not Freud's first category, (a), made possible by incorporating the imago of the mother who is loved according to (b), (c), and (d)—by identifying, in other words, with the object of desire? Self-love, after all, presupposes love of the object in whose image one "finds" oneself.

This reformulation of the early history of female subjectivity gives new meaning to Freud's observation that women generally love according to the narcissistic rather than the anaclitic model,[45] an observation which itself runs completely counter to what he later wrote about woman's felt inferiority, the "scar" to her narcissism.[46] It suggests, that is, that narcissism may at times be less an indication of the female subject's inability to cathect with an external object than an indication of her refusal either to cathect with any object other than the one which was first in her history, or to distinguish desire from object-choice in the way that the positive Oedipus complex teaches her to do. In other words, female narcissism may represent a form of resistance to the positive Oedipus complex, with its inheritance of self-contempt and loathing.

It seems to me that it is this intersection of desire for and identification with the mother, rather than either Irigaray's "two lips" or postmodernism's body without organs, that should constitute the site of feminism's libidinal struggle against the phallus. While this theoretical formulation comes down emphatically on the side of "femininity," it in no way equates that quality or condition with biological identity. On the contrary, as I have already indicated, there may well be an early moment when the male version of the positive Oedipus complex gives rise to a similarly narcissistic desire for the mother, and even within Freud's own summary of the corresponding version of the negative Oedipus complex, maternal identification has an important part to play.[47] Once again, I would argue for the "feminization" of the male as well as the female subject, while at the same time acknowledging that the stakes are very different for these two subjects. (After all, whereas the former has everything to gain through "feminization," the latter appears at first glance to have everything to lose.)

What happens to the girl's narcissism with her entry into the positive Oedipus complex? The answer, I believe, can be found in an essay Freud wrote three years after "On Narcissism," which touches on a number of related issues. That essay, "Mourning and Melancholia," provides a chillingly accurate account of a condition which may be pathological for the male subject, but which represents the norm for the female subject—that condition of melancholia which blights her relations with both herself and her culture. I offer the following passage from that essay as a prefatory epigraph to what I hope will be a compelling demonstration of the connection between female subjectivity and melancholia:

> The patient represents [her] ego to us as worthless, incapable of any achievement and morally despicable; [she] reproaches [herself], vilifies [herself] and expects to be cast out and punished. [She] abases herself before everyone and commiserates with [her] own relatives for being connected with anyone so unworthy . . . [she] declares that [she] was never any better.[48]

Irigaray has also connected melancholia with female subjectivity in an extremely suggestive passage from *Speculum*. Not surprisingly, she locates the inception of woman's melancholia at the castration complex. However, she also mentions in the same context both the girl's love for and her identification with the mother, and in such a way as to indicate that this libidinal configuration constitutes the temporal equivalent of the boy's positive Oedipus complex:

> Unlike the boy—"who exhibits, therefore, two psychologically distinct ties: a straightforward [?] sexual object-cathexis towards his mother and an identification with his father which takes him as his model"—the little girl takes her mother as her first object of love and also as her privileged identificatory reference point for her "ego" as well as for her sex. In point of fact, if all the implications of Freud's discourse were followed through, after the little girl discovers her own castration and that of her mother—her "object," the narcissistic representative of all her instincts—she would have no recourse other than melancholia. (P. 66)

Irigaray goes on immediately after this passage to enumerate the symptoms of melancholia, symptoms which, as she points out, also surface regularly at the site of female subjectivity: "profoundly painful dejection," "abrogation of interest in the outside world," "loss of the capacity for love," "inhibition of all activity," and "fall in self-esteem." For reasons which remain somewhat obscure, however, she abandons this thesis several pages later, giving preference instead to the much more time-honored equation of woman and hysteria, arguing that the former "probably does not have a capacity for narcissism great enough to allow her to fall back on melancholia" (p. 71).

Irigaray is on the verge here of recognizing that the girl enters the

Oedipus complex not through desire for the father, but through desire for the mother,[49] and that this desire coexists for a time with maternal identification. However, because she fails to distinguish, as I have been insisting we must, between symbolic castration and what Freud calls the castration complex—because she is unable to grasp that it is the former rather than the latter which ushers in the first phase of the Oedipus complex—she backs away from her important insight into the melancholic bases of female subjectivity.

At the risk of reiterating what is by now painfully evident, I want to make absolutely clear what is at stake here. It is impossible for the girl to enter into the negative version of the Oedipus complex through that sexually differentiating castration about which Freud writes at length in his essays on female sexuality, for the simple reason that its function is to devalue the mother, and thereby facilitate the displacement of the girl's desire onto the father. It is also impossible under these theoretical conditions to imagine the girl having sufficient narcissistic reserves to become a melancholic, since the only identification with the mother which would be available to her would be one predicated upon lack, insufficiency, and self-contempt.

However, if the girl enters the Oedipus complex through symbolic castration—i.e., through aphanisis of being, and separation from the mother—rather than through the castration of which Freud speaks, then it is possible to conceive of that complex beginning with a period of time during which she would both desire the mother and identify with her, and in which considerable narcissistic reserves would be built up. With the advent of the castration complex, the mother would undergo a devaluation, and the girl would be encouraged to displace her desire onto the father. She would at the same time feel enormous cultural pressure to continue to identify with the mother, and it is here that melancholia enters the picture. But let us look more closely at what Freud has to say about that psychic condition.

Like mourning, Freud tells us, melancholia results from the loss of a loved object. That object may have died, or it may simply have "been lost as an object of love," as I would argue the mother is after she has been deidealized. Freud also stresses that this loss occurs at the level of the unconscious—that, like the negative Oedipus complex, it is "unknown," both to the female subject herself and to the larger cultural order ("In yet other cases one feels justified in maintaining the belief that a loss of this kind has occurred, but one cannot see clearly what it is that has been lost, and it is all the more reasonable to suppose that the patient cannot consciously perceive what he has lost either" [p. 245]).

However, the lost object is not so much surrendered as relocated within the subject's own self—which is, of course, precisely where the mother's imago must be situated if the girl is to identify with her. Through a distinction which is in the final instance irrelevant, since identity is unthinkable apart from incorporation, Freud explains that the reproaches which the melancholic seems to direct against him- or herself are in fact directed against the once-loved object which he or she has internalized:

> An object-choice, an attachment of the libido to a particular person, had at one time existed; then, owing to a real slight or disappointment coming from this loved person, the object-relationship was shattered. The result was not the normal one of a withdrawal of the libido from this object and a displacement of it on to a new one, but something different. . . . The object-cathexis proved to have little power of resistance and was brought to an end. But the free libido was not displaced on to another object; it was withdrawn into the ego. There . . . [it] served to establish an *identification* of the ego with the abandoned object. Thus the shadow of the object fell upon the ego, and the latter could henceforth be judged by a special agency [i.e., the superego], as though it were an object, the forsaken object. In this way an object-loss was transformed into an ego-loss and the conflict between the ego and the loved person into a cleavage between the critical activity of the ego and the ego as altered by identification. (Pp. 248–49)

I want to pause here to make several interjections. First, if we are to assume at least for the moment that this passage describes not only a pathology which sometimes results from a death or an unhappy love affair, but a psychic condition which is somehow endemic to the female version of the positive Oedipus complex, then it does much to explain both the rigorous system of internal surveillance with which the female subject so frequently torments herself—her peculiar tendency to treat herself as an object to be over-seen and over-heard. The passage I have just quoted also puts definitively to rest Freud's extravagant notion that the female subject has a less fully developed superego than her male counterpart.[50]

Significantly, Freud maintains that in order for an object to be incorporated in this way, it must have been loved narcissistically—it must have been loved, in other words, according to that libidinal model which I have associated with the negative Oedipus complex:

> On the one hand, a strong fixation to the loved object must have been present; on the other hand, in contradiction to this, the object-cathexis must have had little power of resistance. As Otto Rank has aptly remarked, this contradiction seems to imply that the object-choice has been effected on a narcissistic basis, so that the object-cathexis, when obstacles come in its way, can regress to narcissism. The narcissistic identification with the object then becomes a substitute for the erotic cathexis, the result of which is that in spite of the conflict with the loved person the love-relation need not be given up. (P. 249)

Freud accounts for the conflict which he mentions here, and which he associates elsewhere in the same essay with sadism, as a turning round upon the subject's own self of anger felt toward the object as a result of having been "slighted, neglected or disappointed" by it. While I do not mean to suggest that the girl's desire for her mother is without ambivalence, or untempered by hatred, it does seem to me that the real force of the hostility which she directs against herself after the conclusion of the negative Oedipus complex has more to do with the devaluation of the original erotic object than with anything else. In effect, the female subject is punishing the mother (and consequently herself) for being inferior and insufficient, unworthy of love.

Freud conceptualizes the internalized object less as a coherent entity than as a network of unconscious memories, all of which have been libidinally invested. In order for the melancholic subject to be cured, each one of these mnemic traces must be emptied of its libidinal investment, and that task is apparently undertaken by the forces of hatred, or, to put it more precisely, by the superego, under the sway of the death drive.[51] Memory after memory is called to the witness stand to be castigated by that punitive agency until it has been rendered worthless:

> In melancholia the relation to the object is no simple one; it is complicated by the conflict due to ambivalence. . . . In melancholia, accordingly, countless separate struggles are carried on over the object, in which hate and love contend with each other; the one seeks to detach the libido from the object, the other to maintain this position of the libido against the assault. The location of these separate struggles cannot be assigned to any system but the *Ucs.*, the region of the memory-traces of *things* (as contrasted with *word*-cathexes). (P. 256)

Freud concludes that the object is discarded once it has been rendered valueless through this process.

This is a dazzling account of the object, and one which has many implications for the operations of desire. However, what Freud describes as the cure—i.e., the devaluation of the object—would seem to be exactly what *causes* female melancholia, which commences when libido begins to be withdrawn from the mnemic traces within which the girl finds both the object and herself. Since the only object capable of inducing melancholia in the subject is one whose significance is "reinforced by a thousand links" or memories (p. 256), I do not believe that the process of devaluation ever reaches a conclusion; certain unconscious memories will inevitably retain their cathexis, and assert the mother's desirability even in the face of the most violent detraction on the part of both culture and the superego. Nevertheless, that detraction would seem capable of diminishing the mnemic reserve, and so both of "shrinking" the beloved object and of making it a less and less pleasurable "mirror" within which to find one's identity. Can the patient be cured? If so, it will most certainly be through a revival or reconstruction of the negative Oedipus complex.

Before returning to Irigaray, I want to make a few concluding remarks about the very different terms under which male and female subjectivity are constituted, remarks which are calculated to underscore the fundamental *impossibility* of the latter. At first glance, the male version of the positive Oedipus complex seems perfectly symmetrical with the female version of that complex. In both cases, after all, identification is sequestered from desire; whereas the girl incorporates the mother and takes the father as her erotic object, the boy incorporates the father and takes the mother as his erotic object. However, desire nevertheless plays a crucial role in the son's imaginary relation to the father— if not his own desire, then that of the mother and the extrafamilial symbolic order. We recall the central place the mother occupies within Lacan's account of (male) subjectivity; it is not merely that the phallus finds its way into the son's unconscious through the mediation of the mother's desire,[52] but that her erotic investment in the father is the precondition for the son's paternal identification. Hamlet, Lacan explains, cannot align himself narcissistically with his dead father because of Gertrude's libidinal failure.[53] No similar desire facilitates the identification of the properly Oedipalized daughter with the mother; on the contrary, that identification must be sustained in the face not only of a general cultural disparagement, but of the most relentless self-castigation, as well. It is no wonder, then, that Freud would suggest that many women are able to love themselves only with "an intensity comparable to that of the man's love for them."[54]

Although Irigaray denies that the mother exercises any hold over her desire in *This Sex Which Is Not One*,[55] elsewhere she stresses both the primariness and the psychic importance of the maternal attachment. Indeed, in "Woman's Exile" she comes very close to formulating that attachment in precisely the terms I have just proposed, remarking that "everything happens as if there were a necessary break between the earliest investments, the earliest desires, the first narcissism of a little girl and those of a 'normal' adult woman" (p. 75). However, like Kristeva she misrecognizes the narcissism and desire she so fortuitously juxtaposes here, assuming them to coincide with the period before the Oedipus complex rather than with that complex's initial phase.

Irigaray conceptualizes the " 'normal' adult woman" as an expatriate or an exile, a metaphor which does much to explain the repeated references in *This Sex Which Is Not One* to proximity and tactility. She sees the female subject's libidinal discontents as the inevitable result of her distance from the mother, and hence conceptualizes closeness as the cure or remedy for those discontents. However, distance from the mother is the precondition not only of subjectivity and language, but of desire itself. The mother emerges as an erotic object for the daughter only after the latter has been separated from her. Thus, what passes in "Woman's Exile" as an alternative model of desire actually points in the direction of desire's abolition. (It is perhaps for this reason that Irigaray was to substitute another woman for the mother in "When Our Lips Speak Together," thereby assuring the all-important gap between subject and object of desire; that she was to locate the inception of lack as early as the severance of the umbilical cord in *Le corps-à-corps avec la mère*;[56] and that she was to envision the mother turning away from the daughter while the latter is still inside the uterus in "And the One Doesn't Stir without the Other,"[57] as if to guarantee that those two figures are never entirely proximate.)

Although Irigaray clings tenaciously to the concept of desire, even in the face of its impossibility, she proves herself quite willing to relinquish subjectivity, regarding it as an impediment to the "two lips" of female sexuality and language.[58] In "Woman's Exile" she maintains both that "female sexuality is not unifiable . . . cannot be subsumed under the concept of subject," and that "[feminine language] has nothing to do with the syntax which we have used for centuries, namely that constructed according to the following organization: subject, predicate, or[:] subject, verb, object" (p. 64). Elsewhere she opts for a "nearness so pronounced" that it would make the "discrimination of identity impossible."[59] Irigaray even comes close to suggesting that woman need not go through the mirror stage, and that she is repressed rather than structured and sustained by the gaze of the cultural Other:

> No need to fashion a mirror image to be "doubled," to repeat ourselves—a second time. Prior to any representation, we are two. . . . You will always have the touching beauty of a first time, if you aren't congealed in reproductions. You will always be moved for the first time, if you aren't immobilized in any form of repetition.[60]

> The predominance of the visual, and . . . the discrimination and individualization of form, is particularly foreign to female eroticism. Woman takes pleasure more from touching than from looking. . . .[61]

In her critique of Irigaray, Plaza stresses that woman has always been a *speaking subject*, even if her words have fallen on deaf ears, or if she has been excluded from certain discursive positions ("Woman has always talked and thought at the same time as man, just as she has participated in history. But she has been excluded from discourses, struck out of the archives" [p. 24]). This is an important and empowering reminder, and a good antidote to the antirationalism of Irigaray's femininity. However, I think it is equally important to remember that woman is also the *subject of speech.* It is not only that the concept of "woman" has been constructed through representation and signification, but that woman "herself" relies upon image and meaning for her identity.

She is also dependent, as is her male counterpart, upon the gaze of the cultural Other. Subjectivity is installed not only through an identification with external images, but through the "click" of an imaginary camera. As Lacan explains it,

> In the scopic field, the gaze is outside, I am looked at, that is to say, I am a picture.
> This is the function that is found at the heart of the institution of the subject in the visible. What determines me, at the most profound level, in the visible, is the gaze that is outside. It is through the gaze that I enter light and it is from the gaze that I receive its effects. Hence it comes about that the gaze is the instrument through which light is embodied and through which . . . I am *photo-graphed.*[62]

There are thus two crucial ways of understanding the subject's relation to visual representation, both of which stress his or her captation— the mirror stage and the "photo session." In the former, he or she incorporates an image, and in the latter, he or she is appropriated as image. (Interestingly, the "photo session" is implicit even within the mirror stage, since the child meets up with its own reflection only through the confirming look of the Other.)[63]

It may be because of its imbrication with the visual that Irigaray shows herself so willing to forgo subjectivity. However, there is no way in which woman can escape specularity by slipping out of subjectivity and into sexuality. As I have already indicated, sexuality is inseparable from fantasy, and all of the "group" fantasies about which Freud writes are scenically organized—laid out, as it were, for the gaze. (At least one of them also deals explicitly with vision [the primal scene], while another implies a certain slippage between seeing and being seen ["a child is being beaten"]). Furthermore, fantasy is all about subject-positioning, and is consequently more a way into identity than a way out of it. Lacan also remarks that it is always when the subject is "sustaining" him- or herself in a "function" of desire[64] that he or she is most likely to be surprised by the gaze—that what seems most intimate and private is in fact structured by the representational constraints of the "photo session."

Moreover, both psychoanalysis and classic cinema suggest that far from being a refuge from specularity, female subjectivity magnifies its effects. The mirror stage and the "photo session" are indeed emblems of femininity, the one attesting to narcissism, and the other to exhibitionism. Since both of these tableaux are central to subjectivity, it is not possible for woman simply to extricate herself from them. I would myself argue for a totally different strategy, which would be to uncover the male subject's own (necessary) narcissism and exhibitionism,[65] and thereby to collapse the scopic regime upon which sexual difference relies. However, whether this strategy is adopted or alternative paradigms are sought, it is crucial for feminism to confront the necessary place of the gaze within the organization of identity.

Although I may seem to have strayed far away from my starting point, the issues upon which I have been focusing during the last two sections of the chapter—narcissism, melancholia, subjectivity, the gaze—complicate woman's relation to her body, making a direct connection between it and language unimaginable. They also impinge in all sorts of ways upon the voice, which cannot speak without assuming an identification, entering into desire, or invoking the Other, and which, as I attempted to demonstrate in chapters 3 and 4, has a complex relationship to fantasy. Finally, these are issues which closely concern both the embodied and the disembodied female voices that inhabit the films I will be discussing in a few moments.

Irigaray's argument on behalf of a "feminine language" becomes even more problematic when it is juxtaposed with classic cinema. As I attempted to demonstrate in chapter 2, Hollywood also holds the female voice to the female body, and through much the same rhetorical mechanism as the one which is so energetically deployed by the author of *This Sex Which Is Not One*, i.e., through analogy. Films such as *Singin' in the Rain, Kiss Me Deadly,* and *Darling* fashion the female voice after that scene of castration which a physical striptease would ostensibly disclose at the site of the female genitals—according, that is, to that model of the female body which is so familiar to Freud's readers. This isomorphism of voice and clitoris is not as far removed from Irigaray's equation of facial and vulval lips as she herself would no doubt like to think, even though the latter is as privileged as the former is deprivileged.

Jones's homology of the female mouth and the vagina is even closer in certain respects to Irigaray's favorite analogy, and it at times supplements the Freudian paradigm within classic cinema. Jones conceptualizes both orifices as "insatiable organ holes" leading to female interior-ity, an interiority which, at least in the case of a film such as *Johnny Belinda*, also conforms closely to the following description from *This Sex Which Is Not One*, with its emphasis upon concentricity:

> It is useless . . . to trap women in the exact definition of what they mean, to make them repeat (themselves) so that it will be clear; they are already elsewhere in that discursive machinery where you expected to surprise them. They have returned within themselves. Which must not be un-derstood in the same way as within yourself. They do not have the interior-ity that you have, the one you suppose they have. Within themselves means *within the intimacy of that silent, multiple, diffuse touch.* And if you ask them insistently what they are thinking about, they can only reply: Noth-ing. Everything. (P. 29)

Whichever of these vocal/corporeal equations is employed within a particular Hollywood film, the end result is to magnify the effects of synchronization, and thereby to hold the female voice more firmly than its male counterpart to the inside of the fiction. Although the latter, like the former, is largely limited to diegetic "appearances," and although most of those "appearances" take the form of synchronous discourse, it does on occasion assume disembodied and extradiegetic forms. From time to time, that is, the male voice speaks from an anonymous and transcendental vantage point, "over" the narrative.

Apart from the documentary, where it is almost an institution, the disembodied male voice-over occurs most frequently in police thrillers and prison dramas of the "B" variety. The foregrounding of criminality in these films (as well as their low production values) would seem to necessitate a kind of "voice on high," whose superior knowledge and diegetic detachment promise eventual justice, despite the vitality of the crooks, the impotence of the cops, and the sleaziness of the *mise-en-scène*. As Bonitzer observes, this voice is a pure distillate of the law; not only does it "forbid questions about its enunciation, its place and its time," but it speaks with an unqualified authority:

> The [voice-over] represents a power, that of disposing of the image and of that which it reflects from a place which is absolutely *other*. . . . Absolutely other and *absolutely indeterminable.* In this sense, transcendent. . . . In so far as it arises from the field of the Other, the voice-over is assumed to know: such is the essence of its power.[66]

Even the *infrequent* sequestration of the male voice from the male body works to align the male subject with potency, authoritative knowl-edge, and the law—in short, with the symbolic father. Since these are the qualities to which he most aspires at the narrative level, but which he never altogether approximates there, we could say that the male subject finds his most ideal realization when he is heard but not seen; when the body (what Lacan would describe as the "pound of flesh"[67] which must be mortgaged in man's relationship to the signifier) drops away, leaving the phallus in unchallenged possession of the scene. Thus, despite its rather rare occurrence in the fiction film, the disembodied voice can be seen as "exemplary" for male subjectivity, attesting to an achieved invisibility, omniscience, and discursive power. However, as I have already demonstrated, the disembodied voice-over is not the only mechanism through which classic cinema manages to associate its male characters with enunciative authority. The same end can be achieved through any textual strategy which delineates the diegesis in terms of "inner" and "outer" spaces, and which locates male speech, hearing, and vision within the latter rather than the former.

The female subject, on the other hand, is excluded from positions of discursive power both outside and inside the classic filmic diegesis; she is confined not only to the safe place *of* the story, but to safe places *within* the story (to positions, that is, which come within the eventual range of male vision or audition).[68] Both constituents of the surveillance system—visual and auditory—must be in effect for it to be really successful. To permit a female character to be seen without being heard would be to activate the hermeneutic and cultural codes which define woman as "enigma," inaccessible to definitive male interpretation. To allow her to be heard without being seen would be even more dangerous, since it would disrupt the specular regime upon which dominant cinema relies; it would put her beyond the reach of the male gaze (which stands in here for the cultural "camera") and release her voice from the signifying obligations which that gaze enforces. It would liberate the female subject from the interrogation about her place, her time, and her desires which constantly resecures her. Finally, to disembody the female voice in this way would be to challenge every conception by means of which we have previously known woman within Hollywood film, since it is precisely *as body* that she is constructed there.

This is all another way of saying that if male subjectivity is most fully realized (or perhaps it would be more accurate to say most fully "idealized") when it is least visible—when it approaches a kind of theological threshold—female subjectivity is most fully achieved (or should I say "deidealized") when it is most visible. Through a curious kind of paradox, man, with his "strikingly visible" organ, is defined primarily in terms of abstract and immaterial qualities such as potency, knowledge, and power, whereas woman, whose genitals do not appeal to the gaze, becomes almost synonymous with corporeality and specularity.

Thus (with the exception of music), there are no instances within dominant cinema where the female voice is not matched up in some way, even if only retrospectively, with the female body. For the most part, woman's speech is synchronized with her image, and even when it is transmitted as a voice-off, the divorce is only temporary; the body connected to the female voice is understood to be in the next room, just out of frame, at the other end of a telephone line. In short, it is fully recoverable. The female voice seldom functions as a voice-over, and when it does it enjoys a comparable status to the embodied male voice-over in film noir—i.e., it is autobiographical, evoking in a reminiscent fashion a fiction within which the speaker figures centrally as a bodily "presence."

It is not surprising, then, that a number of feminist filmmakers have pursued a vocal itinerary which is the obverse of that outlined in Irigaray's writings. Rather than forging closer connections between the female voice and the female body, Bette Gordon, Patricia Gruben, Yvonne Rainer, and Sally Potter have all experimented boldly with the female voice-off and voice-over, jettisoning synchronization, symmetry, and simultaneity in favor of dissonance and dislocation. Some of these filmmakers have devised ways of fracturing the diegesis so as to make it impossible to say whether a particular voice is "inside" or "outside," or have so multiplied and mismatched voices as to problematize their corporeal assignation. Others have assigned the female voice an invisible location within the fiction, or have detached it from the diegesis altogether.

Three of the films I will be discussing here—Rainer's *Film about A Woman Who . . .* , Gordon's *Empty Suitcases,* and, most complexly, Gruben's *Sifted Evidence*—comment interestingly upon synchronization and its relation to the female voice. The other two—Rainer's *Journeys from Berlin/71* and Potter's *The Gold Diggers*—use the female voice to interrogate female subjectivity in ways which would have been impossible without permitting it a certain distance from the image track. *Journeys from Berlin/71* focuses upon that psychic condition which is the most frequent extension of Oedipal normalization—melancholia. It also links melancholia both to what might be called the female subject's "performance anxieties," anxieties which classic cinema can only intensify, and to the obsessive self-referentiality of the female voice. *The Gold Diggers,* on the other hand, explores the transformative potential of the negative Oedipus complex. It represents a quite meticulous working out, at the level of both sound and image, of the reversibility which is inherent within the daughter's narcissistic desire for the mother. *The Gold Diggers* also deals very interestingly with the male version of the negative Oedipus complex, and in terms which are more than a little evocative of Irigaray. I will consequently return at the end of this chapter to her critique of the phallic economy.

Film about A Woman Who . . . (1974) resorts to a number of devices for dislodging the female voice from the female image. One of these devices is silence, or as Rainer herself puts it, "the extreme prolongation of certain soundless images."[69] Another, which is taken even further in *Kristina Talking Pictures* (1976), is the projection of more than one female body to which story and speech can be "pinned." The automatic signifying transfer from image to sound is thus frustrated, and the semic code rendered inoperative by the absence of a proper name, a stable visual representation, and a predictable cluster of attributes. The film's reliance upon voice-over and intertitles further denaturalizes the female voice, also contributing to the jamming of the semic code. The episode entitled "Emotional Accretion in 48 Steps" utilizes both of these strategies, as well as periods of complete silence. It also makes startlingly evident what is at issue for woman in the avoidance of synchronized sound. It thus provides an ideal entry point into my discussion of the female voice in feminist experimental cinema.

In "Emotional Accretion in 48 Steps," a man and a woman lie in bed together, sometimes turning toward each other, and sometimes turning away. Each movement or gesture is separated by a number introducing a new "step," some of which include intertitles, and others of which do not. The intertitles narrate rather than offer direct dialogue, substituting the pronouns *he* and *she* for *you* and *I*.

The intrusion of a fragmented but nonetheless intensely psychological narrative into a cinematic system which provides none of the usual supports for viewer identification results in a good deal of free-floating anxiety. The woman who tosses and turns on the bed, and who is described as first wanting to tell the man to go, and then demanding his attention, seems to be constrained by a discourse (the discourse of the "affair") within which she is not entirely comfortable, and to which, moreover, she does not entirely accede. The use of the pronoun *she,* and of an indirect rather than direct construction, indicates her unwillingness to activate her own subjectivity fully within that discourse, an event which—as Benveniste tells us—requires the articulation of the first-person pronoun.[70]

The climactic moment in this episode involves precisely such an articulation. In the only use of synchronized sound in any of the 48 steps, the woman asks: "Would you hold me?" The contradiction between the discourse to which she here surrenders and her own desires is indicated in steps 43 through 48, where we read:

> She arrives home. She is very angry. She knows the crucial moment was when she said "hold me." Somehow she had betrayed herself. She hadn't wanted to be held. (Do you think she could figure her way out of a paper bag?) She had wanted to bash his fucking face in.

The convergence of synchronization and the first-person pronoun *(me)* is highly significant, emphasizing the part played by the former in the production of a coherent, stable, and "manageable" subject. *Film about A Woman Who . . .* shows the alignment of sound and image to be an agency of entrapment, one of the means by which the female subject can be made to emerge within a discourse contrary to her desires, and to submit at least temporarily to a fixed identity.

Like Rainer's *Film about A Woman Who . . .*, Gordon's *Empty Suitcases* (1980) frustrates the spectator's attempts to connect the sound and image tracks by projecting a diversity of female voices, any one of which could be the "heroine." However, the real mobility of the film—not just the shift from one female representation to another, but the movement from one city to another, and one discourse to another—is an effect of the soundtrack, and its projection of a "traveling" voice.

Near the beginning of *Empty Suitcases,* we shuttle back and forth from New York to Chicago dozens of times in the space of five minutes, as a female voice reads aloud from a stack of postcards, some of which are addressed from one of those cities, and some from the other. Even more spectacular are the transits from one melodramatic mode to another: from the subject-position of the suffering artist to that of the rejected professor, the angry mistress, the terrorist, the teller of Oedipal dreams. Gordon negotiates these constant relocations through a multiplicity of female voices and discursive strategies, including not only the voice-over but the voice-off, synchronized dialogue and monologue, and musical lyrics.

It is through the last of these aural modes that *Empty Suitcases* makes both its wittiest and perhaps its most important statement about the female voice. In the scene to which I refer, a woman lies on a bed lip-synching the words of the Billie Holiday song "All of Me." Although there is a perfect match of the movements of the woman's lips with the lyrics we hear, it is belied by the striking disequivalence between her facial expression and the affect of the music; she remains absolutely impassive as Holiday's voice reaches ever-new crescendos of masochistic ardor. The song is ostensibly about a woman's total surrender of herself to her lover, but it takes the form of a series of auto-references. Holiday's voice offers up her body piece by piece, in an elaborate self-dismemberment ("Take my lips . . . take my arms . . . you took my heart, so why not take all of me?").

This scene parodies classic cinema's rigorous "marriage" of voice to image. It also places an ironic distance between the female viewer and her filmic "stand-in," permitting her to see the semiotics of self-reference through which Hollywood constructs woman. That semiotics, which obliges the female voice to signify the female body, and the female body to signify lack, isolates her from effective political action, prevents her from making investments in a new social order, and guarantees that she will remain in the same place. This scene also places the viewer at a formal remove from that condition of melancholia which I have suggested is somehow endemic to normative female subjectivity, and of which Billie Holiday—both as singer and as "personality"—was such a moving example.

Gruben's *Sifted Evidence* (1981) offers a much more detailed and theoretically inflected commentary on the relationship of the female voice to the female body within cinema.[71] Like the other films I have discussed so far, it relies heavily upon voice-over, using synchronization only to dramatize constraint.[72] It also multiplies bodies and voices in such a way as to call the concept of memory, as well as that of character, quite radically into question.

The introductory scene of *Sifted Evidence* not only locates the present tense of the film at a moment subsequent to its main events, but warns that the past cannot be easily or directly recovered ("To reach that spot," Betts warns, "we must proceed from where we are at the moment"). The same point is made through the casting of the central role; different actresses play Betts within the frame story and the inner narrative, suggesting that the past can be recovered only through representation and reconstruction. The voice of a third actress speaks for her within the inner narrative, intensifying the discontinuity between the film's two temporal registers. Finally, in most of *Sifted Evidence*'s key scenes, the characters' bodies are posed against two-dimensional front-projected images of Mexico, images which can in no way pass for real landscapes or interiors.

Both the introductory scene and the middle section of the film enact a narrative progression at the level of the voice, and it is upon this vocal trajectory that I want to focus most of my remarks. The film opens with a disembodied female voice reading lines which are repeated as rolling titles on the image track, a doubling which seems to locate the voice firmly outside the fictional world which is being introduced to us, on the side of the enunciation. In measured accents, it speaks first about Tlatilco, and then—startlingly—about the production of the cinematic image:

> First priority is to fix the frame. To line the crosshairs as accurately as possible. To set the zoom. Hesitation in the moving hand will cause retrograde motion in the elements, or a slight deflection in the field of vision. But strict attention to the crosshairs is the guiding principle to correct the spiral of wandering attention.[73]

Obligingly, the visual track shows cross hairs firmly in place over an aerial shot of sea and land. This is a very different female voice even from those I have mentioned so far in this chapter. It not only functions as a commentator, but identifies itself with the apparatus. At the same time, the phrase with which its speech concludes—"the spiral of wandering attention"—charts out another itinerary, the itinerary which Betts in fact follows during her journey to the quarries, and so pulls away from the rationalism and ostensible objectivity of the camera instructions.

With the third shot of the film, a closer aerial view of the jungle, the first-person pronoun obtrudes, and it becomes evident that the information we are being given about Mexico is filtered not only through the camera and tape recorder, but through the desires and obsessions of a very particular subjectivity, as well:

> Once I arrived, my whole trip seemed to organize itself around visits to the ruins. I was interested in the female divinities of ancient Mexico.

During the next seven shots, which show photographs of paintings, statues, and religious group scenes all relating in some way to the worship of female saints or divinities, the voice-over reverts to its earlier role of travel guide, although a feminist agenda of sorts seems to be dictating what we hear and see.

These shots are followed by a photo montage of women—primarily Anglo tourists—in public places, and during this montage the female voice not only has recourse once again to the first-person singular pronoun, but slips easily into the first-person plural pronoun. In so doing, it foregrounds its own status both as speaking subject and as object of the gaze. It also inscribes a female viewer as the point of the film's address:

> I know it might seem hard for a woman to travel alone in Mexico. We must always remember the power of archetypes. On the street we have no biographies beyond present behavior. The slight shrug, the turning of the body in a straight-backed chair, the two fists half-clenched under the table are rarely observed. . . . We are billboards on the street.

As yet unlocalized in the image track, and hence beyond the governance of the gaze, the female voice nevertheless feels impelled to speak about woman's constant vulnerability to what I earlier called the "photo session"—to the "click" of a "camera" which is both the manifestation of the Other and the necessary support of a subjectivity grounded in specularity, but which has nevertheless come to be coded as male, and entrusted with a sexually differentiating role. What distinguishes this critique of woman-as-spectacle from that advanced by other feminist filmmakers and theoreticians is that it includes race and class as additionally complicating factors.

> The men on the street called me La Huerra, which means The Blonde, in an insulting way. Don't think it's only desire that makes them feel like that. Don't ever forget what tourists represent. We have money and time to come here for our adventures, the fair-skinned women, the privileged class, our mercy, their sacrifice.

Although the female voice soon resumes its ethnological narrative, its discourse is now much more overtly personal, marked not only by the first-person singular pronoun, but by a continuing preoccupation with the representational uses of the female body. It wonders why the little female figures found by the workmen quarrying gravel in Tlatilco have two faces on the same head, and what their religious value was in the culture that produced them. Then, as the camera tracks across a shelf of German books on philosophy, literature, and archaeology, desire makes itself felt—a desire whose bases are ostensibly intellectual, but which turns in some crucial way upon precisely that entity which has until now functioned simultaneously as structuring absence and dominant thematic—the body:

> I felt that old Teutonic fascination: the body and the spirit, immanence and transcendence, the gap that never can be closed by analysis. Schliemann at Troy, Von Humboldt in the jungles of Veracruz.

This is the first of five German citations in the film. Three of them—of which this is one—are about the impossibility of inhabiting the body, or, to be more precise, about the division of the "spirit" or "heart" from the body. The fourth reiterates, in a mocking way, the connection between Germany and idealism, and the fifth associates dreaming with the German language. Apart from the one ironic citation, they mark moments of great affective intensity, and as a semantic cluster they function to suggest that Betts's visit to the quarries is motivated at least in part by the desire to find a body—and specifically a female body—which would be capacious enough to accommodate the spirit, the heart, or (as the film prefers to conceptualize it) the voice.

The last of the still images over which the female voice delivers its simultaneously academic and personal discourse shows a hand opening a book about Tlatilco. This image is suddenly dimmed, as by the switching on of an overhead light, and the screen goes white. Betts (Susan Huycke) walks into frame, speaking as she does so, and her previously disembodied voice is brought into visual alignment with her moving lips. The preceding images assume the retroactive status of an in-film movie and slide presentation, and we now understand Betts to have been speaking out of frame, but from within the diegesis.

This final part of the introductory scene works complexly with synchronization. Here again Betts moves back and forth between the discourse of ethnology and disclosures of a much more personal sort, but the latter now take on the quality of self-extenuation in the face of an implied critique. The camera "corners" her three times by holding relentlessly on her face as she attempts to explain why she became sidetracked from her search for information about the female divinities of ancient Mexico during her trip to Tlatilco. In the first shot, she explains: "I did reach the village, but I didn't know what I was looking for." In the second one, she says weakly: "I made several *attempts* to get to the ruins in Tlatilco." As the camera "jumps" in to an even closer view of her face, she defensively maintains that "it was difficult to get there, difficult to find out where it was."

These are statements which might well go unremarked if the camera were less aggressively attentive to their speaker, but which, given the look of embarrassment on Betts's face, are tantamount to a confession that self-incriminating information is being withheld. (The camera's persistence is all the more striking in that when Betts talks about the sacrificial rituals once practiced within the Mayan city of Chocen Itza, she walks easily in and out of its line of vision.) Synchronization is here a mechanism for disempowering the female voice— for reducing the authority and indeed the credibility of its words. It is thus a very exact enactment of what, in chapter 2, I described as the "vocal striptease," i.e., the castration of a previously anonymous voice by returning it forcefully to the body, a return which is documented most "satisfactorily" through the incriminating close-up.

The distance between the female voice and the female body is initially even greater in the inner narrative or "flashback" than it is in the introductory sequence. There is, for instance, a complete "non-match" of voice and body at the level of performance, since whereas Maggie Jones plays Betts, Gruben speaks for her. Gruben's voice-over begins, moreover, as a third-person narrator, impersonally describing Betts's visit to the Ciudad Valles bus station and her meeting with the English-speaking man who helps her with directions. Although it almost immediately adopts the speech patterns of that man, Jim Lilly (Doug Innis), and enters freely into what Betts thinks as she listens to him recount his "life story," it nonetheless maintains an ironic detachment from both characters:

> She liked the travelling and she liked people who could tell their stories fast. She liked them to sum up their lives for her in five or ten minutes at the most.

> He said he was a baseball pro from the States, playing winter ball with the Valles Aguilas. Actually, he stayed down there all year round. He could be major league but he preferred the climate. . . . His father was a plastic surgeon in Beverly Hills. He made time stop for people like Hayley Mills and Hugh O'Brian. He owned real estate in four hemispheres.

And a few moments of screen time later, as Betts and Jim Lilly stand before a front-projected roadside scene, Gruben removes her voice even more emphatically from her characters by speaking as the director of the film ("Representationally here she [Betts] should be at right angles facing him [Jim Lilly], because in one channel he filters her data from here on out").

Although the female voice-over invokes directional privilege several more times over the course of the film, closer and closer connections are forged between it and the characters of Betts and Jim Lilly. For a while it continues either to summarize their conversation through a third-person narrative, or to relay it as third-person indirect discourse (e.g., " 'You're a German,' he says. 'Just close your eyes' "), but during the second day in Tlatilco it begins to speak directly for Betts, in the present tense:

> It's light, I missed the bus. They didn't wake me up. He says they wanted to let me sleep because I wasn't feeling well.

Later the same day, it does the same for Jim Lilly, without providing any discursive markers to distinguish his voice from Betts's. This breakdown of verbal differentiation, like that which merges the voice-over with Betts, attests to the latter's increasing confinement both within the inner narrative and within a very traditional female body—one given to modeling bikinis in poses adopted from travelogues, and easily manipulated into situations of helplessness.

The voice-over at times reverts to third-person indirect discourse when relaying Jim Lilly's subsequent words, but it continues to speak directly for Betts until the physical struggle that occurs between them. During this scene, the voice-over gives way to synchronized dialogue as Betts calls for help, and attempts unsuccessfully to persuade Jim Lilly to leave her alone. As in the introductory scene, synchronization works here to strip the female voice not only of discursive authority and flexibility, but of all distance from the body. Betts's screams are virtually wrung out of her by the coercive pressure of Jim Lilly's arms pinning her to the bed, and even after he has released her, she speaks almost entirely in hostile monosyllables.

Only after Betts has extricated herself from the hotel room and Jim Lilly's surveillance does Gruben's voice resume its perch "over" the film's images, and even then it remains emotionally identified with her character. It doesn't regain its earlier distance from the visual track until the moment when there is in effect nothing to see—until the moment when Betts arrives at a deserted area of the quarry in the middle of the night, and finds only rocks, scrubby plants, and a squashed Coke can. At this point, sound and image pull sharply apart once more, the female voice soaring above the impoverished landscape with a quotation from Rilke:

> For our heart transcends us still, as was its wont in Grecian times. Yet we no longer can follow it with our eyes as it enters figures that soothe it, or into the bodies of gods that enhance and restrain it.

At one level, this passage is about what Benjamin would describe as the loss of the auratic object[74]—about the flattening out of spectacle, much like the Coke can, so that it is no longer adequate to the yearnings of desire, or (as Rilke would have it) of the "heart." Recontextualized within *Sifted Evidence*, it is also an obvious reference to the female divinities for whom Betts has been vaguely searching. However, it seems to me that the Rilke quotation addresses, in addition, a more specifically cinematic kind of transcendence—that it alludes in some way to the necessary detachment of the female voice from a body which, rather than "soothing" or "enhancing" it, can only constrain and restrict it. If this literary citation, like the earlier allusion to Schliemann and Von Humboldt, is an acknowledgment of the necessary division of voice from body, it is also a lament. Betts's entire visit to Mexico can be read as her quest for a different kind of female body—one which, to reverse Irigaray's formulation, would be adequate to the possible range, heterogeneity, and complexity of the female voice. But the only body she (re)discovers is the one to which the male gaze, variously represented by Jim Lilly and the Mexicans who call her "La Huerra," returns her.

The female subject's unhappy relation to the gaze is treated at much greater length in what is unquestionably the most remarkable deployment of female voices within the feminist avant-garde, if not within the whole of experimental cinema—Rainer's *Journeys from Berlin/71* (1979). Two of its many voices—that of the "patient," also called Annette, and that belonging to Rainer herself—are synchronized with the image track, while a third—that of the female analyst—connects up with a woman's back. Two other female voices remain completely disembodied, although the persona represented by each is evoked with extraordinary vividness. These voices "belong" to an adolescent girl (Lena Hyun) and to an adult woman (Amy Taubin) who is engaged simultaneously in a conversation about political violence and the preparations for a meal.

One other voice must be included in this list, although it derives from a man. This last voice could best be characterized as a dirty phone-caller, but during his longest and most persistent intrusion, he delivers one of the film's most important female monologues:

> My daddy called me Cookie. I'm really a good girl. I'll go along with anything as long as you'll like me a little. I'll even promise not to bring up all that business about being such a low element, such primeval slime, such an amoeba, such an edible *thing*. I'm not one for fussing. Not like those movie women: Katy Hepburn facing the dawn in her posh pad with stiff upper chin. Merle Oberon facing the Nazi night with hair billowing in the electric breeze. Roz Russell sockin' the words 'n' the whiskey to the best of them. Rita Hayworth getting shot in the mirror and getting her man. . . . I never faced the music, much less the dawn; I stayed in bed. I never socked anything to anybody; why rock the boat? I never set out to get my man, even in the mirror; they all got me. I never smiled through my tears; I choked down the terror. I never had to face the Nazis, much less their night. Not for me that succumbing in the great task because it must be done; not for me the heart beating in incomprehensible joy; not for me the vicissitudes of the class struggle; not for me the uncertainties of political thought. . . .[75]

The dirty phone-caller speaks from the position of the classic female subject brought face to face with cinematic images of "exceptional women"—of women who in some way transcend that representational system through which "the feminine" is constituted in Hollywood cinema, and thereby lay claim to certain phallic prerogatives. "Cookie" speaks about the felt inadequacy of the traditional female viewer in the face of these images, an inadequacy which precipitates intense self-loathing.

It seems to me that there is more at issue here than the inevitable discrepancy that separates cinematic representation from lived "reality." Cookie's speech points to the prior identification which underlies and indeed determines the relationship of the "normal" female subject with all such representations, one which makes it difficult if not impossible for her to see herself in any idealizing "mirror." The identification to which I refer is the one forced upon the female subject by the positive Oedipus complex, with its simultaneous devaluation of mother and self.

Journeys from Berlin/71 explores the relationship of the female subject to the existing symbolic order not only through the voice of the dirty phone-caller, but through those of the adolescent girl, the patient, the cooking woman, and the director herself. Each is located within a context within which women have conventionally been encouraged to talk, contexts which structure and circumscribe their subjectivity. Thus, the adolescent girl addresses her diary, the patient (Annette Michelson) her analyst (Ilona Halberstadt), the cooking woman the man with whom she presumably lives, and Rainer her mother. Each of these discourses is characterized by a high degree of reflexivity; although they all probe the relationship between the personal and the social, the accent falls increasingly on the first of those terms. Toward the end of the film the four voices converge more and more, until they finally seem to be participating in the same solipsistic speech.

The diary entries read aloud by the voice of the adolescent girl range across a wide variety of topics. However, the self is a constant point of reference. The first entry describes a number of events whose common denominator is that they induce in the writer what she calls the "chills" or the "shivers." Subsequent entries return obsessively to the feelings evoked in the adolescent girl by other people and things. The one dated Friday, September 28, is symptomatic:

> The tears are here again. Brush them away. Something just happened. Mama just finished listening to one of those one-hour dramas, a real tragedy. She said, "I shouldn't listen to those stories, they really move me too much. But I don't know what else to do with my time." And the tears came. Sometimes I feel an overwhelming tenderness for her. I don't know if it's love. Right now I am being strangely moved by my feeling for her.

The object is virtually eclipsed in this libidinal economy, whose extensions are all circular.

Events in the external world function as signifiers of the self in much the same way in the patient's discourse. Vietnam provides material for masturbation fantasies, Samuel Beckett finds his way into a story about shopping in Bloomingdale's and the defeat of the patient's hard-won independence, and statistics about political prisoners lead to the seemingly unconnected observation that "rejection and disappointment are the two things that I've always found impossible to take." The most breathtaking assimilation of the public into the private is effected during a reverie about the body:

> Some people don't seem to notice their own body changes. . . . I can predict exactly where new pressures of clothing will occur the next day—buttocks, thighs, belly, breasts—what new topography will appear on my face: creases and barrows as conspicuous as the scars slashed by two world wars into the soil of Europe.

Here all of twentieth-century history and a large portion of the world's geography yield metaphoric precedence to a woman's face and figure, and to the intense self-disgust of which they are the distillate. The patient's voice is synchronized to her image in more ways than one.

The voice associated with kitchen noises speaks about virtually nothing but women anarchists and revolutionaries, reading at length from their letters. However, when asked whether she has read the political writings of Emma Goldman, she responds, "No, I have a collection of her essays, but all I've read is her autobiography." Moreover, near the end of *Journeys from Berlin/71*, this voice talks a good deal about the difficulty she has always experienced in empathizing with oppressed groups. Instead, she gravitates toward radical "stars." Despite this apparent disavowal of the psychic conditions of normative female subjectivity, she is no more capable than "Cookie" of bringing her ego into conformity with these ideal images, and can only brood upon her own insufficiency. (Thus, whereas the figures she most admires all heroically subordinate their private lives to political struggle, she herself despairs of even achieving "correct social behavior".) *Journeys from Berlin/71* conflates this group of "exceptional women" with the earlier group when it shows the female analyst looking through a stack of photographs in which Jane Wyman and Rita Hayworth coexist with Vera Figner, Ulrike Meinhof, and Vera Zasulich.

Finally, there is the voice—and the image—of Rainer, speaking from Europe to her mother about a movie she has just seen, a movie filmed in Berlin before the war. Rainer talks about how affected she and the other viewers were by the shots of a city which no longer exists. Again the emphasis falls on the feelings evoked in the female subject by external occurrences, on sentiment rather than history or the socius. The auto-referentiality of all these voices is periodically accentuated by the appearance against a black background of rolling white titles providing facts and figures about West German postwar politics, i.e., by a discourse traditionally associated with values of "objectivity" and "neutrality," as well as by the interpolation on the soundtrack of other, more strident political statements and accounts (here excerpts from a letter written by Ulrike Meinhof to Hannah Krabbe about the necessity of resisting prison psychiatrification).

In the general conversation about female subjectivity to which all the women's voices contribute during the last third of the film, a conversation which often occurs simultaneously on several registers, the adolescent girl confesses:

> Everything I've written has been put down for the benefit of some potential reader. It is a titanic task to be frank with myself. I fear my own censure. Even my thoughts sometimes appear to my consciousness in a certain form for the benefit of an imaginary mind-reader. And strangely enough, *I* am that reader of these pages; I am that reader of this mind. I have very strong impressions of my childhood *"acting."* Up to a few years ago, whenever I was alone I would "perform." I don't think I did anything unusual or dramatic at these times, but the things I did do I did with the thought in mind that I was being watched. Now this reaction is becoming more and more unconscious, having been transmitted to my actions, speech, writing, and my thoughts. This last is the most unfortunate of all.

What this female voice records is the internalization of the specular and auditory regime upon which classic cinema relies, and which it helps to perpetuate within the larger cultural order. The notion of performance is, of course, an important one in all of Rainer's films,[76] but in *Journeys from Berlin/71* it gains new resonance. It becomes a metaphor for female subjectivity—for the interiorization of discursive demands which must be met at every moment of psychic existence, which carry out the functions of over-seeing and over-hearing the ego even in the most solitary of situations. The rigors of that performance are so severe that they leave the female subject with no capacity for struggle on any other front, and result in extreme cases in suicide. It is also a metaphor, although one upon which the film insists somewhat less strenuously, for the hyperbolic diegeticization of the female body and voice within classic cinema—for the rigorous subordination of the former to the male gaze, and the latter to the male ear, and the confinement of both to textual enclosures and recesses.

Late in *Journeys from Berlin/71*, the woman analyst quotes a passage from Freud's "Mourning and Melancholia" which deals with the psychic circumstances under which suicide is possible:

> The analysis of melancholia now shows that the ego can kill itself only if,
> owing to the return of the object-cathexis, it can treat itself as an object and
> if it is able to direct against itself the hostility which relates to an object and
> which represents the ego's original reaction to events in the external world.
> In the two opposed situations of being most intensely in love and of suicide
> the ego is overwhelmed by the object, though in totally different ways.[77]

This citation is not accidental. It pinpoints precisely what the film's
female voices have in common—the melancholia induced in the female
subject by the positive Oedipus complex, which holds her to an identification with the mother even as it obliges her to withdraw her libidinal
investment from that first and most important of erotic objects.

Journeys from Berlin/71 does more than deconstruct this closed theater of female subjectivity; it also points beyond. Not only does it detach
voice from body, interrupting in the process the coherence upon which
the performance relies, and revealing the degree to which the former
has been obliged to talk about and regulate the latter, but in its final
moments it involves its female speakers in a collective repudiation of
melancholia—of its self-hatred, and of its "failure to imagine a world"
outside. It also broaches, in a tentative and fragmentary manner, the
possibility of moving beyond that psychic condition toward externally
directed action—the possibility, that is, of political struggle. As the adult
woman puts it, "One might conceivably take greater risks . . . in using
one's power . . . for the benefit of others . . . resisting inequities close at
hand."

At the beginning of Potter's *The Gold Diggers* (1984), Potter's own
disembodied voice sings a song called "Seeing Red" over the black-and-
white images of a woman walking down a snowy Icelandic road, the
cropped body of a man entering a rustic cabin with a handful of large
gold nuggets, a woman holding a small girl on her lap, and a woman
laughing wildly in the wind and snow. It is a curious song for a director
to associate with herself, particularly given the centrality of the first-
person pronoun, since its lyrics are about the reception rather than the
production of sounds and images. More specifically, "Seeing Red"—or
at least the first verse of that song—addresses the way in which the
classic cinematic text induces unpleasure in the female spectator, giving
her "the pleasure time blues":

> Went to the pictures,
> For a break,
> Thought I'd put me feet up.

Have a bit of intake;
But then a man with a gun
Came in through the door,
And when he kissed her,
I couldn't take it any more.
Please, please, please,
Give me back my pleasure,
Please give me back my leisure hour.
I've got the pleasure time blues—
I'm seeing red.

A complex series of exchanges takes place between these lyrics and the images that accompany them. The black and white of Babette Mangolte's cinematography contrasts wittily both with the notion of "pleasure time *blues*" and with the idea of "seeing *red*," suggesting that the film we are about to watch will position itself very differently vis-à-vis the female spectator than does classic cinema. The reference to "a man with a gun" coincides with the shot of the man entering a log cabin, a shot which *The Gold Diggers* will retroactively associate with the loss of the mother. The word *pleasure* a few lines later is juxtaposed with the image of the mother and child, while the rhyming *leisure* is superimposed over the image of the woman laughing in the wind and snow—an image which constitutes one of the most important and frequently reiterated maternal inscriptions in the film. The erotics of female spectatorship would thus seem to turn in some crucial way upon the mother.

The images over which Potter sings "Seeing Red" constitute only the first of numerous maternal citations, for *The Gold Diggers* "spirals" back[78] obsessively to the figure of the woman we see walking down the snowy road, and laughing in the wind. Of all the many quests around which the film is organized, the most important is surely Ruby's search for the secret of her own transformation, and that secret is shown to reside in the interaction between her relationship with Celeste (Colette Laffont) and her desire for the mother—to reside, in other words, in the reactivation of the negative Oedipus complex. Celeste urges Ruby (Julie Christie) to look for what might be called the "Philosopher's Stone of female subjectivity" within her own history, and it is precisely there, at the site of her traumatic separation from the mother, that she eventually finds it. (I want to stress that it is to this moment of rupture, which is so fundamental to desire, rather than to the scene of pre-Oedipal unity and plenitude, that *The Gold Diggers* so emphatically returns.)

What stands in the way of Ruby's self-transforming discovery is the loss of (conscious) memory; as she puts it at one point, "I can't remember what I'm supposed to remember." Remaining "in the dark" about her desire for the mother is shown to be the "necessary condition" of her existence as a commodity to be exchanged and speculated upon. Ruby's "recollection" of the negative Oedipus complex, on the other hand, makes it possible for the "goods" to withdraw themselves from the market, and "get together,"[79] as Irigaray would say. *The Gold Diggers* presents as a logical sequence the narrative progression from the theater scene where Ruby recovers her memory to the scene where Celeste rescues her for a second, definitive time, and where the women who are left behind abandon their male partners to dance with each other. (If, as my theoretical alignment of melancholia and female subjectivity suggests, the process of psychically devaluing the mother goes on at an unconscious level, where mnemic trace after mnemic trace is emptied of its libidinal content, conscious "recollection" or reconstruction would indeed seem a way of halting that process. This, at any rate, is how I read *The Gold Diggers's* insistence upon conscious memory. At the same time, it seems to me that "recollection" can take the more displaced and indirect form of living the relation to the mother through another woman—or perhaps even through a man.)

I will have more to say later about the operations of Oedipal desire in *The Gold Diggers,* but I want to return right now to the detail with which I began this analysis—to Potter's inscription of herself as a viewer rather than a filmmaker within the song she sings at the outset. In representing herself in this way, she collapses one of the divisions upon which classic cinema is predicated—the division, that is, between the site of enunciation and that of spectatorship. She also posits an implicit reversibility between the positions of director and viewer, or speaking and spoken subjects.

The distinction between spectator and fictional character is similarly eroded a moment later, through a simple pronominal reconfiguration. A riddle is told twice, once by Ruby's disembodied voice, and once by Celeste's. The form of the riddle remains largely unchanged from the first telling to the second, except that the pronouns *I* and *you* are reversed, and the final question is omitted by Celeste. Here are the two versions:

RUBY	CELESTE
I am borne in a beam of light.	You are borne in a beam of light.
I move continuously yet I'm still.	You move continuously yet you are still.
I'm larger than life,	You're larger than life,
Yet do not breathe.	Yet do not breathe.
Only in the darkness am I visible.	Only in the darkness are you visible.
You can see me but never touch me,	I can see you but never touch you,

I can speak to you but never hear you.	
You know me intimately, and I know you not at all.	You can speak to me but can never listen.
We are strangers, and yet you take me inside of you.	I know you intimately, and yet you know me not at all.
What am I?	We are strangers, yet I take you inside of me.

Although we are given ninety minutes to solve this riddle, it is immediately apparent that the answer to Ruby's question is something like "the celluloid image of Ruby/Julie Christie," or more generally, "cinema." It is equally obvious that the "you" of the first version of the riddle, like the "I" of the second, designates the film viewer. However, because Celeste's voice utters the second of those pronouns, it designates her as well, at least *après coup*, once her character has been introduced. This reading is reinforced by the remark, "We have ninety minutes to solve this riddle and to find each other," since the film concludes with the romantic reunion of Celeste and Ruby. There is thus a way in which Celeste at this moment speaks for the viewer, in her place. A fictional character has in effect taken the viewer inside herself, in a reversal of the process that normally occurs—a process to which the riddle draws our attention. That which is generally assumed to reside outside cinema is inscribed inside, and vice versa, calling radically into question the carefully maintained distinction between interiority and exteriority which organizes the voice in Hollywood film.

Over and over again, the boundary separating spectacle from spectator is shown to be absolutely permeable. Celeste's dream, for instance, begins with a shot of an elderly woman drawing a ceremonial curtain to reveal the backs of a theater audience, who have themselves been put on stage. And although here and elsewhere in the film Celeste functions as a viewer, the moment inevitably comes when she, too, is called upon to perform, and sings the "Empire Song." The men who are repeatedly shown sitting in the theater audience watching women perform are ultimately asked to look at men dancing with each other—men who might as well be themselves, so anonymous and generalized are all the male characters in the film. Even Ruby, who is insistently placed on the side of the spectacle, takes her place as viewer both when Celeste sings and when Lilly dances. However, the interpenetration of image and gaze is most intricately worked out in the theater sequence, upon which I want to comment in somewhat greater detail.

That sequence begins when Ruby, followed by a group of male pursuers, enters an auditorium and sits down. Startled by catching sight of herself as a character within the play that is underway, she rushes backstage, only to be thrust back on the boards once again after she has watched Lilly perform her dance routine. For the moment during which she still remains seated after sighting herself on the elevated platform, she is *simultaneously* spectacle and spectator, both inside and outside the space that is marked "interior" with respect to the film as a whole.

Even more remarkable, the play both replicates and incorporates the larger narrative of *The Gold Diggers*. In dumb show, Ruby, her mother, and the anonymous man enact the story to which the film has itself as yet only cryptically alluded, but which is its most crucial syntagm: Ruby sits on her mother's lap in a primitive cabin in the middle of a desolate landscape. A man enters with some gold nuggets, and tears mother away from daughter. The man and the woman exit, leaving a desolate Ruby behind. At this point the distinction between the play and the film begins to blur altogether, as five shots from Ruby's "real" past are interspersed between shots of the male audience responding, and Ruby herself looking from on-stage. Both ostensibly see what we see—a man and woman leaving the cabin, their heads cropped; a child walking up a rocky incline; a procession of gold miners in the snow; and the same child standing alone by rocks and a stream of water. Miraculously, a character within a play becomes a spectator of "actual" events, events which are somehow folded into the play itself.

As if this were not already a sufficient assault upon our inherited notions of textual limits, the camera cuts away from a shot of the booing male audience to a shot of Ruby in the audience, once again simultaneously on- and off-stage. She gets up hastily and leaves, once again followed by her male pursuers. Temporarily shaking them, she goes through a battered outside door, and suddenly finds herself in the landscape of her past, running toward the by now ubiquitous cabin. A series of shots show Ruby watching herself as a child, first from a distance and then up close, with only a window intervening between the two sets of eyes. She sees her mother laughing in the wind once again, and looks while she and the anonymous man run away together in the snow. Finally, the child runs round and round the cabin, becoming increasingly mature, until she finally merges with the adult Ruby, and goes in through the door. There is a dissolve to a balcony shot of the curtain going down on the play, a shot which extends the perimeters of the stage to encompass the whole of *The Gold Diggers*.

This complete reversibility of female spectator and spectacle must be understood as the obverse of the scopic regime described by Lilly in her backstage conversation with Ruby—a regime within which woman is "frozen" as object of the male look. *The Gold Diggers* acknowledges the specular bases of subjectivity—the necessary place, as it were, of the "photo session"—but it frees the gaze of its sexually differentiating function, making it absolutely reciprocal between any two parties.

The only sound during the pantomime, apart from the musical accompaniment and the prompting whispers of the stage manager, is the laughter of the anonymous man as he displays his gold nuggets and dances with the mother. The dense imbrication of interiority and exteriority is effected entirely at the visual level. However, throughout the film, the female voice moves fluidly in and out of synchronization, sometimes issuing from a visible source and at other times speaking over the image track. Apart from the examples I have already mentioned ("Seeing Red" and the twice-told riddle), no logic governs these vocal vicissitudes; the voice is simply free to roam. Once again *The Gold Diggers* refuses to acknowledge the opposition between "inner" and "outer."

The permeability of the line distinguishing interiority from exteriority—and hence the synchronized voice from the voice-off, and the spectacle from the gaze—is the formal extension of *The Gold Diggers's* concern with the negative Oedipus complex. As I have already had occasion to stress more than once in this chapter, the female version of that complex is predicated upon a *narcissistic* desire for the mother— upon the girl's love for an object which represents both what she was, prior to differentiation, and what she aspires to become (i.e., the mirror in which she sees an idealized version of herself). Within this libidinal economy, there are no hard and fast distinctions between subject and object. Even though the former can never possess the latter, and is indeed separated from it by an irreducible distance, there is an imaginary dimension to their relationship which promotes identification, and which facilitates reversals of the sort that occur over and over again in *The Gold Diggers*. The negative Oedipus complex thus constitutes not only a psychic "Philosopher's Stone," able to effect the transformation of normative female subjectivity, but the model for a different kind of cinema, as well—the path leading away from fixed and hierarchical schematizations to a transversality of spectacle and gaze, diegesis and enunciation, character and viewer, voice "in," "off," and "over."

The Gold Diggers can also be read as a disquisition on the male version of the negative Oedipus complex. Since the same is true of "Women on the Market" and "Commodities among Themselves," and since those two Irigarayan essays provide such an inspired addendum to *The Gold Diggers*, I want to conclude both this analysis and the chapter as a whole by bringing those three texts together.

In her guise as that beauty which, when it is not being kept for safekeeping in the bank, is ritually circulated from one male dancer to another, Ruby is the commodity par excellence. However, her status as commodity has nothing whatever to do with her "intrinsic" qualities (whatever those might be), but is entirely "super-natural" or "supplemental," the effect of "an imprint that is purely social in nature."[80] Irigaray accounts for this supplement or imprint in three ways, each of which can be seen to be determinative of Ruby's "marketability."

To begin with, Irigaray suggests that an object has exchange value only insofar as it "specularizes" man's labor—only to the degree that it functions as "a locus of imprints, marks, and mirage of his activity":

> To be able to incorporate itself into a mirror of value, it is necessary that the work itself reflect only its property of human labor: that the body of a commodity be nothing more than the materialization of an abstract human labor. That is, that it have no more body, matter, nature, but that it be objectivization, a crystallization as visible object, of man's activity.[81]

One thinks immediately in this context of the striking image of Ruby borne aloft on a platform, her very elevation a testimony to the efforts of six men, and her lavish garments a veritable proclamation of the productivity of countless others. In this guise, she is indeed precisely an *artifact*.

A commodity also derives its exchange value, Irigaray argues, from its relation to another, similar commodity, and from the simultaneous relation of both of these commodities to a third, privileged term:

> When women are exchanged, woman's body must be treated as an *abstraction*. The exchange operation cannot take place in terms of some intrinsic, immanent value of the commodity. It can only come about when two objects—two women—are in a relation of equality with a third term that is neither the one nor the other. It is thus not as "women" that they are exchanged, but as women reduced to some common feature—their current price in gold, or phalluses—and of which they would represent a plus or minus quantity.[82]

She goes on in the same passage to link woman's value as the product of human labor with her value as a "plus or minus quantity" of the privileged third term, a connection which is easier to conceptualize if that term is understood to be gold than if it is taken to be the phallus.

The Gold Diggers forges an equally close connection between Ruby-as-commodity and that most precious of all metals, not merely by relegating each for safekeeping to the bank, but by designating both as "assets" to be "frozen." Moreover, whenever Ruby is borne aloft in full regalia, she is always preceded by ten men carrying an enormous tray of gold bricks, as if to trumpet her value to all onlookers.

Finally, and most interestingly, Irigaray suggests that woman derives her value through the exchange which she makes possible—the exchange, that is, between two men. As she puts it in "Women on the Market," woman is the "material alibi for the desire for relations among men" (p. 180). In "Commodities among Themselves," she elaborates much more fully on what these relations entail, suggesting that male homosexuality is the very glue that holds the symbolic order together:

> The exchanges upon which patriarchal societies are based take place exclusively among men. Women, signs, commodities, and currency always pass from one man to another. . . . Thus the labor force and its products, including those of mother earth, are the object of transactions among men and men alone. This means that the very possibility of a sociocultural order requires homosexuality as its organizing principle. Heterosexuality is nothing but the assignment of economic roles: they are producer subjects and agents of exchange (male) on the one hand, productive earth and commodities (female) on the other. (P. 192)

Yet the very symbolic order that is sustained through homosexual desire prohibits the direct expression of that desire, obliging it to assume the censored and circuitous form of heterosexual exchange.

If Irigaray is to be believed—and her argument carries great force—the male version of the negative Oedipus complex must be understood as having primacy, at least at the level of the unconscious, over its positive counterpart.[83] Indeed, the positive Oedipus complex becomes merely the indirect and disguised expression of the male subject's unacknowledged (and unacknowledgeable) desire for the father, the exchange of women being only a pretext for putting man in touch with man. The ultimate extension of Irigaray's argument would be the proposition, dazzling in its simplicity, that the phallus is what the penis becomes when it itself cannot be enjoyed. In fact, Irigaray comes very close to saying this, remarking that "once the penis . . . becomes merely a means to pleasure, pleasure among men, *the phallus loses its power*" (p. 193).

The Gold Diggers moves toward just such a pleasurable implementation. When Ruby and her colleagues refuse to function any longer as "the mediation, transaction, transition, transference, between man and his fellow man, indeed between man and himself,"[84] the male characters are obliged to do what the film suggests they have always wanted to do—to dance among themselves. *The Gold Diggers* thus obliges its male viewer to confront the homosexual desire that holds together the present symbolic order. Meanwhile, Ruby and Celeste, having found the Celestial Ruby or Philosopher's Stone within their own erotic alliance—or, to be more precise, within the negative Oedipus complex upon which that alliance is based—journey away from the city of men toward the woman welder, who knows how to convert base metal into ships.

As the films I have grouped together here flamboyantly demonstrate, the female voice has enormous conceptual and discursive range once it is freed from its claustral confinement within the female body. It is capable of talking about terrorism, anger, melancholia, homosexual as well as heterosexual desire, ancient Mexican divinities, soap operas, Emma Goldman, the circulation of money, and even cinema itself. In the next and final chapter, I will be extending the category of the female voice to encompass authorship, as well. In so doing, I will be abstracting it away from a literal to a metaphoric "speech."

[6]

THE FEMALE AUTHORIAL VOICE

In 1968, Roland Barthes proclaimed the death of the author as an individual and originating force behind the literary text.[1] Within film studies, however, this very male author still seemed to be at least vaguely alive as late as 1973, when Ed Buscombe made a qualified argument on behalf of authorial intention,[2] and "he" made a spectacular comeback in the late seventies in the work of Raymond Bellour.[3] In 1978, Sandy Flitterman offered an argument which would have seemed inconceivable to the Barthes of "The Death of the Author"—the argument that Hitchcock's "assertion of his presence as producer of the look" works not to center his films ideologically, but rather to subvert the operations of dominant cinematic meaning.[4]

The author has also continued to haunt the edges of film theory, feminist cinema, political cinema, and the avant-garde as the possibility of a resistant and oppositional agency, at times in a less masculine guise. I think in all four respects of the "Laura Speaking" section of *Riddles of the Sphinx*, which presents the spectator not only with the moving images of one of the film's two directors, but with the recorded sounds of her voice talking about what she hoped to effect through the thirteen 360-degree pans ("When we were planning the central section of this film, about a mother and a child, we decided to use the voice of the Sphinx as an imaginary narrator. . . .").[5] This is a far more flamboyant authorial inscription than anything to be found in Hitchcock's films, and one which raises the specter of intentionality even more palpably than do any of his cameo appearances.

However, it is not my wish to reinstate the film author as punctual source or transcendent meaning. The purpose of this chapter is quite otherwise. First, I would like to determine the conditions under which

188 THE ACOUSTIC MIRROR

the author has lived on as a discursive category since his biographical demise in 1968, not only in film studies but within the work of Barthes, as well. Second, I would like to carve out a theoretical space from which it might be possible to hear the female voice speaking once again from the filmic "interior," but now as the point at which an authorial subject is constructed rather than as the site at which male lack is disavowed. Finally, I will attempt to trace female authorial desire and subjectivity within the films of the Italian director Liliana Cavani, films which have proved singularly intractable to other kinds of feminist analysis, and have therefore been largely neglected. My preliminary step in this triple project will be to return to the scene of the Barthesian crime, and to search there both for the murder weapon and for the corpse of the deceased author.

There is a certain ambiguity about the terms under which the author meets his unmaker in "The Death of the Author." Where—and when—did this major cultural event occur, and through what means? There is a good deal of equivocation in the way Barthes answers these questions. It is "writing," he tells us, that passed the death sentence on the author, but "writing" turns out to mean three very different things. It refers simultaneously to what Derrida has promoted under the rubric of *écriture,* to modernist literature, and to that activity of productive reading which would be elaborated by Barthes one year later in *S/Z,* a book which is forcefully anticipated in "The Death of the Author" through the quotation from "Sarrasine" with which it begins.[6]

"The Death of the Author" initially characterizes writing as a system of graphic traces cut adrift from all phenomenological moorings—as "the black-and-white where all identity is lost, beginning with the identity of the body that writes."[7] According to this account, writing automatically enacts the death of the author by virtue of its iterability— by virtue of its capacity to be reactivated as discourse in the absence of its writer.[8] Since the figure of the author as a person "behind" the text has never been more than a rationalist, empiricist, and positivist illusion, all that is necessary to dissolve that figure is to repeat the vital lesson of Jakobsonian and Benvenistian linguistics—the lesson that "the speech-act in its entirety is an 'empty' process, which functions perfectly without its being necessary to 'fill' it with the person of the interlocutors: linguistically, the author is nothing but the one who writes, just as *I* is nothing but the one who says *I;* language knows a 'subject,' not a person, and this subject, empty outside of the very speech-act which defines it, suffices to 'hold' language. . . ."[9] However, it is important to note that although Barthes argues for the loss of the author's "identity," he does not entirely erase the authorial figure. The author's body remains as the support for and agency of *écriture*.

"Writing" also designates a very specific group of literary texts, conjured up somewhat paradoxically through a catalogue of talismanic names: Mallarmé, Valery, Proust, Baudelaire. Significantly, this part of Barthes's argument is hedged about with contradictions, contradictions which intimate that the modernist (or premodernist) text may not be as inimical to authorship as he would have us believe. Not only does he rely heavily upon certain proper names, but at one point he suggests that the modernist text does not so much kill the author as move him from the center to the margins of the stage.[10] At another, closely adjacent point, Barthes suggests that if the text *does* murder the author, it also presides over his rebirth. Of course, this new author bears scant resemblance to his precursor; he is voiceless, he is an impersonal scriptor rather than a psychological coherence, and his existence is absolutely coterminous with the text. However, like the author-as-individual-person, the author-as-scriptor would seem capable of assuming a corporeal form, since we are given a quick glimpse of his dismembered hand:

> The modern *scriptor* is born *at the same time* as his text; he is not furnished with a being which precedes or exceeds his writing, he is not the subject of which his book would be the predicate; there is no time other than the speech-act, and every text is written eternally *here* and *now*. . . . the modern *scriptor*, having buried the Author, can therefore no longer believe, according to the pathos of his predecessors, that his hand is slower than his passion . . . for him, on the contrary, his hand, detached from any voice, borne by a pure gesture of inscription (and not of expression), traces a field without origin—or at least with no origin but language itself, i.e., the very thing which ceaselessly calls any origin into question.[11]

Finally, and most definitively, "writing" designates a way of reading which discloses the cluster or "braid" of quotations that make up a text. The author is here subjected to a double displacement: First, the "voices" of culture replace him as the speaking agency behind the text, and as a consequence unitary meaning gives way to discursive heterogeneity and contestation. Second, because this plurality is activated only through and "in" the reader, he or she supplants the author as the site at which the text comes together. Here again the image of (re)generation is closely linked to that of the authorial dissolution: "the birth of the reader," Barthes writes, "must be requited by the death of the Author."[12] Significantly, this newly emergent reader closely resembles the author-as-scriptor produced earlier in the essay; the former, like the latter, has no history, biography, or psychology, but is merely "that *someone* who holds collected into one and the same field all of the traces from which writing is constituted."[13]

Why must the author be killed three times over, each time with a different murder weapon? And why does he nonetheless persist, in the proper names that herald the modernist text, the fragment of the writing hand, and the image of rebirth? Because, as I would argue, Barthes desires not so much the author's dissolution as his recovery in a new guise. This desire would surface emphatically five years after "The Death of the Author," in *The Pleasure of the Text*. That work relinquishes the author once again as a person and an institution, but reinstates him a moment later as a figure inside the text:

> Lost in the midst of the text (not *behind* it, like a *deus ex machina*) there is always the other, the author.
> As an institution, the author is dead: his civil status, his biographical person have disappeared; dispossessed, they no longer exercise over his work the formidable paternity whose account literary history, teaching, and public opinion had the responsibility of establishing and renewing; but in the text, in a way, I *desire* the author: I need his figure (which is neither his representation nor his projection), as he needs mine. . . .[14]

The word *figure* marks the return of the authorial body, grasped now not as biographical or corporeal profile but as the materiality of writing. The body of the author has become the (highly eroticized) body of the text.

However, a subsequent passage indicates that the body of the text has undergone in the process of substitution a quite remarkable anthropomorphization, assuming many of the attributes of the human form. This passage effects an even more dramatic reversal of the earlier essay than the passage I quoted a moment ago, since it exhumes the authorial organ—i.e., the voice—which Barthes was at most pains to bury there. Whereas "The Death of the Author" attempts to deoriginate writing by severing its connection to the voice, *The Pleasure of the Text* argues passionately on behalf of what it calls "writing aloud," or "vocal writing." And in the process it conjures up the vision not only of writing-as-voice but of the word made flesh:

> *Writing aloud* is not phonological but phonetic; its aim is not the clarity of messages, the theater of emotions; what it searches for (in a perspective of bliss) are the pulsional incidents, the language lined with flesh, a text where we can hear the grain of the voice, the patina of consonants, the voluptuousness of vowels, a whole carnal stereophony; the articulation of the body, of the tongue, not that of meaning, of language.[15]

Most astonishing of all, Barthes goes on to compare "vocal writing" to the closely miked sounds of speech at the cinema, sounds which permit us to hear "the breath, the gutturals, the fleshiness of the lips, a whole presence of the human muzzle."[16] He characterizes these sounds as an acoustic close-up, but his panegyric also evokes cinema's visual close-up, with its conventional hold on the magnified features of the face. By the conclusion of *The Pleasure of the Text*, the author "lost in the midst of the text" has thus emerged with all the corporeal and vocal palpability of the author "behind" the text, albeit without the latter's biographical and institutional supports.

By fragmenting the authorial body in the way he does—by giving it to us a section at a time (hand, mouth, breath)—Barthes attempts to hold it outside the perspectival frame of classic representation. He also attempts to sustain it outside gender. However, no discourse of the body can foreclose for very long upon sexual difference, which will at the very least function as a structuring absence. Here it is more than that. Sexual difference is the very ground and terrain of Barthes's battle against the traditional author, and of his struggle to install the "modern scriptor" in the other's place.

Although Barthes never definitively says so, the author he seeks to annihilate occupies a definitively male position. As he observes in *The Pleasure of the Text*, the traditional author's "civil status" and "biographical person" exercise a "formidable paternity" over his work, holding it to phallic rectitude and dominant meaning.[17] Barthes dreams of "dispossessing" this author—of stripping him of his paternal legacy. It is in this context that we must read the opening paragraph of "The Death of the Author":

> In his tale *Sarrasine*, Balzac, speaking of a castrato disguised as a woman, writes this sentence: "She was Woman, with her sudden fears, her inexplicable whims, her instinctive fears, her meaningless bravado, her defiance, and her delicious delicacy of feeling." Who speaks in this way? Is it the hero of the tale, who would prefer not to recognize the castrato hidden beneath the "woman"? Is it Balzac the man, whose personal experience has provided him with a philosophy of Woman? Is it Balzac the author, professing certain "literary" ideas about femininity? Is it universal wisdom? Romantic philosophy? We can never know, for the good reason that writing is the destruction of every voice, every origin. Writing is that neuter, that composite, that obliquity into which our subject flees, the black-and-white where all identity is lost, beginning with the very identity of the body that writes.[18]

The ostensible function of this quotation from "Sarrasine" is to dramatize the way in which language can be said to write itself, even in the most "readerly" of novels, and so to drive a wedge between discourse and its ostensible author. However, that quotation also introduces the metaphor with which Barthes will subsequently characterize the body of the text, and by means of which he will attempt to exorcise the paternal author—the metaphor of a "neuter" or "composite." This

metaphor derives its representational force from the figure of Zambinella, a castrato masquerading as a woman.

What does the metaphor of the neuter tell us about the sexual
identity of the author whose voice Barthes dreams of hearing through
the body of the text? Let us entertain for a moment the most obvious
answer to that question, and assume that Barthes's project is to replace
the male author with an androgynous author. This is in many respects
an exemplary dream, not least because it is self-destructive. One must
not lose sight of the fact that Barthes "himself" was culturally gendered
as male, and therefore qualified to occupy an author-itative position.
Instead, he puts his own sexual and cultural identity under erasure.
Rather than speaking "frontally," from the place of the phallus, he
constructs *The Pleasure of the Text* on the model of "that uninhibited
person who shows his behind to the *Political Father.*"[19] "The Death of
the Author" negates masculinity even more emphatically, since it presents the scriptor as a man who has not only severed his anatomical link
to the phallus, but assumed a feminine persona.[20]

However, the female subject can participate in this fantasy of sexual
and discursive divestiture only in a displaced and mediated way. She
can assist the male subject in removing his mantle of privileges, but she
herself has nothing to take off. Besides, as I attempted to indicate in
chapter 2, the striptease has for too long functioned as the privileged
metaphor by means of which female lack comes to be textually exposed.
Once the author-as-individual-person has given way to the author-as-
body-of-the-text, the crucial project with respect to the female voice is
to find a place from which it can speak and be heard, not to strip it of
discursive rights.

In fact, Barthes's project seems more complex than I have indicated
so far, and more aware of what a feminist reader might see as the pitfalls
of androgyny.[21] To begin with, there is an implicit acknowledgment in
the opening paragraph of "The Death of the Author" that sexual difference can probably be suspended only by modeling both genders on the
accepted logic of one of them, and an insistence that if this be the case,
"woman" will be the preferred standard. Barthes thus inverts what Luce
Irigaray has called the "*hom(m)osexual*" economy of dominant culture.[22]

"The Death of the Author" also facilitates a very different interpretation of Barthes's authorial dream, and one which is closer to my own.
When I read the sentence from "Sarrasine" with which Barthes's essay
begins, I am always struck less by the accomplished fact of the author's
demise than by what would seem to be a crisis within traditional
authorship. The passage in question still bears the marks of male
enunciation (it is, after all, a fragment of what might be called the

Discourse of the Woman as Other), but no male voice comes decisively forward to claim it. This crisis is precipitated in part by the fact that "she" here refers not to "natural" but to "artificial"—or what I would prefer to call "constructed"—femininity. However, it is also motivated by the fact that the voice has taken up residence elsewhere, that it has migrated from a masculine to a feminine position. The castration which Zambinella undergoes not only "unmans" him, making it impossible for him to speak any longer from a masculine position, but it produces a *female* singing voice. Significantly, singing is one of the privileged tropes through which Barthes describes "vocal writing," or the author within the body of the text. The Barthesian fantasy would thus seem to turn not only upon the death of the paternal author, but upon the production of a female authorial voice, as well. It would also seem to insist upon male castration or divestiture as one of the conditions of such a production— to insist that insofar as the female voice speaks authorially, it does so at the expense of the system of projection and disavowal I discussed at the beginning of this book.

I will be talking later in this chapter about a group of films which, although more "readerly" than "writerly," nonetheless both reiterate the connection between male castration and female authorship, and enact in a mediated and displaced way the search for a sexual "neutrality" based not on a male but on a female model. At that juncture I will want to challenge the notion that a radically reconstituted authorship should be theoretically located only at the level of a text's materiality, rather than, for instance, at the level of its narrative or character system. I am in fundamental agreement, however, that the author who should be the chief object of current theoretical concern is the one who occupies the interior of the text, and I will henceforth refer to that figure as the author "inside" the text. I am less prepared than was the Barthes of 1969 to bracket the biographical author altogether, and will instead attempt to propose a new model for conceptualizing the relation between the author "inside" the text and what I will from this point forward designate the author "outside" the text.

I would now like to track a more specifically filmic author through a series of theoretical texts extending from 1962 to 1978. The itinerary I propose to follow will begin with what might be called the "monumental" view of the film author—a view from which he seems to dominate the theoretical landscape like one of the presidential profiles on Mount Rushmore, or the mountain ranges in a John Ford western. However, the road will lead very quickly away from this *auteur*, and as it does he will diminish "like a figure at the far end of the literary stage."[23] As he recedes, he will make way for the "scenery" of the text, within which the outlines of a very different author will begin to be glimpsed. The tour will necessarily be a highly selective one, but extensive enough, I hope, to convey some sense of the terrain.

Andrew Sarris's "Notes on the Auteur Theory in 1962" would seem a logical place to begin our retrospective tour, since it both summarizes the *"politique des auteurs"* and defends it against Bazin's criticisms. It could also be seen to mark the beginning of the authorship debate in English, although that debate had been raging in France for more than a decade.

What is perhaps most noteworthy about Sarris's *auteur* is that he has the heroic proportions of the romantic author; he belongs to a "pantheon" of geniuses who tower over the mere *"metteurs en scène."* This author derives his preeminence from his "personality" or "elan of the soul," which he imprints on his films through "certain recurring characteristics" that provide a kind of "signature."[24] He is also the guarantee of unity and consistency; even in his humblest incarnation, as a technician, he represents "the ability to put a film together with some clarity and coherence," and his films "almost always" run "true to form."[25] Finally, Sarris envisions the *auteur* as both the origin and meaning of the cinematic text, insisting that there is a close relationship between the way an authored film "looks and moves" and the way its director "thinks and feels." Those thoughts and feelings are responsible for the film's "interior meaning."[26]

Significantly, however, the author's feelings and thoughts turn out to be inseparable from the text itself. Sarris argues that the director's personality is "imbedded in the stuff of the cinema and cannot be rendered in noncinematic terms."[27] A curiously unexplained epigraph, from Kierkegaard's *Either/Or* precedes "Notes on The Auteur Theory in 1962," and suggests even more forcefully that the author-as-originating-agency and extratextual significance can be glimpsed only in and through his films:

> I call these sketches Shadowgraphs, partly . . . [because] they derive from the darker side of life, partly because, like other shadowgraphs, they are not directly visible. When I take a shadowgraph in my hand, it makes no impression on me, and gives me no clear conception of it. Only when I hold it up opposite the wall, and look not directly at it, but at that which appears on the wall, am I able to see it. So also with the picture I wish to show here, an inward picture that does not become perceptible till I see it through the external. This external is perhaps not quite unobtrusive, but, not until I now look directly through it, do I discover that inner picture that I desire to show you, an inner picture too delicately drawn to be outwardly visible, woven as it is of the tenderest moods of the soul.[28]

This passage is remarkable for its unabashed idealism. Its account of shadowgraphs conforms closely to the Christian and Platonic account of the cosmos, in which the material world functions as an indirect expression of spiritual truths too ineffable to be directly viewed by fallen eyes. However, its inclusion here also has a very different discursive effect. It works to suggest that even at the farthest reaches of auteurism, the author "himself" cannot be clearly seen—that the author "outside" the text is concealed within an impenetrable shadow, and does not "figure" for all intents and purposes. The intelligence behind the cinematic text, like that behind the Biblical creation, can be deduced only from the "traces" or "signature" it leaves behind, i.e., from the author "inside" the text.

It is fully in keeping with the inaccessibility of this originating intelligence that Sarris would stress cinema's visual properties rather than its scriptural ones—its style and *mise-en-scène* rather than its themes or narrative organization. Sarris himself explains this emphasis by pointing out that most Hollywood directors, at least during the studio period, worked on assigned projects, and were consequently obliged to leave their mark on the "look" of a film rather than on its story.[29] However, the end result is once again to privilege the body of the text over the author-as-transcendental-meaning.

Our next theoretical stop is chapter 2 of the 1969 edition of Peter Wollen's *Signs and Meaning in the Cinema*, where authorship is grasped less as the expression of a personality or "elan of the soul" than as a series of oppositions that recur from one film to another by the same director. Wollen provides an extended discussion of what might be called the "authorial system" of John Ford films, a system which pits garden against wilderness, plowshare against saber, settler against nomad, European against Indian, civilization against savagery, marriage against the single state, and East against West.[30] The author "outside" the text nevertheless continues to haunt the margins of this discussion, and he eventually returns to center stage. Wollen is reluctant to attribute complete conscious control to that author, but he does present him as the mental agency responsible for the primary level of cinematic meaning. He dismisses all competing semantic elements as "noise," and likens the assigned script to a substance which makes a chemical reaction possible but is not itself part of that process. The extratextual author thus emerges once again both as origin and as the assurance of a fundamental coherence:

> What the *auteur* theory demonstrates is that the director is not simply in command of a performance of a pre-existing text; he is not, or need not be, only a *metteur en scène*. . . . Incidents and episodes in the original screenplay or novel can act as catalysts; they are the agents which are

introduced into the mind (conscious or unconscious) of the *auteur* and react there with the motifs and themes characteristic of his work. The director does not subordinate himself to another author; his source is only a pretext, which provides catalysts, scenes which fuse with his own preoccupations to produce a radically new work.[31]

The 1972 postscript to *Signs and Meaning in the Cinema* shifts the terms of the analysis in a number of crucial ways. To begin with, it distinguishes firmly between the author "outside" the text and the author "inside" the text ("Fuller or Hawks or Hitchcock, the directors, are quite separate from 'Fuller' or 'Hawks' or 'Hitchcock,' the structures named after them, and should not be methodologically confused").[32] Wollen does not deny a relation between the director and the cinematic structure that manifests itself in the films that bear his name, but he gives theoretical priority to the latter rather than the former; the author "outside" the text thus becomes a kind of projection of the author "inside" the text, rather than the other way around. Moreover, even as a projected figure, the extratextual author has undergone a diminution; whereas the earlier edition of *Signs and Meaning in the Cinema* describes him as the mental receptacle within which the alchemy of artistic production occurs, here he is only a catalyst within a much larger and more heterogeneous process of production. Wollen leaves no room whatever for intention, insisting several times over upon the unconscious status of the authorial contribution:

> The structure is associated with a single director, an individual, not because he has played the role of artist, expressing himself or his own vision in the film, but because it is through the force of his preoccupations that an unconscious, unintended meaning can be decoded in the film, usually to the surprise of the individual involved. The film is not a communication, but an artefact which is unconsciously structured in a certain way. *Auteur* analysis does not consist of re-tracing a film to its origins, to its creative source. It consists of tracing a structure (not a message) within the work, which can then *post factum* be assigned to an individual, the director, on empirical grounds.[33]

The 1972 postscript also reconceives the author "inside" the text. That figure is no longer identified with the primary level of cinematic meaning, nor is every other textual element considered to be "logically secondary, contingent, to be discarded." Instead, his is only one among the many and disparate voices that "speak" the text, voices that are now associated with discourse rather than "noise." With the authorial structure no longer functioning to unify the film in which it appears, the cinematic text also undergoes a theoretical transformation. It is no longer impossible to conceive of having an "integral, genuine experience" of that text, or to grasp it as a stable or essential entity, since it becomes a different "experience" with different readings.[34] The cinematic text is not only destabilized, but dispersed; the centripetal image of a film centered around authorial meaning gives way to the centrifugal image of codes engaged in an endless dialogue with other codes, a dialogue that transgresses textual boundaries. It is probably not necessary to add that Barthes casts a long shadow over the 1972 postscript.

Psychoanalysis also plays a key role in Wollen's redefinition of authorship. Within the later account of authorship, it is not only the director who is unconscious of his contribution to a given film, but the film, as well. Like a dream, the cinematic text proffers a series of more or less plausible and coherent representations, behind which is concealed the author "inside" the text, now conceived as an organizing cluster of desires:

> What the *auteur* theory argues is that any film, certainly a Hollywood film, is a network of different statements, crossing and contradicting each other, elaborated into a final "coherent" version. Like a dream, the film the spectator sees is, so to speak, the "film facade," the end-product of "secondary revision," which hides and masks the process which remains latent in the film's "unconscious." Sometimes this "facade" is so worked over, so smoothed out, or else so clotted with disparate elements, that it is impossible to see beyond it, or rather to see anything in it except the characters, the dialogue, the plot, and so on. But in other cases, by a process of comparison with other films, it is possible to decipher, not a coherent message or world-view, but a structure which underlies the film and shapes it, gives it a certain pattern of energy cathexis.[35]

Although the notion of the film text as the site of contestation between multiple codes has much in common with *S/Z*, Wollen breaks away from Barthes in positing the authorial signature as the latent, and hence ultimate or final, level of cinematic organization (albeit not, as we are cautioned, of meaning). The 1972 postscript also differs from the Barthes of "The Death of the Author" and *The Pleasure of the Text* in the way it defines that signature; here the author resides not in the body of the text, but rather "behind" or "beneath" it.

Although the word *structure* recurs in this passage, it is overshadowed by a more general emphasis upon process, evoked both through the multiple references to the dream-work, and through the identification of authorship with a "pattern of energy cathexis." A dynamic model of authorship thus takes the place of the earlier structuralist model;[36] desire replaces binary opposition as the element that is seen to persist from work to work within any given authorial corpus. The notion of authorship as a "pattern of energy cathexis" also forces a further reconceptualization of the author "outside" the text, and of his relationship to the author "inside" the text; although the former is for all intents and purposes a projection of the former, he is at the same time the point from which desire issues, and so a kind of absent or empty origin.

Stephen Heath's "Comment on the 'Idea of Authorship,' " also published in 1972, marks a dramatic change of direction in the *auteur* debate. That essay shifts theoretical attention not only away from the author as a creative agent or "personality," but away from the author per se. Heath begins by calling into serious doubt the possibility of any "individual" ever functioning as the source of discourse, given the social basis of all language. He then focuses for the remainder of the essay upon two closely related theoretical categories, both of which he sees as inimical to the "idea" of authorship: subjectivity and ideology.

Heath's concern with subjectivity is at least implicitly a concern with the position which the cinematic text constructs for the spectator— with that text's "subject-effects." "Comment on the 'Idea of Author-ship' " thus follows the trajectory traced by Barthes, the trajectory leading away from the author to the one who reads or views the text. Like "The Death of the Author," it also insists upon the mutual ex-clusiveness of those terms. (Heath argues that an investigation of the ways in which subjectivity is constructed cannot be simply added to the *auteur* theory, but will necessarily function to supplant it.) However, there is a crucial difference between Barthes's reader and Heath's sub-ject; whereas the former can be an active producer of textual meaning, the latter is him- or herself produced through textual meaning.

Within Heath's model, ideology takes the place earlier occupied by the author—the place, that is, of origin or impetus. Cinema is seen no longer as the expression of an individual vision, but rather as an "ideological formation." One of the consequences of that ideological formation, Heath explains, is precisely to account for textual meaning through the appeal to individual vision—to promote the belief that the subject gives rise to meaning rather than being spoken through it:

> The function of the author (the effect of the idea of authorship) is a function of unity; the use of the notion of the author involves the organicisation of the film (as "work") and, in so doing, it avoids . . . the thinking of the articulation of the film text in relation to ideology. A theory of the subject represents precisely an attempt, at one level, to grasp the constructions of the subject in ideology (the modes of subject-ivity); it thus allows at once the articulation of contradictions in the film text other than in relation to an englobing consciousness, in relation now, that is, to a specific historico-social process, and the recognition of a heterogeneity of structures, codes, languages at work in the film and of the particular positions of the subject they impose.[37]

What happens to the author "inside" the text as a result of these various displacements? By emphasizing the ideological basis of the antinomies identified by Wollen in his analysis of Hawks's and Ford's films, Heath seems to efface the author "inside" the text as completely as his biological counterpart. However, that author returns on at least one occasion, albeit fleetingly. Within the context of some general remarks about the "history" of the subject, Heath stresses that "the interrogation of a group of films within that history is not the revelation of the author but the tracing in the series of texts of the insistence of the unconscious."[38] This reference to an unconscious tracing evokes Wollen's "pattern of energy cathexis," and so returns us to the notion of the author as a textual figuration. However, this brief acknowledgment that authorship might somehow persist beyond the intervention of Althusser and Lacan, Heath's primary theoretical touchstones, quickly gives way to a catalogue of the problems attending its analysis, and to a restatement of his primary concern with ideology and (spectatorial) subjectivity:

> Such an interrogation meets difficulties similar to those encountered by the attempt to place literary texts in this perspective—absence of analytical situation, associations, transference, etc.—and it seems clear that the work that needs to be done at the moment is the close analysis of the systems of particular texts . . . in relation to the ideological formations they reflect or articulate and the positions in which they inscribe the subject and, overall, to the whole process of subject and sense in the text.[39]

I will attempt to demonstrate later in this chapter that the categories of the author and the subject are by no means as mutually exclusive as this passage would suggest—that the necessary project is in fact somehow to grasp the author precisely as subject.

Although authorship ceased to be a central issue after 1972, the film text has come increasingly to seem a problem of discourse, and so to beg (from its theoretically reconceived vantage point) the question, "Who (or what) is speaking?" Metz's influential essay "History/Discourse: A Note on Two Voyeurisms" (1975/76) argues that since untheorized classic cinema generally works to efface all signs of its own production, to present itself as a story without a teller, the crucial project is to reconstitute that text as an utterance.[40] The distinction between discourse *(discours)* and story *(histoire)* comes, of course, from Benveniste, as do two other categories that were to prove crucial to the reconceptualization of the film text as an utterance—the categories of the speaking subject *(le sujet de l'énonciation)* and the subject of speech *(le sujet de l'énoncé)*.[41]

In Benveniste's writing, the speaking subject refers to the existential person engaged in discourse, and the subject of speech to the discursive marker through which he or she assumes linguistic identity. Benveniste insists upon the interdependence of these two subjects, since it is only through concrete utterance that a speaker enters into subjectivity, and only through its connection to a speaking subject that the subject of speech comes to have signifying value:

> It is in and through language that man constitutes himself as a *subject*, because language alone establishes the concept of "ego" in reality. . . .
> The "subjectivity" we are discussing here is the capacity of the speaker to posit himself as "subject." . . . "Ego" is he who *says* "ego." That is where we see the foundation of "subjectivity," which is determined by the linguistic status of "person."[42]

The signifier through which subjectivity is most conventionally activated in language is of course the first-person pronoun, which can "shift" its meaning from one discursive situation to another.

Needless to say, Benveniste's model has been applied to cinema only with the greatest difficulty. To begin with, all films foreclose upon the site of their own production by simple virtue of the double absence upon which they are based. The system of suture works to occlude the process of enunciation even more radically, at least in dominant cinema, by folding *"histoire"* over *"discours."* It is thus no easy matter to answer the question: "Who (or what) is speaking?" Second, since cinema is not primarily a linguistic medium—since it generally relegates language and the voice to the interior of the diegesis—the concept of "speech" usually has only a metaphoric application; film's status as discourse must consequently be accounted for in some other way than through linguistic utterance. Finally, it is by no means immediately apparent where to look in cinema for the subject of speech. What is the filmic equivalent of the first-person pronoun?

There is surprising unanimity about the kinds of answers that have been given to the first of these questions. Metz, Nowell-Smith, Baudry, Mulvey, Heath, Dayan, and Oudart have all identified cinema's discursive function with the visual axis, converting the question, "Who (or what) is speaking?" into the query, "Who (or what) is looking?"[43] This reformulated query also elicits a surprisingly uniform response—the answer that it is the camera whose look enunciates the film, and which consequently corresponds most closely to Benveniste's speaking subject. (The camera is here a synecdoche for the cinematic apparatus, albeit not an entirely "innocent" one. That it should be installed in a representative position rather than some other branch of the apparatus, such as the technology of sound recording, attests to the privileged position recent theory has given to cinema's visual transactions.)

Most of the theoreticians listed above also insist upon the ideological implications of the camera's look, which frames, delimits, and organizes space according to monocular perspective. The process whereby a fictional gaze stands in for and covers over the camera's gaze is assumed to be an ideological one, too, since it represents discourse as "a story from nowhere, told by nobody [or at least nobody outside the fiction] but received by someone." Films are thus ideologically as well as cinematographically "spoken."

The author is conspicuously absent from this account of film-as-discourse. He is barred from any overt access to the site of enunciation, although he makes the occasional surreptitious return. Metz goes so far as to characterize the spectator's identification with the camera (i.e., primary identification) as an act of "pure" perception, thereby erecting an insuperable barrier between the speaking subject of the film text and any authorial personage, and inflecting the notion of mechanical reproduction with some very Bazinian idealism.[44] (This is, of course, a much more extreme position than that taken by the other theoreticians listed above, since it also excludes ideology from the first level of cinematic reception. In an essay that accompanied the English translation of "History/Discourse: A Note on Two Voyeurisms" in 1976, Geoffrey Nowell-Smith argues against the possibility of anything approximating Metz's innocent perception. However, he does so by pointing to the connection not between the camera's point of view and the authorial point of view, but between the camera's point of view and that of fictional characters: "the so-called secondary identifications . . . tend to break down the pure specularity of the screen/spectator relation in itself and to displace it onto relations which are more properly intra-textual— i.e. relations to the spectator posited from within the image and in the movement from shot to shot.")[45]

It was in keeping with this general theoretical tendency both to exclude the author from the site of cinematic enunciation and to focus new attention upon the construction of the viewing subject, that I at one point conceptualized the subject of speech in a way that now seems to me rather curious. In *The Subject of Semiotics*, I suggested that it "can best be understood as that character or group of characters most central to the fiction—that figure or cluster of figures who occupy a position within the narrative equivalent to that occupied by the first-person pronoun in a sentence."[46] Moreover, I saw this cinematic subject of speech as a discursive marker or "stand-in" for the viewing subject, rather than as a representative of the authorial subject. While I would still maintain that certain fictional characters have the crucial function of representing and thereby structuring the viewer, it now seems important to me to consider the ways in which the Benvenistian model might help us to rethink authorship, as well.

As will be evident to the reader of earlier chapters of the present book, most particularly chapter 1, I have no intention of putting this newly reconceptualized author in the place of the cinematic apparatus. I want merely to suggest that the director may in certain situations constitute *one* of the speakers of his or her films, and that there may at times be pressing political reasons for maximizing rather than minimizing what might be said to derive from this authorial voice. Since one of the things the author must be understood to speak is precisely his or her own authorial subjectivity, the subject of speech will also prove a necessary theoretical category within my reformulation. In this context, it will figure not as the character who marks the viewer's position within the text, but as any representation or network of representations through which the author is constituted as speaking subject.

Is it necessary to add that I do not mean to resuscitate the author laid to rest by Barthes in 1969, or even the author dreamt by Wollen during the same year? That I have in mind an author who would be subordinate to all the discursive constraints emphasized by Benveniste, who would in fact *be nothing* outside cinema—an author "outside" the text who would come into existence as a dreaming, desiring, self-affirming subject only through the inscription of an author "inside" the text, and not one who could ever lay claim to a radical and self-present exteriority, even though he or she might masquerade in such a guise?

Hitchcock has posed a consistent challenge to those theories that seek to dissolve authorship, both because of his cameo appearances in his own films, and because of the sophisticated verbal apparatuses that he has put in place around those films through interviews and publicity statements.[47] It is therefore not surprising that the theory of authorship should have received fresh impetus in the late seventies through a theorist working closely with that director's films—Raymond Bellour. I would like to conclude this brief and highly selective account of the *auteur* debate with a discussion of two of his essays (or, to be more precise, with an essay and an interview, published in *Camera Obscura* in 1977 and 1979), a discussion which will bring us back emphatically to the problem of sexual difference, and which will indicate the necessity of thinking "authorship" and "subjectivity" in close relation to each other.

Bellour asks of Hitchcock's work the by now familiar question: "Who is speaking (or, to be more precise, looking)?" However, he answers the question rather differently than the theoreticians who posed it before him, showing himself quite prepared to entertain the possibility that Hitchcock "himself" might be said to speak *Marnie* or *The Birds*. I have put quotation marks around the third-person pronoun to distinguish Bellour's Hitchcock from the Hitchcock who surfaces in Sarris's writing, or even Mulvey's, because the former has neither self-presence nor existential reality. Bellour's Hitchcock has at best what Geoffrey Nowell-Smith would call a "notional coherence";[48] he is the imaginary intersection of two subjects who are, in fact, irreducibly disjunctive—the speaking subject or "enunciator," and the subject of speech.

As enunciator, Bellour explains, Hitchcock is both the site "from which the set of representations are ordered and organized," and the site "toward which they are channelled back."[49] He puts things in discursive motion, but he derives his authorial status only from a series of masculine representations, which as a group define the subject of his speech. Bellour illustrates this account of Hitchcockian enunciation through *Marnie*, a film which begins with an overtly voyeuristic rear shot of the title character on a train platform, and which then proceeds in shots 2, 21, and 25 to align that image of woman with three quickly successive male looks—Strutt's, Rutland's, and Hitchcock's (in his guise as a character within the fiction). These intratextual looks refer back to Hitchcock the director as their point of origin, but they also function to construct that figure, who has no authorial identity apart from that which they confer upon him. The result is a structure of refractions and reflections which is sustained in the absence of any original:

> By observing Marnie, object of desire, enigma . . . Hitchcock becomes a sort of double of Mark and of Strutt who have just contributed to the creation of his image but who, at the same time, are caught in it. This is possible because they too are nothing but doubles, irregularly distributed on a trajectory at the origin of which there is Hitchcock, the first among all his doubles, a matrix which allows their generation, and his own representation as duplicate image of himself as pure image-power—the camera-wish, of which the object choice is here the woman.[50]

As in the 1972 postscript to *Signs and Meaning in the Cinema*, Bellour's version of the author "outside" the text is thus both a projection of the author "inside" the text and the point from which desire flows. He is the anthropomorphization of a site which is simultaneously "productive" and "empty."

Bellour conceives of the author as both a gendered and a discursive subject—as someone who cannot speak outside sexual difference, or aspire to identity outside image or word. The name "Hitchcock" would consequently seem to designate not so much a biographical person as a symbolic position—the position occupied by the exemplary male subject, and sustained through phallic identification, the circulation of women, and what might be called "group disavowal." This phallic identification is discursively articulated in *Marnie* through the alignment of Hitchcock's look both with the camera, a synecdoche for the cinematic apparatus, and with a series of more or less idealized fictional male looks (those of Strutt, Rutland, and Hitchcock-as-fictional-character). The agency of that identification is the image of Marnie, which is passed from the camera to Strutt, from Strutt to Rutland, and from Rutland to Hitchcock-as-fictional-character during the opening three scenes of the film. Ironically, it is only through this radically dispersed and decentered *"hom(m)osexual"* economy that Hitchcock-as-director comes to be installed as the point of apparent textual origin, and as the seemingly punctual source of meaning.

Under pressure from Janet Bergstrom, Bellour has acknowledged his own implication in this economy ("It was as the subject whose desire is the prisoner of this machinery that I tried to demonstrate its functioning").[51] He goes on in the same interview to suggest in the strongest possible terms that reading a film is as complexly bound up with gender as is authorship, and that the very "systematicity" which preoccupies his own analysis represents an insurmountable barrier to any analysis which might seek to find a female voice or point of view because it represents the overdetermined expression of male desire and the male gaze:

> The classical American cinema is founded in a systematicity which operates very precisely at the expense of the woman . . . by determining her image, her images, in relation to the desire of the masculine subject who thus defines himself through this determination. Which means that the woman too finds herself involved, for herself, in relation to desire and the law, but in a perspective which always collapses the representation of the two sexes into the dominant logic of a single one. If women want to and are able to do analyses of these films and find representations between the sexes which will satisfy them, by all means let them do so: I would be very eager to see the results, even though I can't help feeling a bit skeptical.[52]

It is good of Bellour to admit women into the inner circles of segmentation, although he seems perhaps too insistent upon the impossibility of performing a transgressively feminist reading of Hollywood cinema, dwelling with undue relish upon the obstacles that would confront any such project (the "indifference" of Hollywood cinema, the female theorist's desires, her abilities, her unpleasure at the results, his own skepticism). Nevertheless, he is correct in assuming that the authorial system of most Hollywood films forecloses upon the female voice. If we were to ask, with Foucault, "Where does [this discourse] come from; how is it circulated; who controls it?" or more precisely, "Who can fulfil these diverse functions of the subject?" the answer would resoundingly be: "The male subject."[53]

Not surprisingly, in light of this answer, feminist film theory and criticism have manifested only an intermittent and fleeting interest in the status of authorship within the classic text. One of the earliest essays to approach authorship through a critique of sexual difference was, of course, Laura Mulvey's "Visual Pleasure and Narrative Cinema" (1975). Although the first half of that essay focuses on spectatorship, its second half uses the notion of the author as a mechanism for distinguishing between two very different specular regimes, regimes which exceed the "intratextual" relations of which Nowell-Smith speaks, and which it associates with Sternberg and Hitchcock. Mulvey argues that there are moments in Sternberg's films when no fictional gaze mediates the spectator's access to Dietrich's image, and where the construction of that image as a fetish cannot be explained through an ideological spillage from the look of a character onto the look of the camera, implying instead an authorial eye behind the visual apparatus:

> Sternberg plays down the illusion of screen depth; his screen tends to be one-dimensional, as light and shade, lace, steam, foliage, net, streamers, etc., reduce the visual field. There is little or no mediation through the eyes of the main protagonist. On the contrary, shadowy presences like La Bessière in *Morocco* act as surrogates for the director, detached as they are from audience identification.[54]

Mulvey also positions Hitchcock as the speaking subject of his films, attributing their voyeurism to the intensity of their author's obsessions, noting that "Hitchcock has never concealed his interest in voyeurism, cinematic and non-cinematic" (p. 15).

In an even earlier essay, "Women's Cinema as Counter-Cinema" (1973), Claire Johnston emphasizes the importance of the *auteur* theory for feminism, suggesting that its polemics have "challenged the entrenched view of Hollywood as monolithic," and have made it possible to see that the "image of woman" does not assume the same status in all films made within that system of production.[55] Johnston also poses the possibility of female authorship within classic cinema by juxtaposing the names of Dorothy Arzner and Ida Lupino with the ubiquitous Howard Hawkes and John Ford.

In a monograph published in 1975, Johnston elaborates more fully upon the notion that Arzner's films bear the marks of female authorship. However, although she argues that what she calls "the discourse of the woman" provides Arzner's work with its "structural coherence," she is far from attributing to that discourse the systematicity which figures so centrally within Bellour's account of male authorship, or even the binary logic which Wollen identifies with the films of certain male *auteurs*. Johnston suggests that the female authorial voice makes itself heard only through disruptions and dislocations within the textual economy of classic cinema—i.e., *through breaks within its systematicity and binary logic*. Significantly, Johnston suggests that these disruptions and dislocations may occur at the level of the *histoire*, as well as at that of the *discours*.

> In Arzner's work, the discourse of the woman, or rather her attempt to locate it and make it heard, is what gives the text its structural coherence, while at the same time rendering the dominant discourse of the male fragmented and incoherent. The central female protagonists react against and thus transgress the male discourse which entraps them.[56]

Sandy Flitterman has also suggested that feminist theory would do well to rethink authorship within the Hollywood text, which she conceptualizes in terms of discourse. In "Woman, Desire, and the Look: Feminism and the Enunciative Apparatus in Cinema" (1978), she stresses the importance of Bellour's work on enunciation in *Marnie*, and argues that any foregrounding of authorship within the classic text functions at least momentarily to subvert "the subject-effect that the apparatus is designed to produce and to conceal" by both raising and answering the question: "Who is speaking?"[57]

However, one looks in vain to the feminist work published in *Camera Obscura* for a further elaboration of this point. Although that work is heavily indebted to Metz's and Bellour's notion of film-as-discourse, it largely occludes the role of the author within dominant narrative cinema. One of the most striking examples of this occlusion is Jacqueline Suter's "Feminine Discourse in *Christopher Strong*." Published in the same issue of *Camera Obscura* as "Alternation, Segmentation, Hypnosis," that essay is in many respects a direct extension of Bellour's work on Hollywood cinema.[58] There is, however, one crucial difference: Suter makes absolutely no room in her discussion for the authorial subject. Indeed, the name "Dorothy Arzner" is mentioned only once, along with the date of *Christopher Strong*. This is surprising, and not only because it marks a point of departure from the Bellourian model. Arzner was, after all, one of only two women to direct sound films in Hollywood during the studio period, a fact that would seem of some relevance to a feminist analysis of one of her films—especially when the stated aim of that analysis is to uncover a feminine discourse. However, instead of looking for ways in which Arzner might be said to "speak" *Christopher Strong* differently from the ways in which Hitchcock "speaks" *Marnie*, Suter focuses on two distinct and seemingly anonymous levels of the text—on what she calls the "patriarchal discourse," and on what she calls the "feminine discourse."

Because of the way she conceptualizes each of these discourses, Suter's feminist reading would have to be characterized as dystopian. In effect, she associates the "patriarchal discourse" with the film's formal and narrative articulation, and its "feminine discourse" with the voices and transgressive desires of two of its female characters, Cynthia and Monica. Because Suter assumes enunciation to be absolutely coterminous with that formal and narrative articulation, the "patriarchal discourse" emerges as a metalanguage, capable of neutralizing any disruptions at the level of character or narrative, while the "feminine discourse" is consigned in a completely unproblematical way to the inside of the diegesis. Suter at no point broaches the possibility that the latter discourse might also provide mechanisms through which an author "outside" the text could "speak" her subjectivity—the possibility, that is, that authorship might be inscribed not merely through the camera, or such an obviously reflexive diegetic indicator as the look, but through those forms of identification and textual organization which are generally assumed to be "secondary," and which hinge upon a variety of characterological and narrative devices. Her theoretical model thus closely replicates the Hollywood model, which identifies the male voice with enunciative exteriority, and the female voice with diegetic interiority.

Suter's textual analysis is extremely persuasive, and it is difficult to argue with the conclusions she draws from it. However, the presupposition that *Christopher Strong* is enunciated like any other classic Hollywood film—i.e., from an exclusively male speaking position—guides and coerces her reading. The very different reading of Arzner's work proposed by Claire Johnston is clearly made possible by the assumption that an emphatically female authorial voice at least to some degree speaks Arzner's films, and that there can never be an absolutely smooth fit between such a voice and the dominant Hollywood model. This may very well be a situation where the cinematic apparatus in its complex totality speaks the film one way, in terms of the systematicity and binary logic that Suter notes, dominating and determining what has been widely taken to be the enunciative level, but where authorial desire seeks out another kind of language, finds a way of expressing itself through diegetic elements. The debate around *Christopher Strong* may also provide the occasion to rethink the absolute priority that recent film theory has given to cinematic specificity, particularly camera distance, angle, and movement and shot-to-shot relationships, and to consider whether there may not be enunciative elements elsewhere, as well—enunciative elements which can best be uncovered through returning to the issue of authorship, and by reposing the question: "Who (or what) is speaking?" To assume, as Suter seems to do, that the cinematic apparatus is the only conceivable "speaker" of a Hollywood film is to risk sealing over all kinds of localized resistance, which—as Foucault tells us—may well be the only form resistance can possibly take.[59]

Not surprisingly, this tendency to think of dominant cinema in monolithically phallic terms leads Suter to reject that cinema altogether:

> Undoubtedly, the fact that we can locate certain formal transgressions in a film advances our knowledge of what might constitute a feminine discourse. But we should be aware that isolated interruptions do not necessarily deconstruct the narrative discourse in any significant way. It seems that a systematic rethinking of the entire terms of narrative logic, a reformulation of its elements into an order different from what has come to be known as the classic text, may allow the feminine to express itself more forcefully.[60]

What Suter proposes in place of *Christopher Strong* is *Jeanne Dielman, 23 Quai du Commerce, 1080 Bruxelles* (1975), a film whose formal as well as thematic operations deviate markedly from the classic paradigm. Significantly, the turn to experimental cinema marks the reemergence of the author. Chantal Akerman figures conspicuously in this part of Suter's analysis, both as the director of *Jeanne Dielman* and as its enunciator ("Akerman, in showing a woman's daily routine in all its banality, breaks with convention because these images do not necessarily function to advance the narrative. . . . Akerman says that she found a plot *because* she wanted to show certain gestures in women's lives that are customarily left out of films").[61]

I have dwelt at such length upon Suter's extremely interesting essay for several reasons. To begin with, it gives new force to Bellour's suggestion that the "systematicity" of classic cinema "operates very precisely at the expense of woman"—in this case, of the woman director. It may well be impossible to locate a female authorial voice within a Hollywood film by means of the strategies Bellour has devised for locating the male authorial voice. No film, after all, is entirely "spoken" by its ostensible author, and in the case of dominant cinema, there are an enormous number of other productive elements, not the least of which is a whole textual system which often persists intransigently from one directorial corpus to another. Only a director "speaking" from a position as smoothly aligned with the cinematic apparatus as Hitchcock—i.e., from a position of phallic dominance—would be able to identify his own "vision" so fully with the textual system of Hollywood that the latter can seem the extension of the former. Other authorial subjects might well find themselves speaking against the weight of the textual system through which their films are largely articulated. What I am trying to suggest is that if authorial enunciation within the classic film text continues to be as insistently equated with that text's macrologic as it is within Bellourian segmentation, the theorist may quite simply be unable to "hear" authorial voices that speak against the operations of dominant meaning, since those voices are much likelier to manifest themselves through isolated formal and diegetic irregularities than through formal systematicity.

A second reason why I have so conspicuously featured the Suter essay is that it dramatizes certain tendencies that are indicative of much recent writing on cinema by women. To the degree that feminist theory and criticism of the late seventies and the eighties have concerned themselves centrally with authorship, they have shifted attention away from the classic text to experimental cinema, and specifically to experimental cinema made by women. The author often emerges within the context of these discussions as a largely untheorized category, placed definitively "outside" the text, and assumed to be the punctual source of its sounds and images. A certain nostalgia for an unproblematic agency permeates much of the writing to which I refer. There is no sense in which the feminist author, like her phallic counterpart, might be constructed in and through discourse—that she might be inseparable from the desire that circulates within her texts, investing itself not only in their formal articulation, but in recurring diegetic elements.

A brief essay by Janet Bergstrom on *Jeanne Dielman* is a case in point.[62] Bergstrom contends that there are two discourses in Akerman's film—one feminist, and the other deriving from a suppressed or "acculturated" femininity. The first of these discourses is that "spoken" by the director herself through the "permissive" look of the camera, and the second is that associated with the character of Jeanne Dielman. Bergstrom argues that in eschewing the logic of the shot/reverse shot, the film works both to foreground the feminist discourse and to keep it separate from the feminine discourse. There would thus seem to be no possibility of "contamination" or slippage from one side to the other. Bergstrom further isolates the author from her central female character by referring to her in quick succession as a "marked controller" and a "controlling eye."[63]

I am not nearly as certain as Bergstrom that Jeanne Dielman manages to distinguish so sharply between feminism and femininity, or that the author "outside" the text occupies the position of a transcendental seer, resting in easy detachment from the woman whose gestures are so meticulously recorded. To do Bergstrom justice, her own language ultimately works to erode the absoluteness of the division she draws, and to suggest that the feminist author is at least partially defined through her female protagonist. She characterizes the relationship between Akerman's stationary camera and Jeanne Dielman as "obsessive" and "fascinated,"[64] adjectives which point to a certain psychic spillage between author and character. That spillage indicates that the ostensible object of speech is in this case also the subject of speech, and as such at least partly constitutive of the author-as-speaking-subject, even though the camera never adopts Jeanne Dielman's point of view.

As with most critiques, there is a barely concealed polemic here. I have been arguing over the last few pages for two rather contrary things—for a greater theoretical attentiveness to the ways in which authorship is both deployed and limited within the experimental text, and for the development of hermeneutic strategies capable of foregrounding rather than neutralizing female authorship within the classic film, where it is in danger of being occluded altogether. Of course, the obvious problem with respect to the second of these goals is that so few Hollywood films carry a female directorial signature. How is the feminist writer to proceed?

One possible solution to this difficulty is suggested by Tania Modleski in a chapter of her book *The Women Who Knew Too Much*. The chapter in question, "Woman and the Labyrinth," focuses on the relationship between Hitchcock's *Rebecca* (1940) and the Daphne du Maurier novel on which it was based. Modleski comments upon Hitchcock's reluctance to claim that film, which was assigned to him by Selznick, as his own, and some of the subsequently deleted scenes in the script through which he attempted to "vomit out" a "whole school of feminine literature."[65] What emerges from this discussion is a sense of the way in which even a classic film might be riven by conflicting authorial systems, in this case one "male" and the other "female." But Modleski pushes her analysis even further than this, arguing that through his forced identification with du Maurier, Hitchcock found one of the great subjects of his later films—the "potential terror involved in identification itself, especially identification with a woman." This observation has important ramifications for our understanding of Hitchcock's status as *auteur*, indicating that his own authorial system may be far more heterogeneous and divided than Bellour can ever have imagined, and that it may, in fact, contain a female voice as one of its constituent although generally submerged elements.

Modleski bases her case not only on Truffaut's interview with Hitchcock, and the exchanges around the making of *Rebecca* that took place between Selznick and Hitchcock, but on the narrative organization of the film itself, which she persuasively shows to hinge upon the whole problematic of identification with the mother. The telling detail which brings this problematic definitively around again to the question of authorship is the fact that the character who most fully represents the mother—Rebecca—figures insistently throughout the film as an "absent one" whose signature dominates the image track, but who herself escapes visibility. As such, it seems to me, she functions as a strikingly literal diegetic surrogate for the speaking subject, and hence very precisely as the subject of speech. What I am suggesting, in other words, is that Rebecca stands in for Hitchcock, in much the same way that Mark Rutland does in *Marnie*, and that in so doing she re-en-genders his authorial subjectivity.

Another strategy, deployed with very interesting results by Lea Jacobs in an article on *Now, Voyager*, is to shift the emphasis so sharply away from systematicity and textual macro-logic to disruption and contradiction as in effect to *reauthor* the classic film from the site of its (feminist) reception. This project has much in common with that Barthesian undertaking whereby the "readerly" text yields to the *writerly* one, in that it shifts productivity away from the ostensible author to the side of the reader, and places itself on the side of heterogeneity and contradiction rather than unity. However, rather than working to disclose the chorus of cultural voices within the text, it strives to install the female voice at the site of a very qualified and provisional origin (and one which, I would argue, is once again defined through the subject of speech)—the voice, that is, of the female critic or theorist.

I speak of this project as though it were an overt and conscious one, but Jacob's reauthorship of Rapper's film can be glimpsed only indirectly, through the interpretive process whereby Charlotte is shown to supplant Dr. Jacquith as the speaker of her "own" subjectivity. Her discussion focuses attention on that sequence in *Now, Voyager* where Charlotte looks at her image in the café window as the camera cuts back and forth between her and the reflected spectacle. This sequence, Jacobs argues, becomes the occasion whereby the female protagonist "takes the enunciating position with respect to herself through an identification with a man," and so becomes "a self-sufficient sexual and discursive configuration"—something which is seen as disturbing both to the shot-to-shot organization of the films, and to the constitution of the couple which is the form of narrative closure.[66] "*Now, Voyager:* Some Problems of Enunciation and Sexual Difference" mimics this disturbance even as it in a sense creates it. Jacobs, in other words, enacts a discursive resistance to dominant cinema precisely through the resistance which she constitutes Charlotte as having. Charlotte thus functions not just as an enunciator within the diegesis, but as the subject of the speech whereby Jacobs rewrites *Now, Voyager,* and hence as a stand-in for the feminist theorist.

In a few pages, I will attempt to establish the textual status of a female author whose preoccupations are neither classically "feminine" nor overtly feminist, and whose work is perhaps as anomalous in relation to dominant cinema as it is with respect to a whole range of experimental practices, or even to what generally passes as the European art film[67]—Liliana Cavani. It is my hope that authorship not only will prove a way into her cinema, which has proved quite resistant to other theoretical and critical paradigms, and has consequently been largely neglected, but will maximize its considerable oppositional value, as well. First, however, I would like to consider some of the guises that can be assumed by the author "inside" the text.

Authorial subjectivity is inscribed into the cinematic text in two primary ways. The first kind of authorial inscription can best be described through a further elaboration of the Benvenistian model, with its distinction between the speaking subject and the subject of speech, but since it hinges upon a psychic mechanism about which linguistics has little to say—the psychic mechanism of identification—it will be necessary to supplement that model with psychoanalysis. The second kind of authorial inscription assumes a rather more dynamic and less easily localized form; it is the libidinal coherence that the films by a particular director can sometimes be said to have—the desire that circulates there, more or less perceptibly.

Insofar as a filmmaker can be said to function as one of the enunciators of the works that bear his or her name, those works will contain certain sounds, images, characterological motifs, narrative patterns, and/or formal configurations which provide the cinematic equivalent of the linguistic markers through which subjectivity is activated. However, the linguistic model is insufficient to account for the relationship which is thereby set up between the author "inside" the text and the author "outside" the text. Let us look, by way of example, at the most obvious of authorial references.

A director may turn the camera on his or her face, or the tape recorder on his or her voice, and incorporate the results into a film in the guise of a visual representation, a voice-over, a voice-off, or a synchronized sound and image "totality." Such an authorial citation would seem the closest of cinematic equivalents to the first-person pronoun. However, it also differs from that shifter in one crucial way: whereas the relation between "I" and the speaker who deploys that signifier is based upon arbitrary convention, the relation between the cinematic image of a filmmaker and the actual filmmaker is based upon similitude; it is an iconic representation, and therefore more easily confused with what it designates.

Of course, this is not to suggest that the image is an ontological extension of the material reality it mimics. This is so far from being the case that it actually facilitates something which is in no way intrinsic to the "original"—authorial subjectivity. Indeed, so far from being a mere reflection of the author "outside" the text, it could reasonably be said to constitute him or her as such, in much the same way that the mirror reflection (retroactively) installs identity in the same child.

It is by now a truism of film theory that movies construct viewing subjects through identification. It seems to me that authorial subjects can be similarly constructed, albeit through a wider variety of textual supports than have been so far adduced for their spectatorial counterparts. Identity is, after all, impossible not only outside the symbolic, but outside the imaginary. Even an image which seems self-evidently part of the individual it depicts—which seems nothing more than his or her reflection or photographic imprint—can be claimed by that individual only through identification. And identification, as the writer of the *Ecrits* cautions us, inevitably turns upon misrecognition.

Through its intimate conflation of the author "inside" the text with the author "outside" the text, this kind of directorial "appearance" often works to promote a second, much less inevitable misrecognition. It is the frequent site, that is, of a narcissistic idealization, through which the filmmaker speaks him- or herself as the point of absolute textual origin. Such is the case in *Marnie*, where Hitchcock not only makes his usual appearance on the image track, but turns to look boldly at the camera and the theater audience, as someone clearly in control of both.

Conversely, an authorial citation of this sort may also become the vehicle for an authorial diminution, a device for representing a film's director as a subject speaking from within history, ideology, and a particular social formation, as it is in *Far from Vietnam* (1967), where Godard turns the camera on himself, rather than "going" to Southeast Asia. As important an authorial critique as this film provides, though, it never really qualifies the filmmaker's ostensible responsibility for its sounds and images, calls his masculinity into question, or suggests that his identity as a speaking subject is radically dependent upon the ways in which it is textually constituted. Although it lacks the reflexive complexity of either *Marnie* or *Far from Vietnam,* Chantal Akerman's voice-over in *News from Home* (1975) deprivileges the authorial voice much more profoundly by rendering it feminine, personal, and informal, and by stripping it of all transcendental pretense.

However, I can think of only one film—the Fassbinder section of *Germany in Autumn* (1978)—in which an authorial "appearance" works not to subordinate the camera and voice-recording apparatuses to the filmmaker, but to subordinate *him* to *them.* It does so by placing at absolute center stage the irrecuperable figure of a director who is not just suffering, desiring, politically conflicted, unjust, and domineering, but a culturally, historically, and *textually* bound subject—by showing that his authorial subjectivity is kept in place only through a compulsive and frenetic productivity. *Germany in Autumn* also hystericizes the body of its author through a veritable theater of grotesque corporeality. This last dimension of the film is as exemplary as the other, since its insistence upon Fassbinder's sagging flesh, putrid breath, and drug and alcohol dependency locates him firmly on the side of a graceless but "readable" spectacle, making it impossible ever again to conflate him with a phallic exteriority. It thus openly declares the author "outside" the text to be nothing more than an effect of discourse.

So far I have focused only on representations which so closely approximate the visual or sonorous features of the filmmaker as to be easily conflated with him or her—with representations which promote the kind of mirror recognition that Lacan associates with "primary narcissism." However, authorial subjectivity can also be brought into play through what both Lacan and Metz would call "secondary identification"—i.e., through identification with an anthropomorphic representation which is not, strictly speaking, his or her "own," but that of an other who also happens in this case to be a fictional character. This kind of psychic alignment is brilliantly dramatized in *Scénario du Passion* (1982), where Godard once again turns the (video) camera on himself as he sits in an editing suite taking apart and recombining sounds and images from the film to which the title refers. At a key moment in the tape, he reaches out to the image of Jerzy, the character of the Polish expatriate filmmaker who is clearly a stand-in for Godard-as-director, and locks him in a narcissistic embrace. With that extraordinary gesture, the author who is sitting outside the text of *Passion* looking in is shown to derive all his subjective sustenance from a character who is firmly inside.

A director's relationship with the fictional character who "stands in" for him or her textually may be predicated, as it is not only within *Marnie* but within many classic films, upon a kind of replication at the level of the fiction of those functions generally attributed to the cinematic apparatus—authoritative vision, hearing, and speech. Secondary identification can thus provide another vehicle leading to imaginary mastery and transcendence. Provided, at least, that the character who sustains this ambition is male, such an identification is completely compatible with dominant cinema. However, a filmmaker's secondary identifications may also depart from that paradigm altogether, and put in place a very different kind of authorial subjectivity—one which, for instance, is much more openly endangered and at risk. I think in this respect of Ulrike Ottinger's fascination with freaks of all sorts, or Marguerite Duras's investment in the figure of the exile. I will have much more to say about "deviant" kinds of secondary identification when I come to Cavani, whose authorial subjectivity relies heavily upon her imaginary relation to her male characters.

Finally, the author "outside" the text may find the mirror for which he or she is looking in the "body" of the text—in the way in which his or her films choreograph movement; compose objects within the frame; craft, disrupt, or multiply narrative; experiment with sound; create "atmosphere"; articulate light and shadow; encourage or inhibit identification; use actors; or work with color. The kind of identification I am talking about here is the narcissistic correlative of that "recognition" which permits a reasonably literate moviegoer to say after looking at several shots of *The Red and the White* that "it's Jancso," or after viewing three or four minutes of a Peter Greenaway film that "it's Greenaway." Although the authorial citation is in this case a formal or narrative "image," it is not any the less complexly imbricated with gender, ideology, or history.

Although directors such as Welles, Fassbinder, and Duras speak themselves through their films in virtually all of the ways in which it is possible to do so, other filmmakers may leave their signature only at random points within the diegesis. It would be a mistake to assume that there is no author "inside" a particular corpus of films simply because they have no distinguishing formal trademark. There is little or nothing about the formal operations of either Arzner's or Cavani's work to distinguish it from other contemporaneous and culturally homogeneous work—little or nothing, indeed, to indicate a particular preoccupation on the part of either director with what generally passes for the level of enunciation. However, even at the level of the fiction, there can be all kinds of authorial spoors.

Of course, tracking these spoors is no simple matter. A reasonably experienced viewer can readily understand a heavy reliance on primary colors, collage techniques, and intertextuality to be devices with which Godard identifies, and even a naive viewer would immediately understand his "appearance" in *Far from Vietnam* or *Scénario du Passion* to be an authorial trace. However, a filmmaker's imaginary relation to a given character is often much less evident, particularly so long as it is theoretically isolated from the closely related issue of desire. The moment has arrived when I must not only turn to the second of my authorial categories, but abandon the pretense that it can be so clearly separated from the first. Identification and desire are complexly imbricated with each other—so much so that it is often possible to uncover the former through the latter.

But what would the theorist be looking for if she wanted to find what gives a particular group of films their libidinal coherence? She would be searching not just for the author "inside" the text, but for the text "inside" the author—for the scenario for passion, or, to be more precise, the "scene" of authorial desire. The "scene" to which I refer is what Laplanche and Pontalis, in an inspired passage from *The Language of Psycho-analysis,* call the "fantasmatic," and which they define as that unconscious fantasy or cluster of fantasies which structures not merely dreams and other related psychic formations, but object-choice, identity, and "the subject's life as a whole."[68] The fantasmatic generates erotic tableaux or *combinatoires* in which the subject is arrestingly positioned—whose function is, in fact, precisely to display the subject in a given place. Its original cast of characters would seem to be drawn from the familial reserve, but in the endless secondary productions to which the fantasmatic gives rise, all actors but one are frequently recast. And even that one constant player may assume different roles on different occasions.

Freud has given us some idea of the kinds of fantasies that most frequently come to organize psychic life in this way. Not surprisingly, although he attempts to ground most of them in phylogenesis, all of his examples clearly derive from the Oedipus complex. The list is not, at first glance, very extensive; it includes only the fantasy of the primal scene, the fantasy of seduction, the fantasy of castration, and the fantasy of being beaten.[69] However, this list becomes extremely rich and varied once we have grasped the possible permutations of each fantasy—once all the instinctual vicissitudes have been factored in, the negative as well as the positive Oedipus complex has been taken into account,[70] and theoretical allowance has been made for the fantasizing subject to occupy more than one position in the imaginary tableau. Freud explores the multiple forms which the beating fantasy is capable of assuming for both the male and the female subject in "A Child is Being Beaten," but we have barely begun to calibrate the textual range of any of the others.[71] And, of course, there may well be other fantasmatics than those to which Freud draws our attention.

Insofar as authorial desire manages to invade a particular corpus, it will be organized around some such structuring "scene" or group of "scenes." It seems to me, for instance, that Fassbinder's cinema revolves around the beating fantasy, and that much of Bertolucci's work is libidinally motived by the male fantasy of maternal seduction. However, these generalizations indicate very little about the actual workings of desire in either body of work, since there are so many ways in which these two fantasies can be elaborated, each with its own consequences not only for object-cathexis, but for identity.

It is at this last juncture that my earlier distinction between authorial identification and authorial desire most completely collapses, since an author's identification with a fictional character will be determined by the subject-position the latter occupies not only within the narrative, but within the fantasmatic "scene" which that narrative traces in some oblique and indirect way. This means that authorial identification and authorial desire are indeed mutually referential—that an investigation of one will sooner or later open on to the other.

Since the subject-position which the author occupies within the cinematic *"mise-en-scène* of desire"[72] may well transgress the biological gender of the author "outside" the text, the question of whether the latter speaks with a "male" or a "female" voice can be answered only through an interrogation of the sort I have been urging. At the same time, this libidinal masculinity or femininity must be read in relation to the biological gender of the biographical author, since it is clearly not the same thing, socially or politically, for a woman to speak with a female voice as it is for a man to do so, and vice versa. All sorts of cultural imperatives dictate a smooth match between biological gender and subject-position, making any deviation a site of potential resistance to sexual difference. As stage 3 of the female version of the beating fantasy would indicate, where the subject sees herself as a group of boys being treated as if they were girls (i.e., occupying an erotically passive position in relation to the father),[73] biological gender can also figure in complex ways within the fantasmatic "scene."

Although this might seem the end point for an investigation of authorial desire, it is in many ways only the beginning. Laplanche and Pontalis make the crucial point that the fantasmatic is "constantly drawing in new material" (p. 317), thereby indicating that it is far from closed—that, on the contrary, it is always absorbing the world outside. I would go even farther, and argue that it is being continually drawn into new social and political alignments, which may even lead to important "scenic" changes. It is thus important to ask of any authorial desire: How has it assimilated history? And how might it be seen to have acted upon history?

One possible point of entry into the libidinal economy that helps to organize an authorial corpus would be through its nodal points. A nodal point might take the form of a sound, image, scene, place, or action to which that work repeatedly returns, such as Parma and its environs within the films of Bertolucci, dancing within the films of Yvonne Rainer or Sally Potter, or undressing within the films of Cavani. It might also assume the guise of a sound, image, scene, or sequence which is marked through some kind of formal "excess," indicating a psychic condition such as rapture (the revolving door shot with which Leandro Katz's *Splits* concludes),[74] fixation (the frequent close-ups of Terence Stamp's crotch in Pasolini's *Theorem*), or intoxication (the vertiginous play of camera, set, and back projection during the final kiss in Hitchcock's *Vertigo*).

The authorial fantasmatic can also be tracked at the level of the story, at least within those films where story can be said to play even a vestigial role. Like Teresa de Lauretis, I believe that there is always desire "in" narrative,[75] and that in certain cinematic instances that desire can reasonably be attributed to the author "outside" the text. (There is also narrative in desire, or, to put it slightly differently, a fundamentally narrative bent to desire, which is so fully sustained by retrospection and anticipation.) Sometimes the fantasmatic "scene" is sketched by the larger narrative trajectory which is repeatedly mapped by films with the same authorial signature. At other times, as in Duras's *India Song*, or in the films of Mark Rappaport, the fantasmatic "scene" may give rise to an insistently scenic narrative structure.

We have seen that in a film such as *Marnie*, which is in many ways emblematic of classic cinema, authorial subjectivity is constructed through an identification with mastering vision, and with those male characters who might be said to embody that vision. Cavani's films enact a very different narcissistic drama, and one which is uncannily similar to that staged in the opening paragraph of Barthes's "The Death of the Author." Authorial subjectivity is delineated through a series of young men who renounce power and privilege—who sever their relation to the phallus.

Authorial desire, as I have already indicated, is always closely bound up with authorial subjectivity, but in Cavani's films the two are almost impossible to separate. There is no object as such, to be yearned for or to be possessed; there are only models to imitate, replicate, or incorporate, or intersubjective "spaces" to be shared. This is a cinema of "being," not of "having." In attempting to summarize Cavani's authorial desire, I am thus obliged to repeat what I have already said about her authorial subjectivity: That desire finds expression through the repeated narrative figuration of phallic divestiture—through the fantasmatic "scene" of male castration. But before embarking upon a discussion of this strangely narcissistic desire, I want to confront the difficulties which I imagine most feminist viewers would have with the films within which it is inscribed.

Cavani has to date made nine features,[76] yet not one of them overtly addresses the topic of sexual oppression, or charts any of the usual avenues of reaction against or resistance to that oppression. Nor can any of her films be said to be "about" women in any of the ways that *Riddles of the Sphinx*, Ulrike Ottinger's *Madam X*, or Sally Potter's *The Gold Diggers* might be said to be. This apparent inattentiveness to sexual difference seems all the more perverse given the sorts of female characters who inhabit Cavani's films (Antigone in *The Cannibals*, Lou-Andreas Salome in *Beyond Good and Evil*, a female concentration camp inmate in *The Night Porter*, a Japanese/German lesbian couple in *The Berlin Affair*)—characters who virtually invite feminist analysis.[77]

Moreover, instead of moving her female characters beyond masochism, Cavani demonstrates the fatal lure of that position for her *male* characters. *Francesco d'Assisi, Milarepa*, Antigone's male comrade in *The Cannibals*, Max in *The Night Porter*, and Paul Ree in *Beyond Good and Evil* all occupy subject-positions which are more classically "feminine" than "masculine"—subject-positions demanding of them passivity, suffering, and renunciation. Since the interiority of these characters is often objectified in domestic settings and rituals, and since it is privileged over action, they also seem to have appropriated the cinematic space traditionally reserved for the female subject.[78]

Cavani's cinema proves politically intractable in other respects, as well. While never for a moment relaxing her critique of the existing symbolic order, she generally makes men rather than women the vehicle of that critique. Francesco, Galileo, Milarepa, Nietzsche, and the male novelist in *The Guest* are all discursively at odds with the culture in which they find themselves, and thus function to varying degrees as spokesmen for change. Figures such as Lou-Andreas Salome or the female patient in *The Guest,* on the other hand, seem absorbed in much more private forms of resistance (indeed, Antigone in *The Cannibals* is the only one of Cavani's women who could be said to be "politically engaged").

Men enjoy a privileged place in Cavani's extracinematic discourse, as well. She invariably talks about her films in terms of their central male actors (Lou Castel, Pierre Clementi, Lajos Belazsovits, Dirk Bogarde), actors who she insists "become" the parts they play (thus she is fond of asserting that the character of Max in *The Night Porter* "stole" Bogarde's "soul," and that Castel identified with the figure of Francesco so completely that he also gave away all his possessions).[79] These condensations point to Cavani's intense investment in the subject-positions occupied by certain of her male characters, as does another of the recurrent tropes in her extracinematic discourse—her remarkable claim that "each of my [male]actors looks a bit like me," a claim which points with startling clarity to the imaginary relation at the heart of that investment.[80]

However, it is a striking fact that the male characters who dominate Cavani's films retreat from power rather than accede to it; that they entertain a highly problematic relation to discourse; and that they interact with women in ways which defy the usual heterosexual conventions. Indeed, these figures exist on the margins or at the limits of their culture. Francesco gives away his large patrimony and embraces a life of poverty, humility, and (increasingly over the course of the film that bears his name) silence. Milarepa abandons the power-knowledge which he has mastered, and by means of which he has destroyed an entire village, for a discursive apprenticeship that demands of him the utmost self-abnegation. Galileo aligns himself with a discourse which is completely disruptive of the symbolic order within which he resides, while the Pierre Clementi figure in *The Cannibals* speaks a language which no one else knows, and which involves tokens rather than linguistic signs. The male protagonist of *The Night Porter* not only declines to have his crimes erased, and his lost privileges restored to him, but abandons the present, language, and eventually life itself.[81] Finally, one of the male characters in *Beyond Good and Evil*—Paul Ree—chooses to occupy a female subject-position, while the other—Nietzsche—lapses into madness. These figures are thus in some peculiar way simultaneously "male" and "not-male." What desire finds expression through this constant return to and preoccupation with male subjectivity? And what dream is fulfilled through the stipulation that this subjectivity be impaired in some radical way—that it be located at the boundaries of sexual difference, beyond the phallic pale?

The second of these questions can perhaps best be answered through a brief look at the earliest of Cavani's male characters, Francesco d'Assisi. Since the film which is named after him is structured around a series of quite literal divestitures, each of which marks a stage in Francesco's constantly intensifying cultural estrangement, it makes unusually explicit Cavani's obsession with the self-mutilating male subject, and maps out that narrative trajectory through which her authorial desire will be repeatedly inscribed in the films she directed in the sixties and early to mid-seventies.

The first of Francesco's divestitures occurs near the beginning of the film, when he gives away a rich coat of armor to a less wealthy friend, and almost immediately thereafter abandons his knightly service and his chivalric ambitions. It is quickly followed by another deliberate self-loss: Francesco goes to Rome on a religious pilgrimage, but once he arrives, he finds himself completely preoccupied with the dispossessed—with the beggars, the lepers, the orphans. Turning away from the riches of the Church, he trades clothing with one of the derelicts and sits down among the rest of them to beg. An even more extreme dislocation of Francesco from his symbolic legacy occurs in a courtroom, where he is on trial for filial disobedience (he has given large sums of money to a church in need of restoration, and his father considers the gift a theft). At a key moment in the proceedings, when his patrimony becomes an issue, he strips off his garments and hands them to his father with the words: "Your goods. Now I can say, 'My Father, who art in *heaven.*' " With this gesture, Francesco divests himself of his worldly possessions, his merchant class, and his phallic legacy. (Throughout Cavani's cinema, the removal of clothing functions as an insistent metaphor for the renunciation of power and privilege.) He also assumes a very different kind of paternal lineage, one predicated on negation and suffering.

A later scene emphasizes the *jouissance* that accompanies such voluntary sacrifices. In that scene, Francesco and two of his followers dispose of all their remaining possessions in the marketplace, handing out furniture, clothing, and gold coins. After everything has been relinquished and the townspeople have disappeared with their new wealth, the three men are almost capsized with laughter. That laughter attests to the collapse of social hierarchy and distinction, and consequently conforms in certain key respects to Bakhtin's description of medieval humor. Like the merriment generated by carnival, that induced by Francesco's deliberate self-loss attests to a dispersed subjectivity, and to a "social consciousness of all the people":

Man experiences this flow of time in the festive marketplace, in the carnival crowd, as he comes into contact with other bodies of varying age and social caste. He is aware of being a member of a continually growing and renewed people. That is why festive folk laughter . . . means the defeat of power, of earthly kings, of the earthly upper classes, of all that oppresses and restricts.[82]

The final and in many ways the most important of all Francesco's divestitures takes place near the end of the film, on the occasion of a rare feast. The now-numerous Franciscans sit down at a table and begin enthusiastically demolishing a chicken. Francesco, disguised as a beggar, keeps holding out his hand to the diners, but he is given only bones and scraps of skin. Finally the others notice that he is not at the table, and begin looking around for him. When they discover the identity of the beggar, they are horrified at their previous miserliness, and lavish food upon him.

The point is that in the wake of one symbolic order, another has already sprung up—one in which priests are more important than beggars. In order to challenge that new hierarchy, Francesco has been obliged to situate himself on the side of the dispossessed, which in effect means divesting himself of himself. The speech which he makes on this occasion is central to any understanding not merely of this film, but (as I will attempt to show) of the whole of Cavani's cinema and the authorial desire that circulates within it as well: "Who do you think you are? To treat a poor person badly is like throwing a bone to Christ. . . . Your hand is equal to mine—look! The same with the eyes and mouth. His hunger is like yours. . . . There is no difference. None. No difference." During the entire last half of the film, Francesco struggles to make good that utopian assertion, to insist upon the equality between himself and those around him by steadfastly refusing power, privilege, and discursive authority.

One facet of that refusal is an absolutely literal reading of the Scriptures. The cultural regime disclosed to us at the beginning of *Francesco d'Assisi* is one in which all access to the discourse of Christianity is tightly controlled by the Church. That control takes the form of an elaborate hermeneutic mediation, whereby scriptural passages are available only as signifiers within a second order of signification, their denotative value having been almost completely effaced. In other words, an endlessly proliferating commentary intervenes between the Bible and the layperson. Cavani's film suggests that this commentary has three important effects. It functions to contain any potentially disruptive elements within the original discourse, and so to render it at all points compatible with the existing symbolic order. It also closes that discourse to all but a few select users. Finally, this interpretive scheme provides the means by which difference—hierarchy, class, division—is introduced into the world.

Francesco adopts a radically opposed approach to the Scriptures. For him the Bible as a whole enjoys the status of the logos, and he struggles constantly to reenact that linguistic transmutation in his own life—to incarnate its words through action and gestures. Thus, he not only insists upon a purely denotative reading of scriptural passages, but he refuses to distinguish between signifieds and referents. For instance, when two of his followers come to him for guidance, he opens the Bible at random and reads: "If you want to be perfect, take all that you have and give it to the poor . . . take with you neither silver, nor gold, nor change of tunic, nor belt, nor sandals." Examining his own clothing, Francesco discovers it to be incompatible in several details with this recipe for perfection, and promptly removes his belt and sandals.

It is, of course, extremely significant that this passage, to which Francesco frequently returns, describes a divestiture which leads to the abolition of difference. Increasingly, as the film progresses, it becomes clear that only a discursive divestiture is really capable of effecting such an abolition. For a time Francesco attempts to forestall difference through a kind of punctilious repetition—to close the gap between discourse and the materiality of day-to-day life by conforming his physical existence to the text of the New Testament—but he is ultimately obliged to confront the fact that his everyday activities have acquired the status of signifiers to the people who surround him. The other Franciscans gravitate to him as the representative of a new discourse, the purveyor of a new form of power-knowledge; against his will, they transform his casual utterances and gestures into *exempla*. When, during a large convocation of Franciscans, he is asked to write down the rules of their order, and to supplement the Gospels with a commentary, he flees from the appeal, whispering to himself: "You will be held responsible for all vain words."

This linguistic paranoia is a constant feature of Cavani's films. In *Galileo,* for instance, discourse is grasped precisely as power-knowledge, while in *The Cannibals* and *The Night Porter,* language is virtually synonymous with dominant culture. In the second of these films, the two representatives of a failed revolution communicate without words, relying instead on a rhetoric of food, clothing, and gestures. Their silence assumes an overtly political dimension during a torture session, in which the military police attempt to extract speech from Antigone. In *The Night Porter,* language functions as a fascist tool, a mechanism for "binding" guilty and unpleasurable memories. The central characters, Max and Lucia, refuse any such solution, immersing themselves instead in the sensory and affective intensity of their shared past. However, it is to *Beyond Good and Evil* that we must turn in order to glimpse clearly the desire which, as I will attempt to show, motivates this constantly reenacted drama of discursive divestiture—the desire, that is, to exceed sexual difference. That film focuses on a philosophically inflected *ménage à trois* whose aim is the collapse of traditional sexual boundaries. In an interview with the French press immediately before its release, Cavani described *Beyond Good and Evil* in very much the terms through which the film presents itself to me, i.e., as a story about sexual reversibility:

> This life between three people [involves] a transgression of what might be termed the "masculine" and the "feminine"; sometimes the man seems to be Lou, and Fritz and Paul the woman. . . . The major interest of this . . . enounter is finally that they come together to create a new species of three-headed creature.[83]

At least two of Cavani's other films—*The Cannibals* and *The Night Porter*—work in a similar if less overt way to erase the boundaries separating male from female subjectivity, positing highly transversal and unstable heterosexual relationships. Antigone and her male companion, for example, undergo a series of identical clothing changes, each of which affirms their mutual identity. Because the clothing is in two instances a parody of patriarchal dress (Antigone and her friend don black-and-white clerical robes on one occasion, and the uniforms of military police on another), it is disruptive of sexual difference at another level, as well. *The Night Porter* effects a parallel disruption whenever it shows Max and Lucia trading parts in their sadomasochistic drama.

In each case, the negation of difference is made possible only through the willingness of a male character—Paul Ree in *Beyond Good and Evil*, Clementi's nameless character in *The Cannibals*, Max in *The Night Porter*—to divest himself of the phallus, just as Francesco does in the courtyard scene. The recurrence of these marginal men inscribes into the narrative of Cavani's films the desire for a kind of zero-degree subjectivity, a subjectivity which escapes full symbolic structuration, and which in so doing slips through the defiles of gender.

Cavani's cinema would consequently seem to be fueled by the dream of androgyny. I believe that this is indeed ultimately the case, but as in "The Death of the Author," there is another more immediately pressing goal. Significantly, what we see enacted over and over again in that cinema is a narrative event nearly identical to that through which Barthes dramatizes the demise of the traditional (male) author, and the production of a feminine singing voice. Here, too, male castration becomes the agency not merely whereby the masculine subject is forced to confront his own lack, and is remade in the image of woman, but whereby the female author constructs herself as a speaking subject, and emerges as a figure "inside" the text.

The preceding discussion accounts at least in part for the continuing preoccupation of Cavani's cinema with divestiture, but it does not even begin to address the first of the questions posed above—the question as to why that preoccupation requires the support of a male representation. I will pursue the answer to that question through the film in Cavani's corpus which is both most superficially resistant to a feminist reading and most explicitly concerned with the loss of difference: *Milarepa*.

Milarepa is ostensibly the story of a Tibetan yogi and his reincarnation as a British student of philosophy in the late sixties. The film is problematic in a variety of ways, most particularly in its emphasis once again upon the figure of a young man, and in its inability to confront any of its female characters in a direct or sustained manner. Indeed, the camera seems largely incapable of looking at one of those characters, the young man's sister, and at a certain juncture she simply disappears. Another of the film's women, whose meaning seems almost entirely circumscribed by her role as the grand master's wife, functions in such a subordinate and nursing capacity that I find myself barely able to look at her even when the camera does. The final female character, the mother, seems at first glance to play both a very minor and a very unsympathetic part.

At the same time, I would argue that this is the film in which Cavani's authorial subjectivity and authorial desires are most oppositionally inscribed—the film in which both work most insistently against sexual difference. Indeed, I am prepared to state the case even more forcefully: The centrality of the male protagonist works to facilitate rather than to obstruct the author's (as well as the viewer's) identification with a female subject position.

The principle of reversibility is encoded into the film at every level, working to deny the differences between mother and son, male character and author "outside" the text, and authorial and spectatorial subjectivity. The film's plot consists of two closely connected and mutually mirroring narratives, in both of which the same five actors prominently figure. There is also a marked visual similarity between mother and son, a similarity which is compounded by the rather "masculine" features and voice of the former, and the "feminine" appearance

and manner of the latter. Finally, the narrative organization works to
promote on the part of the viewer the same intense identification
through which the author constructs herself as speaking subject, i.e.,
identification with the central male character.

The first of the two narratives revolves around the shared obsession
of a student, Lumley (Lajos Belazsovits), and his professor, Bennett
(Paolo Bonacelli), with a book about Milarepa, a Tibetan yogi. The
professor, his wife, Karin (Marcella Michelangeli), and Lumley decide
to retrace the itinerary of the yogi, and set off for the Orient. On the way
to the airport, they have an automobile accident. The professor's wife is
sent for help, and in her absence the two men talk about Milarepa. Their
conversation—or, rather, their meditation—gradually gives way to the
second narrative, in which Lumley appears as Milarepa; the professor as
Marpa, the grand master from whom Milarepa learns yoga; and the
professor's wife as Damema, Marpa's wife. At the end of the second
narrative, help arrives for the two men in the first narrative, and the
critically injured professor is taken away in an ambulance. The film
concludes with several brief parallel shots of Lumley walking along the
side of the highway, and Mila moving in a solitary fashion through the
Tibetan landscape.

The other important relationship articulated by the frame narrative
is that between Lumley and his mother. There are only two exchanges
between them, but both are characterized by a high degree of intimacy.
The first of these exchanges occurs in the kitchen, around a table
holding Lumley's translation of the book about Milarepa. Lumley
makes some coffee for his mother, who has just returned from work,
and the two have an emotionally charged conversation about the possibility of moving beyond difference to a condition of intersubjectivity:

> LUMLEY: You remember the story of Milarepa?
> MOTHER: How could I forget? I may be ignorant, but I never forget the
>   things you tell me. Then there are all those coincidences with us. . . .
> LUMLEY: Some. Perhaps that's why I'm so fond of it.
> MOTHER: The episode of the farewell made me cry, do you remember?
> LUMLEY: You're a sentimentalist, mother. Listen: "The idea of the void
>   generates piety/Piety abolishes the difference between us and others/The
>   interpenetration of the self and others achieves community. . . ."[84]

This scene establishes not only the intense identification of Lumley
and his mother with the characters of Mila and his mother, but the
imaginary basis of their own relationship, a relationship which permits
the transfer of his desires onto her, and later—within the second narrative—hers onto him. It unfolds through a number of the lengthy
medium and medium-long shots of which Cavani is so fond, panning

rather than cutting from mother to son as the two move around the room and Lumley makes some coffee. However, seven sets of medium-close shot/reverse shots, each of very brief duration, provide the visual analogue to the conversation quoted above. This dense cluster of what is a relatively rare shot formation within Cavani's cinema effects at the formal level what the strong physical similarity between the two characters achieves at the level of the fiction—it blurs the distinctions between them, binding them in a way that affirms their fundamental unity. Moreover, the literal displacement of the camera from one face to another points to the psychic transfer at the center of Cavani's cinema: the transfer from female to male and, ultimately, back again.[85]

(This scene is followed by a shot which further underscores the importance of imaginary replication within *Milarepa's* visual and psychic economy. That shot focuses in close-up on a bronze plaque attached to the door of Bennett's apartment, so highly polished that it reflects the street in front, with its cars and trees. The camera holds on the plaque as Lumley comes into frame, mirroring his face back at him and us.)

The second of the exchanges between mother and son in the frame narrative takes place at night, after Lumley has paid a visit to the Bennetts. He walks into the bedroom where she is sleeping with his young sister, and awakens her. She lights a cigarette and talks sleepily with him about his proposed journey. He asks: "Would you like to go?" and she responds: "Go on! You know it would please me." After a moment Lumley puts out her cigarette, turns off the light, and leaves. His performance of the gestures conventionally associated with motherhood projects her into the symbolic position of a child, once again pointing to the reversibility of their relationship. This scene also relies heavily upon the shot/reverse shot formation, cutting back and forth between mother and son nine times.

Although the mother does not make the trip to the airport with the others the next day, she does reappear, as Mila's mother, in the inner narrative. She has in a sense been incorporated into Mila's fantasy, just as she will later be incorporated into his body. Thus, although she is shown to be enclosed within precisely that confined space within which classic cinema always attempts to hold woman—although she is literally left behind to wait for the hero's return as he sets out upon his journey—she at the same time makes that journey *through* him, much as the author herself does. Much more is at issue here than vicarious experience; Mila's mother is actually *reborn* narratively through the force of his imagination, which is itself based upon his extraordinary psychic community with her. We are consequently given to understand that these two characters come to realize the intersubjectivity about which they earlier converse, and that Lumley carries his mother with him into their shared dream. (Significantly, that dream gives rise to another, into which the mother is once again transported.)

The mother's desires are much more fully foregrounded in the second narrative than in the first, as is her social and economic position. That narrative begins with the reading of her husband's will, a document which makes no mention of either her or her daughter. It bequeaths half the dead man's property to his brother, and half to his son upon maturity. The mother does not challenge the will; she asks only that it be carried out—that Mila's uncle relinquish the property which rightfully belongs to his nephew. However, her seeming compliance in her own disenfranchisement is belied by the intensity of her appeal, and by her murderous rage when the uncle ignores what she has to say. She sends Mila off to master a discourse capable of leveling their village, selling her few possessions to finance the journey. She tells him: "You must learn an oath with which you can move things."

Mila studies magic with a holy man, and eventually succeeds in destroying the uncle's house and killing everyone inside. The film makes it clear that in so doing, he opens himself up to his mother's desires—that those desires have been displaced onto him as the agent of their fulfillment. After Mila has successfully employed his destructive powers, the holy man remarks that "she alone [exercised] this power," and two sets of corroborating images lend credence to his assertion.

The first of these sets of images begins with a frontal shot of Mila sitting cross-legged in a cell with upraised fingers, meditating on the spell which will level the uncle's house. A brief medium close-up of the mother opening the door of her hut follows. She looks directly at the camera. The film cuts from her gaze to Mila in his cell, suggesting that he is what she sees. These three shots constitute an "impossible" three-way shot/reverse shot formation, denying the physical distance separating mother from son, and affirming their psychic continuity. Thus, as in the frame narrative, the mother is shown to be confined within the closed space of the home only to have that confinement denied at a more complex level of the narrative organization. Once again she in fact journeys far away from her native village, in and through Mila.

The second set of corroborating images reveals the mother jubilantly shaking her walking stick in front of the ruins of the uncle's house, while shouting: "Glory to the gods! Glory to the Holy Lama, to the Buddha, to the Darhma! I am happy, I am happy, I am happy! I've waited so many years!" The extremity of her joy, and the suggestion of a gratification long deferred, identify the mother as the diegetic point of origin for the desire which finds fulfillment in the collapse of the village—in the collapse, that is, of a cultural order in which woman figures as lack, and from whose privileges she is entirely barred.

Mila's brief return home after the death of his uncle is the last time we see his mother alive. However, after he has mastered a much higher level of the yoga discourse, he visits the village again, and finds her decomposing skeleton. He takes away some fragments of that skeleton, worn inside his garments, against the skin. When he comes to a waterfall, he pulverizes them, pours them into a vessel of water, and drinks the mixture. Through this cannibalistic ingestion, Mila completes the condensation of himself and his mother toward which all of the earlier imaginary alignments have pointed. He eradicates the differences between them, achieving that interpenetration of self and Other about which Lumley and his mother dream in the frame narrative. This maternal incorporation stands in oppositional contrast to the literal paternal incorporation fantasized by Freud in *Totem and Taboo,* as well as to the psychic one by means of which the superego comes into existence. Through it Mila not only takes the voice and desires of his mother into himself, but he becomes the subject of Cavani's authorial speech, the one identification facilitating the other.

It is important to note that before this can happen, Mila must become in certain respects "not male"—he must divest himself of his destructive power and of the privileges which that power confers, and step into a more classically female subject position. As with Max in *The Night Porter* and Paul Ree in *Beyond Good and Evil,* this shift is effected through a ritual submission to pain. Between his two visits to his old village, Mila undergoes a lengthy and extremely severe ordeal at the hands of Marpa, the grand master of the yoga discourse. Mila seeks out Marpa in order to be educated by him in the next level of that discourse. Hoping to persuade the reluctant master that he will be a worthy apprentice, Mila employs his destructive magic a second time, toppling a nearby structure. Marpa refuses to impart any knowledge to Mila until the latter rebuilds the structure, stone by stone. Significantly, it is now the male subject who is associated with the interiority of a bound space.

During the extended restoration, Mila is denied access not only to the discourse of yoga, but to the master's tent and the various other privileges enjoyed by the elect. He works from sunrise to sunset, and the labor he performs leaves his back bruised and bleeding. He is neither clothed nor fed adequately, and Marpa frequently reviles him and forces him to begin all over. Mila is thus obliged to occupy a completely subordinate and suffering position, and one given over to repetition and closure rather than narrative movement. An exchange which occurs in the script, although not in the film, suggests that he is in the process stripped of all the phallic attributes of male subjectivity.

This exchange takes place between Mila and his lost sister, who disappears abruptly from the film after her brother's initial departure. She has been searching for him since her mother's death, but when she finally encounters him, bathing in the waterfall where he drinks the maternal potion, she fails to recognize him. He has undergone a profound transformation since she last saw him, a transformation which seems to have involved a kind of demasculinization. Not only does she look in vain for the signifiers which would permit her to acknowledge Mila as her brother, but she is disconcerted by the seeming disjunction between his anatomy and his subject-position:

> SISTER: I'm looking for Mila, my brother. You can't be he. . . . My brother was powerful. . . . (She covers her face in embarrassment over his nakedness.)
>
> MILA: Sister, maiden inheriting chasteness, you blush over something which is not shameful. . . . if you stop to distinguish the sex of a body, do not look at it with impure eyes.
>
> SISTER: Don't you do great feats any more?
>
> MILA: I feed like the birds, I warm myself like a bear. . . .
>
> SISTER: Holy men are covered with silk . . . they have gold and servants.
>
> MILA: I am not a holy man, or anything else.
>
> SISTER: What are you then?
>
> MILA: I don't know how to define myself . . . Buddha has smiled on me. Renounce all the laws of this world, and let us go to Laphis on the snow.[86]

As this deleted passage makes clear, the discourse of yoga is a metaphor in *Milarepa* for the collapse of all the binary oppositions that support the present symbolic order, and that keep power and privilege in place— particularly those bearing upon sexual difference, with its "impure" or culturally coercive vision of biological distinction. These are the "laws" whose complete abolition Mila urges his sister to help him effect. But why should the appeal be delivered by him rather than by her? By a voice which, while it is no longer phallic, and perhaps no longer even "male," nevertheless issues from a biologically masculine body? Why, in other words, would the author "outside" the text speak at this critical juncture of the script through a male rather than a female character?

Let us return, for a moment, to Mila's mother. Her absence from her husband's will, her marginal existence within the village, and her confinement to the family hut are surely emblematic of female subjectivity as most women live it within the present social and cultural regime, both in the East and in the West, as are the conditions under which she functions in her more contemporary incarnation: unskilled labor during the day, domestic labor in the evening, relegated by both to a life of what she herself characterizes as "ignorance." This exclusion from symbolic privilege can only generate, with all the force of a historical imperative, the desire for discursive power—for what the mother calls "an oath with which you can move things."

The film suggests that this is a necessary desire for the female subject, even as it dreams of a moment beyond it: of the moment when, having acceded to power, the female subject can divest herself of it. In *Milarepa,* as in *Francesco d'Assisi* and to some degree *The Cannibals,* Cavani is obliged to rely upon male characters to express this dream because they alone occupy a position from which divestiture is possible. Her constant return to male subjectivity speaks to the desire to participate in a renunciation which is not yet possible for the female subject (which indeed can be seen only as a dangerous lure at this moment in her history)—the renunciation of power, in all its many social, cultural, political, and economic guises.

The extraordinary invitation held out by Mila to his sister in the conversation quoted above contains the utopian vision of a subjective space beyond sexual difference—a space made possible not only by male, but by female divestiture. One can only guess at the psychic and political constraints which resulted in its excision. However, that vision persists at the latent level of the text, and is quite easily exhumed from what remains of the waterfall scene. Mila's cannibalistic incorporation of his mother permits her to participate in his liberating divestiture, and with him to transcend sexual difference. Together they make the journey to "the snows of Laphis," a journey that leads definitively away from both narrative and ideological closure.

The recurrence in Cavani's films of the marginal male subject constructs her authorial subjectivity at the site of that divestiture. Through its extensive use of doubles and reflecting narrative elements, *Milarepa* makes that construction unusually explicit, foregrounding the imaginary relation not only of Lumley and Mila, Bennett and Marpa, but of mother and son, and Cavani and her male protagonist. The film's equalizing drift also clarifies precisely what is at stake in this imaginary relation. However, at the same time that it points definitively beyond sexual difference, male divestiture in *Milarepa* has a quite opposite immediate effect: It allows us to hear a voice which neither originates nor defers, but which articulates a narrative and characterological system through which it constructs itself both as author and—in the most denatured sense possible—as female.

But what is the fantasmatic "scene" toward whose recovery we have been moving, and which is at the basis of this quite remarkable authorial inscription? It seems to me that it is a variant of the fantasy Freud codified in "A Child Is Being Beaten," a variant which might be titled "A Child Is Being Castrated." What justifies me in substituting the action of castration for that of whipping is not only Freud's observation in "The Economic Problem of Masochism" that masochistic fantasies frequently signify castration,[87] but his suggestion in "A Child Is Being Beaten" that "punishments and humiliations of another kind may be substituted for the beating itself"[88] *during the transformation of the second phase into the third phase.* Let us look briefly at all three phases.

Freud transcribes the first phase of the beating fantasy told to him by his female patients with the following linguistic formula: "My father is beating the child [whom I hate]." The second phase reads: "I am being beaten by my father," and the third phase: "Some boys are being beaten [by a paternal representative. I am probably looking on]."[89] Freud explains that the first phase is really only a vague memory, and that fantasy proper begins with the second phase, which substitutes the subject herself for the anonymous child. Positive Oedipal desire inter-venes between phase 1 and phase 2, with the latter functioning simul-taneously to punish that desire and to satisfy it through a regression from genital to anal sexuality. Because phase 2 anchors desire to maso-chism, it might be said to be the most exemplary of all female fantasies. However, because it is so deeply repressed, it is recoverable only as a "construction of analysis." What takes its place as a conscious fantasy is phase 3, in which a group of boys fill in for the female subject as the targets of pleasurable parental punishment.

Freud maintains that this gender change is motivated only by the demands of censorship—that it is a simple disguise. However, as I have argued at length elsewhere,[90] the final phase of the girl's beating fantasy is capable in addition of satisfying at least three transgressive desires— the desire that it be boys rather than girls who are loved/disciplined in this way; the desire to be a boy while being so treated; and, finally, the desire to occupy a male subject-position, but one under the sign of femininity rather than of masculinity. Since the fantasmatic "scene" is constantly assimilating "new material," it is presumably possible for these desires to be historically activated, and it seems to me that this is precisely what has happened within Cavani's cinema.

For what is the exchange that occurs between Cavani as author "outside" the text and those male characters who represent her within the text if not a restaging of that fantasmatic drama whereby a girl turns herself into a group of boys only in order to position them as female subjects, i.e., to "castrate" them? Cavani's cinema not only reenacts phase 3 of the beating fantasy, it also (as I have attempted to indicate) makes it the libidinal basis for a radical attack on sexual difference, the agency whereby the phallus is dethroned, and "femininity" made the very norm of subjectivity. A fantasy which would seem to lead inexorably to the maintenance of existing gender categories, and to a permanent investment in the present symbolic order, is thus reworked in such a way as to transform both utterly, at least within the cinematic fiction. Is it necessary to add that it is through feminism that history can be seen to have worked in this way upon the *mise-en-scène* of masochistic desire?

In *The Archaeology of Knowledge*, Foucault suggests that if a group of signs can be called a "statement," it is because "the position of the subject can be assigned":

> To describe a formulation *qua* statement does not consist in analysing the relations between the author and what he says (or wanted to say, or said without wanting to); but in determining what position can and must be occupied by an individual if he is to be the subject of it.[91]

Until now I have stressed precisely what Foucault seems prepared to dismiss here—the relations between the author and what s/he has to say, or, to put it rather differently, between the author "outside" the text and the author "inside" the text. I have attempted, in other words, to demonstrate the key role played within the libidinal economy of Cavani's films by the recurring figure of the marginal male subject, a figure who functions as a kind of nodal point for the authorial dream, and who casts onto the director "herself" the image of what she would like to be. (It is through a curious reversal of this operation that Cavani can be heard to say: "Each of my actors looks a bit like me.")

However, the structuring force of this authorial dream extends beyond the site occupied by Cavani-as-speaking-subject. Foucault is correct to suggest that there is a more crucial project than determining the relation between the author and what he or she says, and that is to establish the position which the reader or viewer will come to occupy through identifying with the subject of a given statement. That position is indeed "assignable" (or reassignable). All of this is another way of saying that the reader or viewer may be captated by the authorial system of a given text or group of texts.

My own fascination with Cavani's marginal male characters attests to precisely such a captation—suggests, that is, that I in some way participate in the desire for divestiture that circulates through *Francesco d'Assisi* and *Milarepa,* and that my own authorial subjectivity in some way reflects or replicates the one those texts project. I have, in fact, pursued the image of a lacking or impaired male subjectivity across the breadth of this book, and through a diverse group of texts: Freud's essays on fetishism and sexual difference, Powell's *Peeping Tom,* Chion's *La voix au cinéma,* Coppola's *The Conversation,* Barthes's "The Death of the Author" and *The Pleasure of the Text,* and (finally) Cavani's *Francesco d'Assisi* and *Milarepa.* I can trace my obsession with this image back a long way, and it undoubtedly goes back much farther. However, the moment when it first imposed itself upon my consciousness was while I was watching and writing about another film by Liliana Cavani—*The Night Porter.* In some curious way, my own authorial voice is thus precisely an "assigned" one, from her to me.

But I have also found myself in a variety of more properly "acoustic" mirrors over the course of writing this book—in Helen's questioning voice in *Peeping Tom,* the loathingly self-referential voices in *Journeys from Berlin/71,* Potter's pleasure-seeking voice in *The Gold Diggers,* and the voice "apart" which narrates *Riddles of the Sphinx,* to name but a few. The preceding pages have thus been a self-analysis of sorts, and like Freud's own self-analysis, mine has led inexorably to the castration crisis and the Oedipus complex. However, both of those organizing concepts have undergone a curious metamorphosis in their displacement from the male to the female subject. Freud's anatomical castration has given way to an insistence upon the crucial importance of symbolic castration, effected through separation from the mother and the entry into a linguistic order which anticipates and exceeds the subject. And the positive Oedipus complex has yielded theoretical priority to its "feminine" counterpart, the negative Oedipus complex, site both of desire for and identification with the mother, and thus generative not only of narcissism, but—as I have attempted to demonstrate—of feminism as well. Of course I am assuming, much like Freud before me, that my self-analysis has been simultaneously an analysis of female subjectivity—that the reader of this book will also have found herself within some of the acoustic mirrors which it has placed before her.

Notes

Preface

1. *The Classical Hollywood Cinema: Film Style and Mode of Production to 1960* (New York: Columbia University Press, 1985).

1. Lost Objects and Mistaken Subjects: A Prologue

1. Jean-Louis Comolli, "Machines of the Visible," in *The Cinematic Apparatus*, ed. Teresa de Lauretis and Stephen Heath (New York: St. Martins, 1980), p. 141.

2. In "Ste Anne," Lacan writes that "every male is a slave to the phallic function" (*Semiotext [e]* 4, no. 1 [1981]: 217).

3. Hugo Munsterberg, *The Film: A Psychological Study* (New York: Dover, 1970), p. 69.

4. Andre Bazin, "The Virtues and Limitations of Montage," in *What Is Cinema?* trans. Hugh Gray (Berkeley: University of California Press, 1967), vol. 1, p. 50.

5. "The Evolution of the Language of Cinema," *What Is Cinema?* vol. 1, p. 37.

6. "The Ontology of the Photographic Image," in *What is Cinema?* vol. 1, p. 15.

7. Ibid., pp. 23–40.

8. *What Is Cinema?* vol. 2, p. 29.

9. "Bicycle Thief," in *What Is Cinema?* vol. 2, p. 59.

10. Christian Metz, *The Imaginary Signifier: Psychoanalysis and the Cinema*, trans. Celia Britton, Annwyl Williams, Ben Brewster, and Alfred Guzzetti (Bloomington: Indiana University Press, 1982), p. 63.

11. "The Evolution of the Language of Cinema," in *What Is Cinema?* vol. 1, p. 38.

12. Peter Wollen notes the affinities between this passage from Bazin and Freud's essays on fetishism in " 'Ontology' and 'Materialism' in Film," *Screen* 17, no. 1 (1976): 9.

13. Stephen Heath, "Lessons from Brecht," *Screen* 15, no. 4 (1970): 107.

14. Lacan's essay on the mirror stage is included in *Ecrits: A Selection*, trans. Alan Sheridan (New York: Norton, 1977), pp. 1–7.

15. See "Where to Begin?" in *Reading Lacan* (Ithaca: Cornell University Press, 1985), pp. 74–92, for an excellent analysis of the ways in which anticipation and retroactivity organize the mirror stage.

16. Jacques Lacan, "Seminar of 21 January 1975," in *Feminine Sexuality*, ed. Juliet Mitchell and Jacqueline Rose (New York: Norton, 1983), p. 164.

17. Jacques Lacan, *The Four Fundamental Concepts of Psycho-analysis*, trans. Alan Sheridan (New York: Norton, 1978), p. 103.

18. Jacques Lacan, "The Subject and the Other: Aphanisis," in *Four Fundamental Concepts*, p. 218.

19. Ibid., pp. 211–13.

20. Siegfried Kracauer, *Theory of Film* (London: Oxford University Press, 1960), pp. 169 and 164.

21. Serge Leclaire, *Démasquer le réel: un essai sur l'objet en psychanalyse* (Paris: Editions du Seuil, 1971), p. 50.

22. Metz, *The Imaginary Signifier*, p. 45.

23. Kracauer, *Theory of Film*, p. 171.

24. Jean-Pierre Oudart, "Cinema and Suture," *Screen* 18, no. 4 (1977/78): 41, 44.

25. Daniel Dayan, "The Tutor Code of Classical Cinema," in *Movies and Methods*, ed. Bill Nichols (Berkeley: University of California Press, 1976), pp. 438–51. For additional readings on suture, see Stephen Heath, "Notes on Suture," *Screen* 18, no. 4 (1977/78): 48–76; Claire Johnston, "Towards a Feminist Film Practice: Some Theses," *Edinburgh Magazine*, no. 1 (1976): 50–59; Kaja Silverman, "Suture," in *The Subject of Semiotics* (New York: Oxford University Press, 1983), pp. 194–246; and Leslie Stern, "Point of View: The Blind Spot," *Film Reader*, no. 5 (1979): 214–36.

26. See Metz, "Story/Discourse (A Note on Two Kinds of Voyeurism)," in *The Imaginery Signifier*, pp. 89–98; and Jean-Louis Baudry, "Ideological Effects of the Basic Cinematographic Apparatus," trans. Alan Williams, *Film Quarterly* 28, no. 2 (1974/75): 39–47, and "The Apparatus," trans. Jean Andrews and Bertrand Augst, *Camera Obscura*, no. 1 (1976): 104–128.

27. See Comolli, "Machines of the Visible," in *The Cinematic Apparatus*, pp. 124–127; Metz, *The Imaginary Signifier*, pp. 49–52; and Baudry, "Ideological Effects of the Basic Cinematographic Apparatus," pp. 41–42.

28. Oudart, "Cinema and Suture," p. 36.

29. Dayan, "The Tutor Code of Classical Cinema," p. 448.

30. Sigmund Freud, "Some Psychical Consequences of the Anatomical Distinction between the Sexes," in *The Standard Edition of the Complete Psychological Works*, trans. James Strachey (London: Hogarth Press, 1953), vol. 19, p. 252.

31. See "Fetishism," in *The Standard Edition*, vol. 21, pp. 152–57.

32. For a discussion of sublimation and its relation to intellectual activity, see "Leonardo da Vinci and a Memory of His Childhood," in *The Standard Edition*, vol. 11, pp. 53–55, 80–81.

33. Jacqueline Rose, "The Cinematic Apparatus: Problems in Current Theory," in *The Cinematic Apparatus*, p. 182.

34. *The Standard Edition*, vol. 17, p. 84.

35. "Some Psychical Consequences of the Anatomical Distinction between the Sexes," p. 252.

36. "The Unconscious," in *The Standard Edition*, vol. 14, p. 184.

37. J. Laplanche and J.-B. Pontalis, *The Language of Psycho-analysis*, trans. Donald Nicholson-Smith (New York: Norton, 1973), p. 354.

38. "Instincts and Their Vicissitudes," in *The Standard Edition*, vol. 14, p. 136.

39. "Some Psychical Consequences of the Anatomical Distinction between the Sexes," p. 252.

40. "Fetishism," p. 155.

41. "The Uncanny," in *The Standard Edition*, vol. 17, p. 220.

42. Ibid., p. 234.

43. Julia Kristeva, *Powers of Horror*, trans. Leon S. Roudiez (New York: Columbia University Press, 1982), p. 63.

44. "Fetishism," p. 155.

45. Roland Barthes, "Upon Leaving the Movie Theater," trans. Bertrand Augst and Susan White, in *The Cinematic Apparatus: Selected Writings*, ed. Theresa Hak Kyung Cha (New York: Tanam Press, 1980), p. 2.

46. Metz, *The Imaginary Signifier*, pp. 50–51.

47. Ibid.

48. Rose suggests a very similar formulation in the second introduction to *Feminine Sexuality*, where she writes: "As the place onto which lack is projected,

and through which it is simultaneously disavowed, woman is a 'symptom' for the man" (p. 48).

49. J. C. Flugel, *The Psychology of Clothes* (London: Hogarth Press, 1930), pp. 117–19. For a more extended discussion of Flugel, and one more specifically concerned with fashion, see my "The Fragments of a Fashionable Discourse," in *Studies in Entertainment: Critical Approaches to Mass Culture*, ed. Tania Modleski (Bloomington: Indiana University Press, 1986), pp. 139–52.

50. Silverman, *The Subject of Semiotics*, pp. 222–25.

51. See Laura Mulvey, "Visual Pleasure and Narrative Cinema," *Screen* 16, no. 3 (1975): 8–18; Teresa de Lauretis, *Alice Doesn't: Feminism, Semiotics, Cinema* (Bloomington: Indiana University Press, 1984), pp. 1–36; Linda Williams, "Film Body: An Implantation of Perversions," *Ciné-Tracts* 3, no. 4 (1981): 19–35; Lucy Fischer, "The Image of Woman as Image: The Optical Politics of *Dames*," in *Genre: The Musical*, ed. Rick Altman (London: Routledge and Kegan Paul, 1981), pp. 70–84; and Sandy Flitterman, "Woman, Desire, and the Look: Feminism and the Enunciative Apparatus in Cinema," *Ciné-Tracts* 2, no. 1 (1978): 63–68.

52. Laura Mulvey provides an interesting discussion of the ways in which classic cinema facilitates the female viewer's identification with male as well as with female characters in "Afterthoughts . . . Inspired by *Duel in the Sun*," *Framework*, nos. 15/16/17 (1981): 12–15.

53. Freud, "The Uncanny," p. 241.

54. For a rather different account of authorship, see chapter 4.

55. "Theater and Cinema—Part Two," in *What Is Cinema?* vol. 1, p. 97.

56. Lacan, "Seminar of 21 January 1975," p. 186.

57. See Linda Williams, "When the Woman Looks," in *Re-vision: Essays in Feminist Theory*, ed. Patricia Mellencamp, Mary Ann Doane, and Linda Williams (Los Angeles: American Film Institute, 1984), pp. 83–99, for an extremely interesting discussion of the way in which Mark seeks to trap his female victims in attitudes of narcissism and exhibitionism.

58. "Lessons from Brecht," p. 106.

59. Ian Christie provides an excellent summary of those reviews in "The Scandal of *Peeping Tom*," published in *Powell, Pressburger, and Others*, ed. Ian Christie (London: BFI, 1978), pp. 53–59.

60. Ibid., p. 57.

61. Ibid.

62. Michel Foucault, *The Order of Things: An Archaeology of the Human Science* (London: Tavistock Publications, 1970), p. 387.

2. Body Talk

1. Béla Balázs, *Theory of the Film: Character and Growth of a New Art* (New York: Dover, 1970), p. 216.

2. Christian Metz, "Aural Objects," *Yale French Studies*, no. 60 (1980): 29.

3. Jean-Louis Baudry, "Ideological Effects of the Basic Cinematographic Apparatus," trans. Alan Williams, *Film Quarterly* 28, no. 2 (1974/75): 47.

4. Alan Williams, "Is Sound Recording Like a Language?" *Yale French Studies*, no. 60 (1980): 51–66; Tom Levin, "The Acoustic Dimension: Notes on Cinema Sound," *Screen* 25, no. 3 (1984): 55–68.

5. Williams, "Is Sound Recording Like a Language?" p. 58.

6. Charles Affron, "Voice and Space," in *Cinema and Sentiment* (Chicago: University of Chicago Press, 1982), p. 105.

7. See Jacques Derrida, *Speech and Phenomena and Other Essays on Husserl's Theory of Signs*, trans. David B. Allison (Evanston: Northwestern University Press, 1973), and *Of Grammatology*, trans. Gayatri Chakravorty Spivak (Balti-

more: Johns Hopkins University Press, 1976), for a critique of the concepts of presence and self-presence, and their philosophical imbrication with speech and the voice.

8. Jacques Lacan, "Function and Field of Speech and Language," in *Ecrits: A Selection*, trans. Alan Sheridan (New York: Norton, 1977), p. 86.

9. See Roland Barthes, "The Grain of the Voice," in *Image, Music, Text*, trans. Stephen Heath (New York: Hill and Wang, 1977), pp. 179–89.

10. Denis Vasse, *L'ombilic et la voix: deux enfants en analyse* (Paris: Éditions du Seuil, 1974), p. 21.

11. For a discussion of this point, see chapter 3.

12. Jean-Louis Comolli, "Machines of the Visible," in *The Cinematic Apparatus*, ed. Teresa de Lauretis and Stephen Heath (New York: St. Martins, 1980), p. 132.

13. The phrase "sonorous *vraisemblable*" comes from Michel Marie, *Lectures du film* (Paris: Éditions Albatros, 1975), p. 209.

14. Jacques Rancière, "The Image of Brotherhood," *Edinburgh Magazine*, no. 2 (1977): 28.

15. See, in particular, Mary Ann Doane, "The Voice in the Cinema: The Articulation of Body and Space," *Yale French Studies*, no. 60 (1980): 33–50.

16. In *Questions of Cinema* (Bloomington: Indiana University Press, 1981), p. 55, Heath describes "the regime of sound as voice in the cinema" as "that of the 'safe' place," and adds that "the safe place is carefully preserved in fiction films. Voice and sound are diegetic (with music following the images as an element of dramatic heightening), generally 'on screen' but equally defined in their contiguity to the field in frame when 'off screen.' "

17. See Rudy Behlmer, *America's Favorite Movies: Behind the Scenes* (New York: Ungar Press, 1982), pp. 267–68.

18. Heath discusses this operation, which he calls the "metonymic lock," in *Questions of Cinema*, pp. 38–54.

19. As Doane puts it, the voice-off "*accounts* for lost space" ("The Voice in the Cinema: The Articulation of Body and Space," p. 40).

20. There is another disembodied female voice-over in *Letter to Three Wives*—the voice that issues from the radio on the evening of the birthday party. That voice, which is associated with the power to invade people's minds and cheapen their thoughts, is ridiculed and discredited by the film.

21. Pascal Bonitzer, *Le regard et la voix* (Paris: Union Générale d'Éditions, 1976), pp. 31–32.

22. Michel Chion, *La voix au cinéma* (Paris: Éditions de L'Étoile, 1982), pp. 32–33.

23. Significantly, while the striptease—and hence synchronization—is interpreted through reference to the primordial "discovery" of woman's difference, that discovery is invoked only *after* the striptease, *retrospectively*. What Chion gives us, then, is a three-way analogy in which each term derives its meaning entirely through its metaphoric relation to the other terms, a relation which takes the form of a ceaseless deferral. Female lack is thus at no point "present."

24. Sarah Kozloff discusses this last voice in detail in "Humanizing 'The Voice of God': Narration in *The Naked City*," *Cinema Journal* 23, no. 4 (1984): 41–53. Her analysis seems to me to be rather too dependent upon narrative literary models, and too quick to assume that the individuating features of Mark Hellinger's voice undercut the privileged position that voice occupies.

25. Bonitzer, *Le regard et la voix*, p. 33.

26. In the first of these examples, a disembodied male voice-over with a Canadian accent introduces the Nova Scotia town where the story is set, much like a travelogue, before abruptly disappearing. In the second, the voice of the

law provides both a prologue and an epilogue. In the third example, a disembodied male voice-over gives a "humorous" account of the battle of the sexes from primitive times to the present, and then exits.

27. The embodied male voice-over figures much more prominently on American television. It is a standard feature of at least two current dramatic series, "Magnum P.I." and "Mickey Spillane's Mike Hammer." However, even here that voice-over functions nostalgically, as a signifier for an earlier textual system. It would seem important to explore the reasons for this nostalgia, although it falls beyond the limits of the present study to do so.

28. Doane, "The Voice in the Cinema: The Articulation of Body and Space," p. 41.

29. What seems to warrant our violation of Cecile's privacy is the compulsion with which she revisits her own past. As her voice-over says at the outset of the film, "I try to stop remembering, but I can't."

30. For a very different, but extremely interesting, reading of *Letter from an Unknown Woman*, see Tania Modleski, "Time and Desire in the Woman's Film," *Cinema Journal* 23, no. 3 (1984): 19–30. Modleski argues that Stefan's "feminine" qualities make him a figure onto whom the female subject's desire for freedom from patriarchy can be projected. She also suggests that the film's preoccupation with repetition and return is a manifestation of *"another* relationship to time and space, desire and memory" than that which characterizes either hysteria or obsessional neurosis.

31. Bonitzer, *Le regard et la voix*, pp. 31–32.

32. *The Standard Edition of the Complete Psychological Works of Sigmund Freud*, trans. James Strachey (London: Hogarth Press, 1953), vol. 5, p. 536.

33. For a discussion of the "medical discourse" in the "woman's film," see Mary Ann Doane, "Paranoia and the Specular," in *The Desire to Desire* (Bloomington: Indiana University Press, 1987), pp. 123–54.

34. For a reading that stresses the disruptive force exercised by the female voice in this film, see Carol Flinn's insightful essay "Sound, Woman, and the Bomb: Dismembering the 'Great Whatsit' in *Kiss Me Deadly*," *Wide Angle* 8, nos. 3/4 (1986): 115–27.

35. See Ernest Jones, "The Early Development of Female Sexuality," *International Journal of Psycho-analysis* 8, no. 4 (1927): 459–72, "The Phallic Phase," *International Journal of Psycho-analysis* 14, no. 1 (1933): 1–33, and "Early Female Sexuality," *International Journal of Psycho-analysis* 16, no. 3 (1935): 263–73; Bela Grunberger, "Outline for a Study of Narcissism in Female Sexuality," in *Female Sexuality: New Psychoanalytic Views*, ed. Janine Chasseguet-Smirgel (Ann Arbor: University of Michigan Press, 1970), pp. 68–83; and Michèle Montrelay, *L'ombre et le nom* (Paris: Éditions de Minuit, 1977). The key chapter of *L'ombre et le nom*, "Recherches sur la féminité," has been translated into English by Parveen Adams; see "Inquiry into Femininity," *m/f*, no. 1 (1978): 83–101.

36. Jones, "Early Female Sexuality," p. 267.

37. Montrelay, "Inquiry into Femininity," pp. 90–91.

38. Jones, "Early Female Sexuality," p. 265.

39. This is very much the position that Daniel Charles takes on the female voice in *Le temps de la voix* (Paris: Jean-Pierre Delarge, 1978), pp. 167–82.

40. Heath, *Questions of Cinema*, p. 189.

41. Jones, "Early Female Sexuality," p. 273.

42. One can detect at least a trace of anxiety in *Johnny Belinda* lest the maternal "instinct" it so insistently summons encroach too decisively upon the laws of men (Belinda is, after all, released by the judge into the protection of a doctor, whose erotic interest takes a decidedly scientific and paternalistic form). However, a scene which occurs between the discovery of Belinda's pregnancy

and her trial for murder indicates that there is no real cause for alarm, since her inner territories have been not only penetrated, but colonized. I refer to the scene where she conducts the Lord's Prayer in sign language over the body of her dead father. Whereas in the courtroom scene Belinda is associated with a biological order outside of and in potential opposition to the paternal law, here she invokes that law, and subordinates herself to it ("Our father, who art in heaven: Hallowed be thy name. Thy kingdom come, thy will be done . . ."). Belinda's prayer indicates that the phallus is where it "ought" to be—i.e., in a privileged place within her psychic economy—and that what will later be characterized as a maternal instinct is in fact an Oedipal construction.

43. Of course, these two theoretical paradigms remain resolutely opposed to each other at one crucial level: Whereas Jones sees female sexuality as an inherent condition, Freud insists that it is constructed through the castration crisis and the Oedipus complex. Hollywood does not intersect with the Freudian model at this level, appropriating the notion that the female subject is castrated without incorporating the theoretical conclusions that Freud draws from that assumption—conclusions which feminism has done much to maximize. (See, for example, Juliet Mitchell, *Psycho-analysis and Feminism: Freud, Reich, Laing, and Women* [New York: Vintage, 1975].)

44. Jacques Derrida, "Living On: Border Lines," in Harold Bloom et al., *Deconstruction and Criticism* (New York: Seabury Press, 1979), p. 97.

45. For a critique of some of Derrida's sexual metaphors, see Gayatri Chakravorty Spivak, "Displacement and the Discourse of Woman," in *Displacement: Derrida and After,* ed. Mark Krupnick (Bloomington: Indiana University Press, 1983), pp. 169–95.

3. The Fantasy of the Maternal Voice: Paranoia and Compensation

1. Guy Rosolato, "La voix: entre corps et langage," *Revue francaise de psychanalyse* 37, no. 1 (1974): 81; Mary Ann Doane, "The Voice in the Cinema: The Articulation of Body and Space," *Yale French Studies,* no. 60 (1980): 33–50.

2. Julia Kristeva, "Place Names," *Desire in Language: A Semiotic Approach to Literature and Art,* trans. Thomas Gora, Alice Jardine, and Leon S. Roudiez (New York: Columbia University Press, 1980), p. 282.

3. Didier Anzieu, "L'enveloppe sonore du soi," *Nouvelle revue de psychanalyse,* no. 13 (1976), p. 173; Claude Bailblé, "Programmation de l'écoute (1)," *Cahiers du cinema,* no. 293 (1978): 53–54.

4. Michel Chion, *La voix au cinéma* (Paris: Éditions de L'Etoile, 1982), p. 57.

5. Rosolato, "La voix: entre corps et langage," p. 81; Chion, *La voix au cinéma,* p. 57.

6. Jean Laplanche, *Life and Death in Psychoanalysis,* trans. Jeffrey Mehlman (Baltimore: Johns Hopkins University Press, 1976), p. 45.

7. Gilles Deleuze and Felix Guattari, *Anti-Oedipus: Capitalism and Schizophrenia,* trans. Robert Hurley, Mark Seem, and Helen R. Lane (New York: Viking, 1977), pp. 56–68.

8. Jean Laplanche and J.-B. Pontalis, "Fantasy and the Origins of Sexuality," *International Journal of Psycho-analysis* 49, no. 1 (1968): 11.

9. Chion, *La voix au cinéma,* p. 57.

10. Rosolato, "La voix: entre corps et langage," pp. 80–81; Anzieu, "L'enveloppe sonore du soi," pp. 167–68.

11. Jacques Hassoun, *Fragments de langue maternelle: esquisse d'un lieu* (Paris: Payot, 1979), p. 35.

12. Chion, *La voix au cinéma,* p. 47.

13. Ibid., p. 68.

14. Since the completion of this chapter, Amy Lawrence has published an extremely interesting essay on the relation of sound and image in this film, arguing that as the "organizing Subject," Leona "supplies the faces that go with the voices she hears, the rooms they occupy, the clothes they're wearing," temporarily inverting the usual image/sound hierarchy. See "*Sorry, Wrong Number:* The Organizing Ear," *Film Quarterly* 40, no. 2 (1986–87): 20–27.

15. J. L. Austin, *How to Do Things with Words* (Cambridge, Mass.: Harvard University Press, 1962), p. 5.

16. This is how Lacan describes the child at the time of the mirror stage (see "The Mirror Stage," in *Ecrits: A Selection,* trans. Alan Sheridan [New York: Norton, 1977], p. 2).

17. Rosolato, "La voix: entre corps et langage," p. 79.

18. Ibid., p. 80.

19. Julia Kristeva, *Powers of Horror: An Essay on Abjection,* trans. Leon S. Roudiez (New York: Columbia University Press, 1982).

20. Ibid., p. 65.

21. Christine Gledhill also comments upon the ways in which *Klute* discredits Bree's voice, noting two occasions when the image contradicts Bree's voice-over—once when she complains to her analyst about Klute's intrusion into her life, and a second time, at the very end of the film, when she asserts that she could never become a housewife in Tuscarora. See "Feminism and *Klute,*" ed. E. Ann Kaplan (London: BFI, 1978), pp. 123–24. This essay argues that the film works to recuperate the "would-be emancipated woman" through a rewriting of the film noir genre. Gledhill's essay is in part a response to an earlier essay, Diane Giddis's "The Divided Woman: Bree Daniels in *Klute,*" in *Women and the Cinema,* ed. Karyn Kay and Gerald Peary (New York: Dutton, 1977), pp. 26–36, which reads *Klute* as "the story of a woman and her battle . . . *with* love," and which sees the characters of Klute and Cable as extensions of Bree's own psychic conflicts.

22. Rosolato, "La voix: entre corps et langage," p. 81.

23. Ibid.

24. Jacques Lacan, *The Four Fundamental Concepts of Psycho-analysis,* trans. Alan Sheridan (New York: Norton, 1978), p. 62.

25. Denis Vasse, *L'ombilic et la voix: deux enfants en analyse* (Paris: Éditions du Seuil, 1974), pp. 13–14.

26. Chion offers an extremely interesting discussion of the ways in which Kane coerces Susan's voice in *La voix au cinéma,* pp. 78–79.

27. See Richard Lang, "Carnal Stereophony," *Screen* 25, no. 3 (1984): 70–77, for a much more extended discussion of sound in *Diva.* Lang argues that the film initially situates Cynthia Hawkins within the mirror stage, but that it dramatizes her eventual entry into the symbolic, via the agency of Jules and his tape recorder.

28. For a discussion of voyeurism in *The Conversation,* and of the way in which that scopic activity complicates the viewing process, see Robert Phillip Kolker, *A Cinema of Loneliness: Penn, Kubrick, Coppola, Scorsese, Altman* (New York: Oxford University Press, 1980), pp. 194–205.

29. Rosolato, "La voix: entre corps et langage," p. 77.

30. *The Standard Edition,* vol. 19, p. 24.

31. *The Standard Edition,* vol. 22, p. 78.

32. Otto Isakower, "On the Exceptional Position of the Auditory Sphere," *International Journal of Psycho-analysis* 20, nos. 3–4 (1939): 345.

33. Lacan, "The Mirror Stage," p. 2.

34. While Freud in *The Ego and the Id* at times suggests that the superego is formed through the internalization of the "higher natures" of *both* parents, he consistently stresses that psychic agency's *primary* connection with the father.

4. The Fantasy of the Maternal Voice: Female Subjectivity and the Negative Oedipus Complex

1. Julia Kristeva, "Motherhood According to Giovanni Bellini," in *Desire in Language: A Semiotic Approach to Literature and Art*, trans. Thomas Gora, Alice Jardine, and Leon S. Roudiez (New York: Columbia University Press, 1980), pp. 241–42.

2. "From One Identity to An Other," in *Desire in Language*, p. 133. In "Julia Kristeva: Take Two," Jacqueline Rose points out that if Plato characterizes the *chora* as maternal, that is because "the mother was seen as playing no part in the act of procreation, [as being] a receptacle or empty vessel *merely* for the gestation of the unborn child" (see *Sexuality in the Field of Vision* [London: Verso, 1976], p. 154). This essay provides an impressive overview of Kristeva's writings.

3. This is how Kristeva states the opposition between the semiotic and the symbolic in "The Novel As Polylogue," in *Desire In Language*, p. 206.

4. "Place Names," in *Desire in Language*, p. 283.

5. Ibid., pp. 283–86.

6. Ibid., p. 282. Here Kristeva associates the mother/child relationship with primary narcissism, a concept which undergoes a dramatic transformation in "Freud and Love: Treatment and Its Discontents," where it is associated instead with the father/child relationship. See below.

7. See chapter 3 for a discussion of this text.

8. "Place Names," p. 282.

9. "Freud and Love: Treatment and Its Discontents," trans. Leon S. Roudiez, in *The Kristeva Reader*, ed. Toril Moi (New York: Columbia University Press, 1986), p. 257. For a good general introduction to Kristeva, see both Moi's introduction to this volume and her chapter on Kristeva in *Sexual/Textual Politics: Feminist Literary Theory* (London: Methuen, 1985). I would also like to mention two other useful essays here: Claire Pajaczkowska, "Introduction to Kristeva," *m/f*, nos. 5/6 (1981): 149–57, and Domna C. Stanton, "Language and Revolution: The Franco-American Dis-connection," in *The Future of Difference*, ed. Hester Eisenstein and Alice Jardine (New Brunswick: Rutgers, 1985), pp. 73–87.

10. *Revolution in Poetic Language*, trans. Margaret Waller (New York: Columbia University Press, 1984), p. 25.

11. Ibid., p. 27.

12. Ibid., p. 28.

13. *The Daughter's Seduction: Feminism and Psychoanalysis* (Ithaca: Cornell University Press, 1982), p. 124.

14. "Place Names," p. 289.

15. See Freud's account of the *fort/da* game in *Beyond the Pleasure Principle*, trans. James Strachey (New York: Norton, 1961), pp. 8–11, where the linguistic/gestural game is characterized as a device at the service of instinctual renunciation.

16. See "Julia Kristeva on Femininity: The Limits of a Semiotic Politic," *Feminist Review*, no. 18 (1984), pp. 56–73. Moi offers a similar critique of Kristeva's politics in *Sexual/Textual Politics*, pp. 170–71.

17. "Place Names," p. 278.

18. Ibid., pp. 278–79.

19. "Motherhood According to Giovanni Bellini," p. 240.

20. See "Negation," in *The Standard Edition of the Complete Psychological Works of Sigmund Freud*, trans. James Strachey (London: Hogarth Press, 1953), vol. 19, pp. 235–39.

21. This is the very precise definition offered by J. Laplanche and J.-B. Pontalis in *The Language of Psycho-analysis,* trans. Donald Nicholson-Smith (New York: Norton, 1973), p. 261.

22. "Motherhood According to Giovanni Bellini," p. 239.

23. *"Dora* and the Pregnant Madonna," in *Reading Woman: Essays in Feminist Criticism* (New York: Columbia University Press, 1986), p. 154. This essay offers an extremely insightful discussion of Kristeva and the place of the mother within psychoanalysis.

24. See Mary Russo, "Notes on 'Post-feminism,' " in *The Politics of Theory,* ed. Francis Barker, Peter Hulme, Margaret Iverson, and Diana Loxley (Colchester: University of Essex Press, 1983), pp. 27–37, for an excellent discussion of Kristeva's relation to feminism.

25. For a critique of the heterosexual bias of this essay, see Teresa de Lauretis, "The Female Body and Heterosexual Presumption" (forthcoming in *Semiotica*).

26. "Stabat Mater," trans. Leon S. Roudiez, in *The Kristeva Reader,* p. 178.

27. "Oscillation du 'pouvoir' au 'refus,' " an interview by Xaviere Gauthier, *Tel quel,* no. 58 (1974). This passage is included in *New French Feminisms,* ed. Elaine Marks and Isabelle de Courtivron (Amherst: University of Massachusetts Press, 1980), p. 166. It is translated there by Marilyn A. August.

28. "Freud and Love," p. 257.

29. Ibid., pp. 243–46.

30. *The Ego and the Id,* trans. Joan Riviere and James Strachey (New York: Norton, 1962), p. 23.

31. "Female Sexuality," in *The Standard Edition,* vol. 21, p. 225.

32. "Femininity," in *The Standard Edition,* vol. 22, p. 119.

33. Ibid., p. 120.

34. See Freud, *An Autobiographical Study,* in *The Standard Edition,* vol. 20, p. 34.

35. "The Evolution of the Oedipus Complex in Women," in *Psychoanalysis and Female Sexuality,* ed. Hendrik M. Ruitenbeek (New Haven: College and University Press, 1966), pp. 40–41.

36. Freud interprets the *fort/da* game as a symbolic strategy for overcoming the pain of separation from the mother (see n. 15 above). Lacan reads it as an allegory about the entry into language, and the loss of the subject's own "being" (see "The Agency of the Letter in the Unconscious," in *Ecrits: A Selection,* trans. Alan Sheridan [New York: Norton, 1977], pp. 146–78). For a commentary on this reading, see my *The Subject of Semiotics* (New York: Oxford University Press, 1983), pp. 167–78.

37. One cannot help but note that the diagram with which Lacan most forcefully makes this point fails to distinguish between the boy and the girl. See "On the Possible Treatment of Psychosis," in *Ecrits,* p. 200.

38. Needless to say, this formulation does not give as much primacy to the paternal intervention as a properly Lacanian reading of the Oedipus complex would do. But then I do not give the same weight that he does to the Name-of-the-Father. I would even be prepared to argue that the female subject's entry *only* into the negative Oedipus complex would not impair her relation to language. I will also be arguing, through *Riddles of the Sphinx,* that the third term need not be male. (On this last point, see my discussion of *Riddles of the Sphinx* below.)

39. In "Femininity," Freud writes: "The girl is driven out of her attachment to her mother through the influence of her envy for the penis and she enters the Oedipus situation as though into a haven of refuge. In the absence of fear of castration the chief motive is lacking which leads boys to surmount the Oedipus

complex. Girls remain in it for an indeterminate length of time; they demolish it late and, even so, incompletely" (p. 129).

40. "Female Sexuality," p. 241.

41. Freud insists quite strenuously that when the girl displaces her affections from her mother to her father, she begins to *hate* her mother (see "Femininity," p. 121).

42. "Women's Time," trans. Alice Jardine and Harry Blake, in *The Kristeva Reader*, p. 205.

43. For instance, she writes in "Stabat Mater" that "a mother is a continuous separation, a division of the very flesh. And consequently a division of language—and it has always been so" (p. 178). See Jacobus, "*Dora* and the Pregnant Madonna," pp. 147 and 169–70, for a discussion of this view of motherhood. Jacobus argues that the image of motherhood as unity works to guarantee "a masculine representation and sexual economy," but that the mother's role "in an alternative feminist economy might be to provide an emblem of the subject's difference from itself and its division by, and in, both language and the unconscious" (p. 147). I am in particularly strong agreement with the second of these points.

44. See Christian Metz, *The Imaginary Signifier: Psychoanalysis and the Cinema*, trans. Celia Britton, Annwyl Williams, Ben Brewster, and Alfred Guzzetti (Bloomington: Indiana University Press, 1982), pp. 89–97.

45. All quotes from the film have been taken from the script of *Riddles* published in *Screen* 18, no. 2 (1977): 61–77.

46. For an interesting discussion of the 360-degree pans, as well as the film's "pyramidal structure," see Keith Kelly, "*Riddles of the Sphinx:* One or Two Things about Her," *Millennium* 1, no. 2 (1978): 95–100. For a more general introduction to the film, see "Textual Riddles: Woman as Enigma or Site of Social Meanings?" *Discourse,* no. 1 (1979): 86–127—a fine interview with Laura Mulvey conducted by Sandy Flitterman and Jacquelyn Suter; Lester D. Friedman, "An Interview with Peter Wollen and Laura Mulvey on *Riddles of the Sphinx,*" *Millennium,* nos. 4/5 (1979): 14–32; and E. Ann Kaplan, "Mothers and Daughters in Two Recent Films," in *Women and Film: Both Sides of the Camera* (New York: Methuen, 1983), pp. 171–81.

47. Laura Mulvey, "Visual Pleasure and Narrative Cinema," *Screen* 16, no. 3 (1975): 7.

48. "Desire in Narrative," in *Alice Doesn't: Feminism, Semiotics, Cinema* (Bloomington: Indiana University Press, 1984), p. 157.

49. For a trenchant discussion of woman as commodity, see Luce Irigaray, "Women On the Market," in *This Sex Which Is Not One,* trans. Catherine Porter and Carolyn Burke (Ithaca: Cornell University Press, 1985), pp. 170–91.

50. I would also like to note that the 360-degree pans offer a constant challenge to the categories of "on-screen" and "off-screen." The slowly revolving camera joins voices to bodies only to separate them a moment later. This dialectic of union and division is radically accelerated in shot 12, with its play of reflections, and the distinction between on-screen and off-screen elements which becomes visible near the end of the shot.

5. Disembodying the Female Voice:
Irigaray, Experimental Feminist Cinema, and Femininity

1. *Parole de femme* (Paris: Éditions Grasset and Fasquelle, 1974).

2. For Cixous's account of writing, see "Sorties: Out and Out: Attacks/ Ways Out/Forays" and "Exchange," in Hélène Cixous and Catherine Clement, *The Newly Born Woman,* trans. Betsy Wing (Minneapolis: University of Minneso-

ta Press, 1986), pp. 63–260; "Castration or Decapitation?" trans. Annette Kuhn, *Signs* 7, no. 1 (1981); 41–55; "La venue à l'écriture," in Hélène Cixous, Madeleine Gagnon, and Annie Leclerc, *La venue à l'écriture* (Paris: Union Générale d'Éditions, 1977), pp. 9–62; "The Laugh of the Medusa," trans. Keith Cohen and Paula Cohen, *Signs* 1, no. 1 (1976): 875–99. For a discussion of Cixous's work, see Toril Moi, *Sexual/Textual Politics: Feminist Literary Theory* (London: Methuen, 1985), pp. 102–126; Verena Andermatt Conley, *Hélène Cixous: Writing the Feminine* (Lincoln: University of Nebraska Press, 1984); Ann Rosalind Jones, "Writing the Body," *Feminist Studies* 7, no. 2 (1981): 247–63; Annette Kuhn, "Introduction to Hélène Cixous's 'Castration or Decapitation?' " *Signs* 7, no. 1 (1981): 36–40; Domna C. Stanton, "Language and Revolution: The Franco-American Dis-connection," in *The Future of Difference*, ed. Hester Eisenstein and Alice Jardine (New Brunswick: Rutgers University Press, 1985), pp. 73–87.

3. These two essays are included in *This Sex Which Is Not One*, trans. Catherine Porter (Ithaca: Cornell University Press, 1985), pp. 23–33 and 205–218.

4. See, for instance, "Changing the Subject: Authorship, Writing, and the Reader," in *Feminist Studies/Critical Studies*, ed. Teresa de Lauretis (Bloomington: Indiana University Press, 1986), pp. 102–120, and "The Text's Heroine: A Feminist Critic and Her Fictions," *Diacritics* 12, no. 2 (1982): 42–53.

5. "French Feminism in an International Frame," *Yale French Studies*, no. 62 (1981): 155–84.

6. "Female Paranoia: The Case for Psychoanalytic Feminist Criticism," *Yale French Studies*, no. 62 (1981): 204–219. One of the many things that distinguish this essay from the others with which I have grouped it is that it argues for a metaphoric relation between the female body and a rigorously *theoretical* feminist discourse.

7. *Speculum of the Other Woman*, trans. Gillian G. Gill (Ithaca: Cornell University Press, 1985), pp. 26–27.

8. "Some Psychical Consequences of the Anatomical Distinction between the Sexes," trans. James Strachey, in *Sexuality and the Psychology of Love*, ed. Philip Rieff (New York: Collier Books, 1963), p. 187.

9. Irigaray stresses the positive Oedipus complex in *Speculum*, arguing that the mother remains the male subject's erotic object for the duration of his life (see especially pp. 31–32 and 81). However, in *This Sex Which Is Not One*, as I will indicate later in this essay, she emphasizes much more the male subject's desire for his sexual like, i.e., the negative Oedipus complex.

10. " 'Phallomorphic Power' and the Psychology of 'Woman,' " trans. Miriam David and Jill Hodges, *Ideology and Consciousness*, no. 4 (1978): 13–14.

11. For de Beauvoir's discussion of woman as Other, see *The Second Sex*, trans. H. M. Parshley (New York: Alfred A. Knopf, 1952).

12. *This Sex Which Is Not One*, p. 28.

13. "Woman's Exile: Interview with Luce Irigaray," trans. Couze Venn, *Ideology and Consciousness*, no. 1 (1977): 65.

14. *This Sex Which Is Not One*, p. 24.

15. Ibid., p. 29.

16. "Woman's Exile," p. 62.

17. For an interesting counter-argument, see Jane Gallop *"Quand nos lèvres s'écrivent:* Irigaray's Body Politic," *Romanic Review* 74, no. 1 (1983): 77–83. Gallop maintains that Irigaray is "metaphorizing" the body in language, and in so doing setting it "momentarily" free from "phallomorphic Law." However, she also concedes that there is a strong referential pull in Irigaray's account of the female body.

18. *Le corps-à-corps avec la mère* (Montréal: Les éditions de la pleine lune, 1981), pp. 28–29.

19. For a brief discussion of Irigaray's concept of mimicry, see Moi, *Sexual/ Textual Politics*, pp. 140–42.

20. In "Irigaray through the Looking Glass," *Feminist Studies* 7, no. 2 (1981), Burke writes: " 'When Our Two Lips Speak Together' may be described as a love poem in prose and a fable of female relations in the optative mood: it is written 'as if' we could forget the logical and emotional requirements of the phallic economy" (p. 300).

21. *This Sex Which Is Not One*, p. 211.

22. Ibid., p. 212.

23. Ibid., p. 216.

24. For a fuller discussion of the relation between discursive and real bodies, see my *"Histoire d'O:* The Story of a Disciplined and Punished Body," *Enclitic* 7, no. 2 (1983): 63–81.

25. "Writing the Body: Toward an Understanding of *L'écriture feminine,"* pp. 257–58.

26. See "French Feminism in an International Frame," pp. 179–84. Teresa de Lauretis also speaks very compellingly about the differences between women in "Feminist Studies/Critical Studies: Issues, Terms, and Contexts," in *Feminist Studies/Critical Studies* (Bloomington: Indiana University Press, 1986), pp. 1–19.

27. *This Sex Which Is Not One*, p. 24.

28. *"Histoire d'O:* The Story of a Disciplined and Punished Body," pp. 74–77.

29. "A Child Is Being Beaten," in *Collected Papers of Sigmund Freud,* trans. James and Alix Strachey (London: Hogarth Press, 1924), pp. 172–201. For a lengthy discussion of this essay, see my "Masochism and Subjectivity (II)," in *Male Subjectivity at the Margins* (forthcoming).

30. For an analysis of the place of reminiscence and *après-coup* in fantasy, see Jean Laplanche, *Life and Death in Psychoanalysis,* trans. Jeffrey Mehlman (Baltimore: Johns Hopkins University Press, 1976), pp. 25–47, and Jean Laplanche and J.-B. Pontalis, "Fantasy and the Origins of Sexuality," *International Journal of Psycho-analysis* 49, no. 1 (1968): 1–18.

31. *Speculum,* pp. 82f.

32. *This Sex Which Is Not One*, p. 79.

33. See "Woman's Exile," p. 64. For a fuller elaboration of the relation between vision and the penis, see *Speculum,* p. 47.

34. *The Imaginary Signifier: Psychoanalysis and the Cinema,* trans. Celia Britton, Annwyl Williams, Ben Brewster, and Alfred Guzzetti (Bloomington: Indiana University Press, 1982), p. 59.

35. *This Sex Which Is Not One*, pp. 29, 31, 79.

36. See *The History of Sexuality,* trans. Robert Hurley (New York: Pantheon, 1978), for a critique of the "repressive hypothesis."

37. "Woman's Exile," p. 70.

38. Ibid.

39. "Femininity," in *The Standard Edition of the Complete Psychological Works,* trans. James Strachey (London: Hogarth Press, 1953), vol. 22, p. 126.

40. Note, for instance, Freud's insistence that Dora occupies the position of a young man in the first part of her second dream, particularly when entering the woods and attempting to reach the station, i.e., at those moments when she seems to be connecting erotically with images which in some way represent femininity. *Fragment of an Analysis of a Case of Hysteria,* in *Case Histories,* vol. 1 trans. James Strachey (London: Penguin, 1977), pp. 133–40.

41. *Speculum,* p. 32.

42. "The Psychogenesis of a Case of Homosexuality in a Woman," in *The Standard Edition,* vol. 18, p. 170.

43. "Female Sexuality," in *The Standard Edition*, vol. 21, p. 226; "Femininity," p. 119.

44. "On Narcissism: An Introduction," trans. Cecil M. Baines, in *General Psychological Theory*, ed. Philip Rieff (New York: Collier Books, 1963), p. 71.

45. Ibid., pp. 69–70.

46. "Some Psychical Consequences of the Anatomical Distinction between the Sexes," p. 188.

47. *The Ego and the Id*, trans. Joan Riviere and James Strachey (New York: Norton, 1962), p. 23.

48. "Mourning and Melancholia," in *The Standard Edition*, vol. 14, p. 246.

49. Irigaray in fact suggests at one point in *This Sex Which Is Not One* that the negative Oedipus complex comes first in the history of female subjectivity, drawing as I have upon Jeanne Lampl-de Groot's pioneering essay, and locating the transition from the negative to the positive phase at the castration complex: "Before arriving at a 'positive' desire for the father, which implies the advent of receptive 'passivity,' the girl wishes to possess the mother and supplant the father, and this wish operates in the 'active' and/or 'phallic' mode. The impossibility of satisfying such desires brings about a devaluation of the clitoris, which cannot stand up in comparison with the penis. The passage from the negative (active) phase to the positive (passive) phase of the Oedipus complex is thus achieved through the intervention of the castration complex" (p. 58).

50. In "Some Psychical Consequences of the Anatomical Distinction between the Sexes," Freud writes: "I cannot escape the notion . . . that for women the level of what is ethically normal is different from what it is in men. Their super-ego is never so inexorable, so impersonal, so independent of its emotional origins as we require it to be in men" (p. 193).

51. "Mourning and Melancholia," p. 256.

52. See "On the Possible Treatment of Psychosis," in *Ecrits: A Selection*, trans. Alan Sheridan (New York: Norton, 1977), p. 200.

53. "Desire and the Interpretation of Desire in *Hamlet*," trans. James Hulbert, *Yale French Studies*, nos. 55/56 (1977): 11–52.

54. "On Narcissism," p. 70.

55. In "When Our Two Lips Speak Together," Irigaray addresses her lover in this way: "I love you who are neither mother (forgive me, mother, I prefer a woman) nor sister. . . . What need have I for husband or wife, for family, persona, role, function? Let's leave all those to men's reproductive laws" (*This Sex Which Is Not One*, p. 209).

56. *Le corps-à-corps avec la mère*, p. 23.

57. "And the One Doesn't Stir without the Other," *Signs* 7, no. 1 (1981): 66.

58. Interestingly, Irigaray's earlier work is centrally concerned with subjectivity. See Jean-Jacques Lecercle, *Philosophy through the Looking-Glass: Language, Nonsense, Desire*, ed. Alan Montefiore and Jonathan Ree (London: Hutchinson, 1985), pp. 55–62, for a summary of her discussion of a linguistic mirror stage in *Le language des déments*.

59. *This Sex Which Is Not One*, p. 31.

60. Ibid., p. 216.

61. Ibid., pp. 25–26.

62. *The Four Fundamental Concepts of Psycho-analysis*, trans. Alan Sheridan (New York: Norton, 1978), p. 106.

63. In *The Four Fundamental Concepts of Psycho-analysis*, Lacan writes: "By clinging to the reference-point of him who looks at him in the mirror, the subject sees appearing, not his ego ideal, but his ideal ego . . . (p. 257).

64. Ibid., p. 86.

65. I argue this case in some detail in "Fragments of a Fashionable Dis-

course," in *Studies in Entertainment: Critical Approaches to Mass Culture*, ed. Tania Modleski (Bloomington: Indiana University Press), pp. 139–54.

66. Pascal Bonitzer, *Le regard et la voix* (Paris: Union Générale d'Éditions, 1976), p. 30.

67. "Desire and the Interpretation of Desire in *Hamlet*," p. 28.

68. Stephen Heath describes the insertion of the voice into the diegesis as its preservation within a "safe place," and adds that this place is carefully maintained in the fiction film in "Narrative Space," *Screen* 17, no. 3 (1976): 100.

69. "Yvonne Rainer: Interview," *Camera Obscura*, no. 1 (1976): 89.

70. In *Problems in General Linguistics*, trans. Mary Meek (Coral Gables: University of Miami Press, 1971), p. 227, Emile Benveniste writes that "language is . . . the possibility of subjectivity, and discourse provokes the emergence of subjectivity because it consists of discrete instances. In some way language puts forth 'empty' forms which each speaker, in the exercise of discourse, appropriates to himself and which he relates to his 'person,' at the same time defining himself as *I* and a partner as *you*. The instance of discourse is thus constitutive of all coordinates that define the subject, and of which we have briefly pointed out only the most obvious [i.e., pronouns, verb forms, etc.]."

71. Although *Sifted Evidence* is one of the most important experimental films of the last ten years, it is unfortunately less well known than the other films I discuss in this chapter. For that reason, I am providing the following "synopsis," even though the film itself militates against any summary: A well-educated North American woman, Betts, goes to the ancient Mexican village of Tlatilco in search of information about the female divinities who were worshiped there three thousand years ago. Although she does eventually arrive at the gravel quarries where figurines of those divinities have been found, she never finds what she is looking for. Most of her time in Tlatilco is spent ostensibly trying to make her way to the quarries, but actually engaged in an "archaeological dig" at the site of her own subjectivity. What she discovers there is an inexplicable passivity in the face of a very authoritarian and manipulative masculinity. While she is looking for a bus to take her to Tlatilco, she is waylaid by a smooth-talking black man, who says he is from the States, but who speaks Spanish like a native. From that point on, he orchestrates her journey and mediates all her interactions with the landscape and people of Mexico. He also negotiates her, with her tacit acceptance, into a sexually vulnerable position. Only after a physical struggle has taken place between them does she muster the necessary resolve to slip out of the hotel room where he has been keeping her, visit the gravel quarries, and leave Tlatilco. *Sifted Evidence* can be rented from Film-Makers' Cooperative, 175 Lexington Ave., New York, NY 10016.

72. For a rather different reading of *Sifted Evidence*, see Kay Armatage, "About to Speak: The Woman's Voice in Patricia Gruben's *Sifted Evidence*," in *Take Two*, ed. Seth Feldman (Toronto: 1984), pp. 298–303. Armatage argues that the film is about woman's troubled relation to language and the symbolic. She also places the film very usefully within the context of Gruben's other work.

73. All quotations have been taken from the unpublished script of *Sifted Evidence*, given me by Gruben.

74. See "The Work of Art in the Age of Mechanical Reproduction," in *Illuminations*, trans. Harry Zohn (New York: Harcourt, Brace and World, 1968), pp. 219–54.

75. All quotations have been taken from the unpublished script of *Journeys from Berlin/71*, made available to me by Rainer.

76. B. Ruby Rich treats this metaphor at some length in *Yvonne Rainer* (Minneapolis: Walker Art Gallery, 1981).

77. "Mourning and Melancholia," p. 246.

78. Sally Potter describes the narrative structure of *The Gold Diggers* as a

NOTES FOR PAGES 179–92

spiral in the fine interview conducted with her by Pam Cook. See *Framework*, no. 24 (1984): 12–30.

79. "When the Goods Get Together" is how Claudia Reeder translates the title to the essay "Des marchandise entre elles," in *New French Feminisms*, ed. Elaine Marks and Isabelle de Courtivron (Amherst: University of Massachusetts Press, 1980), p. 107.

80. *This Sex Which Is Not One*, p. 179.

81. Ibid.

82. Ibid., p. 175.

83. Jane Gallop makes a similar point with respect to the *daughter's* relation to the father in *The Daughter's Seduction: Feminism and Psychoanalysis* (Ithaca: Cornell University Press, 1982), p. 71: "Any feminist upheaval, which would change woman's definition, identity, name as well as the foundation of her economic status, must undo the vicious circle by which the desire for the father's desire (for his penis) causes her to submit to the father's law, which denies his desire/penis, but operates in its place. . . ."

84. "This Sex Which Is Not One," p. 193.

6. The Female Authorial Voice

1. Roland Barthes, "The Death of the Author," in *The Rustle of Language*, trans. Richard Howard (New York: Hill and Wang, 1986), pp. 49–55.

2. Edward Buscombe, "Ideas of Authorship," *Screen* 14, no. 3 (1973): 75–85.

3. See Raymond Bellour, "Hitchcock, the Enunciator," trans. Bertrand Augst and Hilary Radner, *Camera Obscura*, no. 2, pp. 66–92, and Janet Bergstrom, "Alternation, Segmentation, Hypnosis: Interview with Raymond Bellour," *Camera Obscura*, nos. 3/4, pp. 71–103. Bellour's author is definitively male.

4. Sandy Flitterman, "Woman, Desire, and the Look: Feminism and the Enunciative Apparatus in Cinema," in *Theories of Authorship*, ed. John Caughie (London: Routledge and Kegan Paul, 1981), p. 248. *Theories of Authorship* is an excellent anthology, with authoritative commentary by Caughie.

5. See *Screen* 18, no. 2 (1977): 61–77, for the script to *Riddles of the Sphinx*.

6. Barthes, "The Death of the Author," p. 49.

7. Ibid.

8. See Jacques Derrida, "Signature, Event, Context," trans. Samuel Weber and Jeffrey Mehlman, *Glyph*, no. 1 (1977): 172–97, for a discussion of iterability.

9. Barthes, "The Death of the Author," p. 51.

10. Ibid., pp. 51–52.

11. Ibid., p. 52.

12. Ibid., p. 55.

13. Ibid., p. 54.

14. Roland Barthes, *The Pleasure of the Text*, trans. Richard Miller (New York: Hill and Wang, 1975), p. 27.

15. Ibid., pp. 66–67.

16. Ibid., p. 67.

17. Ibid., p. 27.

18. Barthes, "The Death of the Author," p. 49.

19. Barthes, *The Pleasure of the Text*, p. 53.

20. For a rather different account of Barthes, see Naomi Schor, "Dreaming Dissymmetry: Barthes, Foucault, and Sexual Difference," in *Men in Feminism*, ed. Alice Jardine and Paul Smith (New York: Methuen, 1987), pp. 98–110.

Schor finds in Barthes's fascination with the figure of the castrato or neuter a refusal to deal with sexual difference.

21. For one presentation of the feminist case against androgyny, see Jean Bethke Elstain, "Against Androgyny," *Telos,* no. 47 (1981): 5–21.

22. In *This Sex Which Is Not One,* trans. Catherine Porter (Ithaca: Cornell, 1985), Luce Irigaray argues at length that the "use and traffic in women subtend and uphold the reign of masculine hom(m)o-sexuality . . . in speculations, mirror games, identifications, and more or less rivalrous appropriations, which defer its real practice. Reigning everywhere, although prohibited in practice, hom(m)o-sexuality is played out through the bodies of women, matter, or sign, and heterosexuality has been up to now just an alibi for the smooth workings of man's relations with himself, of relations among men" (p. 172).

23. Barthes, "The Death of the Author," pp. 51–52.

24. Andrew Sarris, "Notes on the Auteur Theory in 1962," in *Film Theory and Criticism: Introductory Readings,* 3d ed., ed. Gerald Mast and Marshall Cohen (New York: Oxford University Press, 1985), pp. 537–38. See Caughie, *Theories of Authorship,* for a good summary of the simultaneous work on authorship in England in the journal *Movie,* pp. 48–60.

25. Sarris, "Notes on the Auteur Theory in 1962," pp. 539–40.

26. Ibid., p. 538–39.

27. Ibid., p. 538.

28. Ibid., p. 527.

29. Ibid., p. 538.

30. Peter Wollen, *Signs and Meaning in the Cinema* (Bloomington: Indiana University Press, 1972), pp. 94–102.

31. Ibid., pp. 112–13.

32. Ibid., p. 168.

33. Ibid., pp. 167–68.

34. Ibid., pp. 169–70.

35. Ibid., p. 167.

36. See Brian Henderson, *A Critique of Film Theory* (New York: Dutton, 1980), pp. 206–217, for a poststructuralist critique of both the 1969 version of *Signs and Meaning in the Cinema* and the 1972 postscript. While I am in fundamental agreement with Henderson's remarks about the first of these texts, it does seem to me that the second does much to shift the discussion of authorship in the direction Henderson would like it to move.

37. Stephen Heath, "Comment on the 'Idea of Authorship,' " *Screen* 14, no. 3 (1973): 89.

38. Ibid., p. 90.

39. Ibid., pp. 90–91.

40. Christian Metz, "Story/Discourse (A Note on Two Kinds of Voyeurism)," in *The Imaginary Signifier: Psychoanalysis and the Cinema,* trans. Celia Britton, Annwyl Williams, Ben Brewster, and Alfred Guzzetti (Bloomington: Indiana University Press, 1982), pp. 89–97.

41. See Emile Benveniste, "The Nature of Pronouns" and "Subjectivity in Language," in *Problems in General Linguistics,* trans. Mary Elizabeth Meek (Coral Gables: University of Miami Press, 1971), pp. 217–29.

42. Benveniste, "Subjectivity in Language," p. 224.

43. See Metz, *The Imaginary Signifier,* pp. 42–88; Geoffrey Nowell-Smith, "A Note on History/Discourse," *Edinburgh Magazine* no. 1 (1976): 26–32; Jean-Louis Baudry, "Ideological Effects of the Basic Cinematographic Apparatus," trans. Alan Williams, *Film Quarterly* 28, no. 2 (1973/74): 39–47, and "The Apparatus," trans. Jean Andrews and Bertrand Augst, *Camera Obscura,* no. 1 (1976): 104–28; Laura Mulvey, "Visual Pleasure and Narrative Cinema," *Screen* 16, no. 3 (1975): 6–18; Stephen Heath, "Narrative Space," in *Questions of Cinema* (Bloomington: Indiana University Press, 1981), pp. 19–75; Daniel

Dayan, "The Tutor Code of Classical Cinema," in *Movies and Methods*, ed. Bill Nichols (Berkeley: University of California Press, 1976), pp. 438–51; and Jean-Pierre Oudart, "Cinema and Suture," *Screen* 18, no. 4 (1977/78): 35–47.

44. Metz, *The Imaginary Signifier*, pp. 95–96.

45. Nowell-Smith, "A Note on History/Discourse," p. 31.

46. *The Subject of Semiotics* (New York: Oxford University Press, 1983), p. 47.

47. See in particular Francois Truffaut, *Hitchcock* (New York: Simon and Schuster, 1967).

48. Geoffrey Nowell-Smith, "Six Authors in Pursuit of the Searchers," *Screen* 17, no. 1 (1976): 30.

49. Bergstrom, "Alternation, Segmentation, Hypnosis: Interview with Raymond Bellour," p. 94.

50. Bellour, "Hitchcock, the Enunciator," p. 73.

51. Bergstrom, "Alternation, Segmentation, Hypnosis: Interview with Raymond Bellour," p. 95.

52. Ibid., p. 97.

53. Michel Foucault, "What Is an Author?" in *Language, Counter-Memory, Practice: Selected Essays and Interviews*, trans. Donald F. Bouchard and Sherry Simon (Ithaca: Cornell University Press, 1977), p. 138.

54. "Visual Pleasure and Narrative Cinema," p. 14.

55. Claire Johnston, "Women's Cinema as Counter-Cinema," in *Notes on Women's Cinema*, ed. Claire Johnston (London: BFI, 1975), p. 26.

56. Claire Johnston, "Dorothy Arzner: Critical Strategies," in *The World of Dorothy Arzner: Towards a Feminist Cinema* (London: BFI, 1975), p. 4. For another "antisystematic" reading of Arzner's work, see Pam Cook's essay "Approaching the Work of Dorothy Arzner" in the same volume (pp. 9–18).

57. Flitterman, "Woman, Desire, and the Look," p. 248.

58. Jacquelyn Suter, "Feminine Discourse in *Christopher Strong*," *Camera Obscura*, nos. 3/4 (1979): 135–50.

59. See Michel Foucault, *The History of Sexuality*, trans. Robert Hurley (New York: Pantheon, 1978), pp. 92–102, for a discussion of localized resistance.

60. Suter, "Feminine Discourse in *Christopher Strong*," pp. 147–48.

61. Ibid., p. 148.

62. Janet Bergstrom, "*Jeanne Dielman, 23 Quai du Commerce, 1080 Bruxelles*," *Camera Obscura*, no. 2 (1977): 114–18.

63. Ibid., p. 117.

64. Ibid., p. 118.

65. Modleski, "Woman and the Labyrinth," in *The Women Who Knew Too Much: Hitchcock and Feminist Film Criticism* (New York: Methuen, 1987).

66. Lea Jacobs, "*Now, Voyager*: Some Problems of Enunciation and Sexual Difference," *Camera Obscura*, no. 7 (1981): 89–109.

67. Teresa de Lauretis has frequently commented on the way in which Cavani's work fails to "fit" into any of our critical categories. See, for instance, "Now and Nowhere," in *Alice Doesn't: Feminism, Semiotics, Cinema* (Bloomington: Indiana University Press, 1984), p. 87.

68. J. Laplanche and J.-B. Pontalis, *The Language of Psycho-analysis*, trans. Donald Nicholson-Smith (New York: Norton, 1973), p. 317.

69. Freud calls the first three of these "primal fantasies" in "A Case of Paranoia Running Counter to the Psycho-analytic Theory of the Disease," in *The Standard Edition*, vol. 14, p. 269. I have taken the liberty of adding the beating fantasy to the list. In *Introductory Lectures on Psycho-analysis*, Freud suggests that the primal fantasies were once "real occurrences in the primaeval times of the human family," but have since become psychic reality (see *The Standard Edition*, vol. 16, p. 371).

70. For a discussion of the female version of the negative Oedipus complex, see chapters 4 and 5.

71. See "A Child Is Being Beaten," in *Collected Papers of Sigmund Freud*, trans. James and Alix Strachey (London: Hogarth Press, 1924), pp. 172–201. For an extended discussion of this essay, as well as the male version of the negative Oedipus complex, see my "Masochism and Subjectivity (II)," in *Male Subjectivity at the Margins* (forthcoming).

72. This phrase comes from Laplanche and Pontalis, *The Language of Psycho-analysis*, p. 318.

73. See "A Child Is Being Beaten."

74. For an analysis of this film, see my "Changing the Fantasmatic Scene," *Framework*, no. 20 (1983): 27–36.

75. For an extended discussion of the relationship between desire and narrative, see Teresa de Lauretis, "Desire in Narrative," in *Alice Doesn't*, pp. 103–157.

76. Cavani has directed the following feature films:
    Francesco d'Assisi (1966)
    Galileo (1968)
    The Cannibals (1969)
    The Guest (1971)
    Milarepa (1973/74)
    The Night Porter (1974)
    Beyond Good and Evil (1977)
    The Skin (1981)
    Beyond the Door (1983)
    Affair in Berlin (1986)

She has also made the following documentary films for Italian television:
    Story of the Third Reich (1962–63)
    The Age of Stalin (1963)
    The House in Italy (1964)
    Philippe Petain: Trial at Vichy (1965)
    Women of the Resistance (1965)
    Jesus, My Brother (1965)
    The Day of Peace (1965)

I will be focusing here on the work prior to 1975, which I have been able to study much more closely than the subsequent work, and which seems to me considerably more interesting and "distinctive" than the films which were made later. I would like to thank Liliana Cavani for arranging for me to screen her first five feature films, and most of her documentaries.

77. Cavani tried without success to raise the necessary money to make a film about Simone Weil. It is, of course, impossible to predict what the end result would have been, but the script gives a more central position than usual to its female protagonist. See Liliana Cavani and Italo Moscati, *Letters dall'interno: Racconto per un film su Simon Weil* (Turin: Einaudi, 1974).

78. Rituals of eating and drinking play an important part in *Francesco d'Assisi*, *The Cannibals*, and *The Night Porter*, functioning in all three cases to express psychic resistance to dominant culture. In addition, the most emotionally charged moments in *Francesco d'Assisi*, *Galileo*, *The Guest*, *The Night Porter*, and *Beyond Good and Evil* also occur within closed spaces—churches, mental institutions, concentration camps, and (most frequently) homes. The frame narrative in *Milarepa* also gives a privileged position to the family domicile, and to certain oral activities (coffee drinking, smoking) which take place there.

79. During an interview conducted by Claire Clouzot, for instance, Cavani returned again and again to the immersion of Lou Castel in the part of Francesco: "Lou Castel . . . loved the part so much that he completely identified with it. His revolutionary attitude can be attributed [to that identification, as can] the fact that he gave away all his money to an extra-parliamentary political party . . . little by little, Lou Castel became Francesco. It was strange, but sometimes one forgot which was which."

80. Cavani dwelt at great length upon this point in two private interviews she granted me in December 1980. See also pp. 53–54 of the comments she published along with the script of *Milarepa*, ed. Italo Moscati (Bologna: Cappeli Editore, 1974): "Lou Castel, Pierre Clementi, Peter Gonzales and Lajos Belazsovitz. These are not only good actors, they are for me truly the corporeal embodiment of the four films: *Francesco, Cannibali, L'Ospite, Milarepa*. Four poets, four fools, four troubled and sweet faces, with *which I am myself identified, and in which I find my epoch identified* [my emphasis]. These haven't taken 'the part of'; they are physically the four characters. "

81. Teresa de Lauretis was the first to suggest that *The Night Porter* might be more than usually adaptable to a feminist reading, in "Cavani's *Night Porter:* A Woman's Film?" *Film Quarterly* 30, no. 2 (1976/77): 35–38. For an extended discussion of the treatment of memory and language in that film, see my "Masochism and Subjectivity," *Framework,* no. 12 (1980): 2–9.

82. Mikhail Bakhtin, *Rabelais and His World,* trans. Helen Iwolsky (Cambridge: MIT Press, 1968), p. 92.

83. This interview, which was conducted by Simon Mazrahi and Martine Marignac, was published in the Cannes publicity booklet for *Beyond Good and Evil*.

84. Cavani, *Milarepa*, p. 60. Translation of this and other excerpts from the script were done by Michael Silverman.

85. Jacqueline Rose connects the shot/reverse shot formation with the imaginary register in "Paranoia and the Film System," *Screen* 17, no. 4 (1976/77): 85–104.

86. Cavani, *Milarepa*, pp. 113–14.

87. "The Economic Problem of Masochism," in *The Standard Edition*, vol. 19, p. 27.

88. "A Child Is Being Beaten," p. 180.

89. Ibid., pp. 178–86.

90. See "Masochism and Subjectivity (II)."

91. Michel Foucault, *The Archaeology of Knowledge,* trans. A. M. Sheridan Smith (New York: Pantheon, 1972), pp. 95–96.

Index

254